池本幹雄

This is a continuation from the previous volume, but while I was buying up *Australopithecus boisei* on Mercari, I discovered a new ape-man.

Its name: *Australopithecus afarensis*.

It seems to be part of a sequel series from Kaiyodo, who had also sculpted the Boisei. Boisei's craftsmanship is brilliant, but Afarensis is of even higher quality. And it appears to be chewing on a zebra leg... In addition, there are even two hair color varieties, black and red. This is bad news.

Why do I like ape-men so much? I'm gonna keep collecting them.

**–Mikio Ikemoto, 2020**

小太刀右京

I'm sure, during the course of your life, there have been times that you felt all alone, or lonely, or helplessly anxious.

Times when you felt like you were in darkness, unable to see the way out, and not sure what to do. But even during such times, manga are always by your side. No matter what is going on, Boruto and the others are your friends. It may be a truly faint glimmer, but we create these books with the intent that they light your path even a little.

**–Ukyo Kodachi, 2020**

W9-BMC-598

# BORUTO
## -NARUTO NEXT GENERATIONS-

## VOLUME 11

**SHONEN JUMP MANGA EDITION**

**Creator/Supervisor MASASHI KISHIMOTO**
**Art by MIKIO IKEMOTO**
**Script by UKYO KODACHI**

Translation: Mari Morimoto
Touch-up Art & Lettering: Snir Aharon
Design: Alice Lewis
Editor: Alexis Kirsch



Printed in the U.S.A.

Published by VIZ Media, LLC
P.O. Box 77010
San Francisco, CA 94107

10 9 8 7 6 5 4 3 2 1
First printing, May 2021

viz.com

**PARENTAL ADVISORY**
BORUTO is rated T for Teen and is recommended for ages 13 and up. This volume contains fantasy violence.

ratings.viz.com
RATED T TEEN

# BORUTO
## -NARUTO NEXT GENERATIONS-

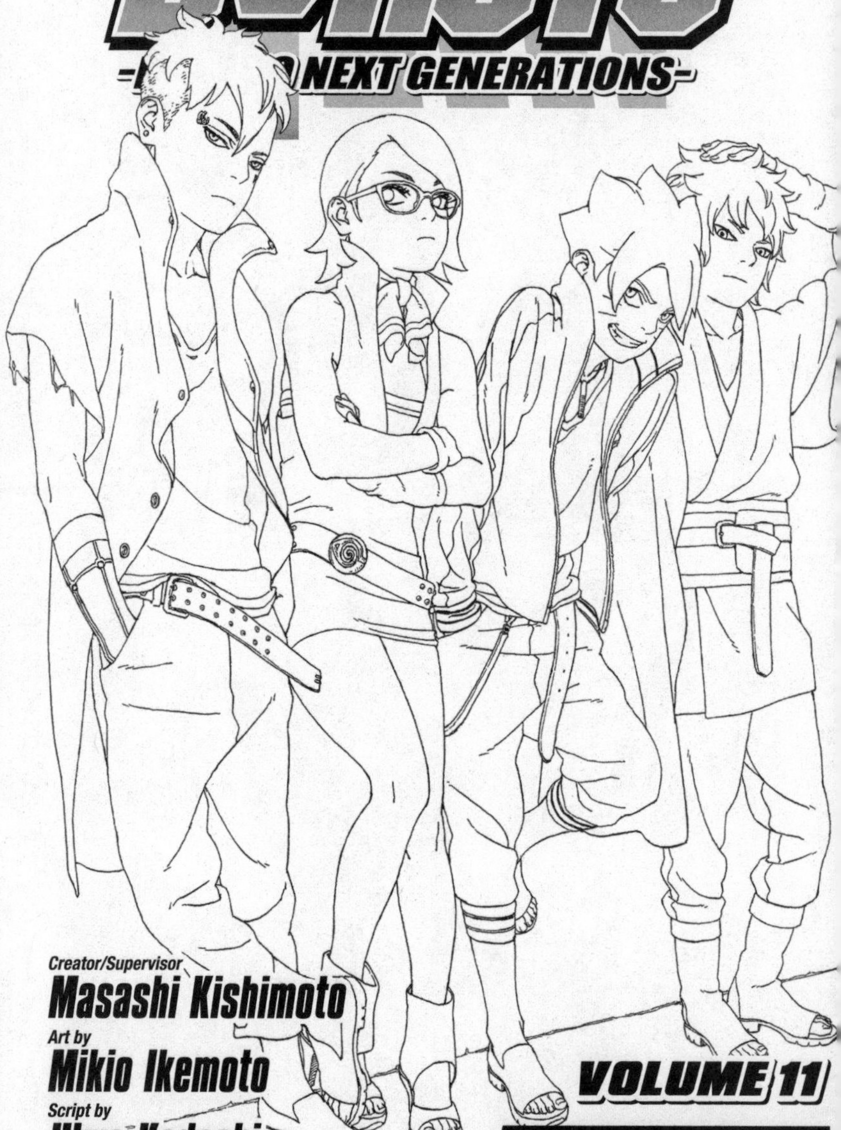

Creator/Supervisor
**Masashi Kishimoto**
Art by
**Mikio Ikemoto**
Script by
**Ukyo Kodachi**

**VOLUME 11**

**The New Team Seven**

# BORUTO -NARUTO NEXT GENERATIONS- CHARACTERS

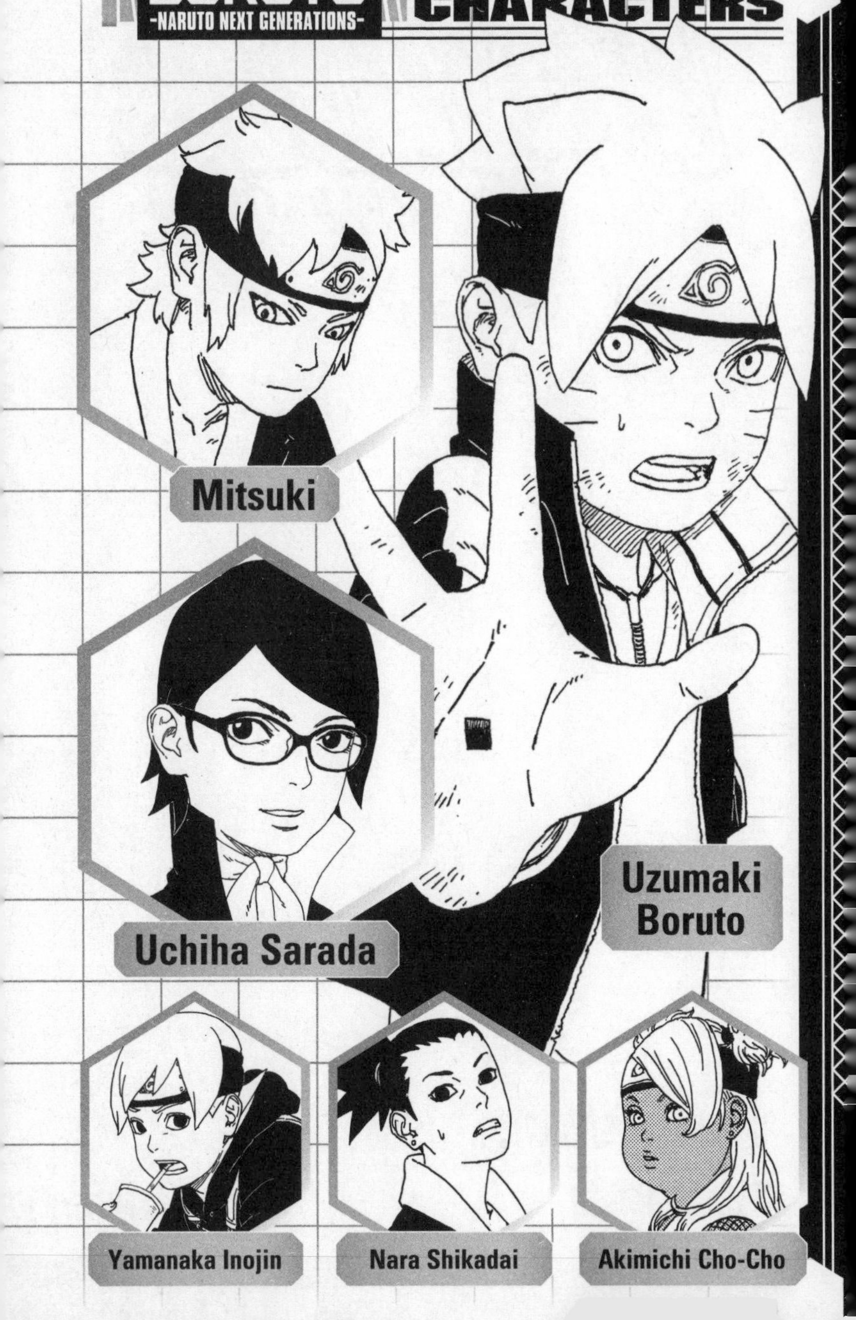
Uzumaki Boruto
Mitsuki
Uchiha Sarada
Akimichi Cho-Cho
Nara Shikadai
Yamanaka Inojin

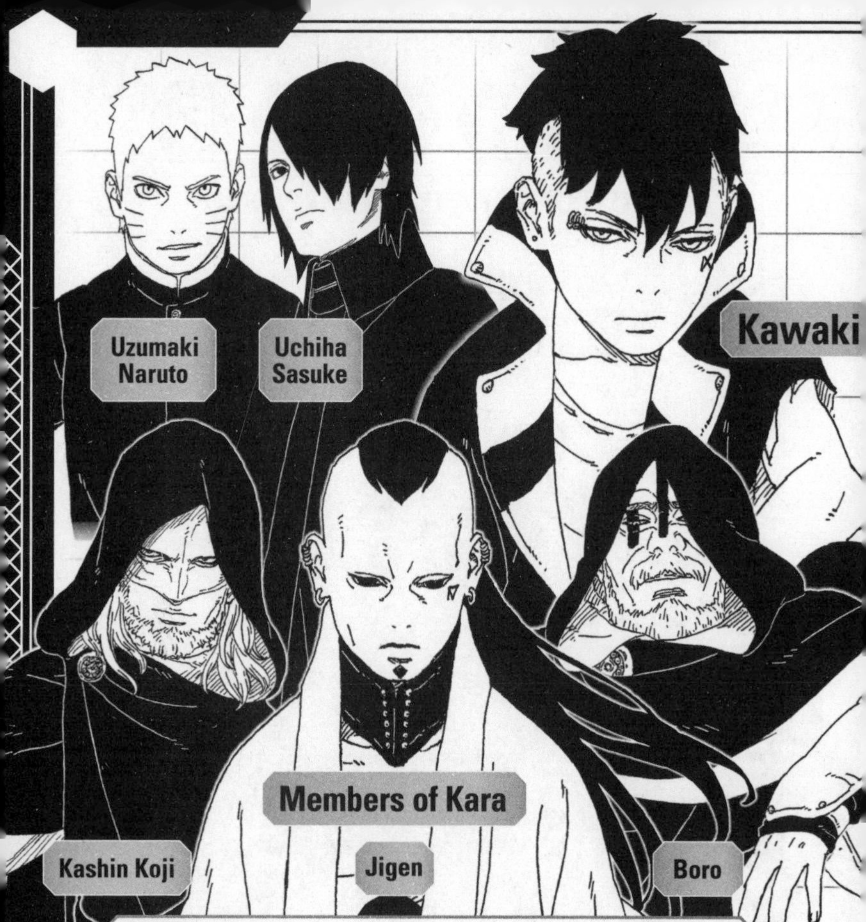
Kawaki
Uchiha Sasuke
Uzumaki Naruto
Members of Kara
Boro
Jigen
Kashin Koji

# STORY

The Great Ninja War that shook the world and shed much blood is now history. Naruto has become the Seventh Hokage, and the people of Konohagakure Village are enjoying peace. Yet Naruto's son Uzumaki Boruto has a glum life, perhaps due to his father's too-great influence.

Rebelling against Naruto while simultaneously craving his praise, Boruto decides to enter the Chunin Exam along with his teammates Sarada and Mitsuki. However, Boruto ends up secretly using a prohibited Scientific Ninja Tool and is stripped of his shinobi status by his father.

Just then, members of the Ohtsutsuki Clan attack the arena! Boruto faces off against them alongside Naruto, Sasuke and others, and they achieve victory with a Rasengan that father and son weave together. However, a strange mark appears on Boruto's right palm…

Afterward, Boruto happens upon a young man named Kawaki who bears the same Karma as himself. And it is he who is proven to be what Kara has been calling the Vessel.

In order to place Kawaki under his protection, Naruto moves him into his own home. However, Delta's attack brings Kara's leader Jigen, who takes Naruto prisoner in another dimension. Kawaki, Boruto, Mitsuki and Sarada head to rescue Naruto using space-time ninjutsu. Another Kara member, Boro, lies there in wait…

# BORUTO

## -NARUTO NEXT GENERATIONS-

## VOLUME 11
### THE NEW TEAM SEVEN

# CONTENTS

# Number 40: The Invisible Jutsu

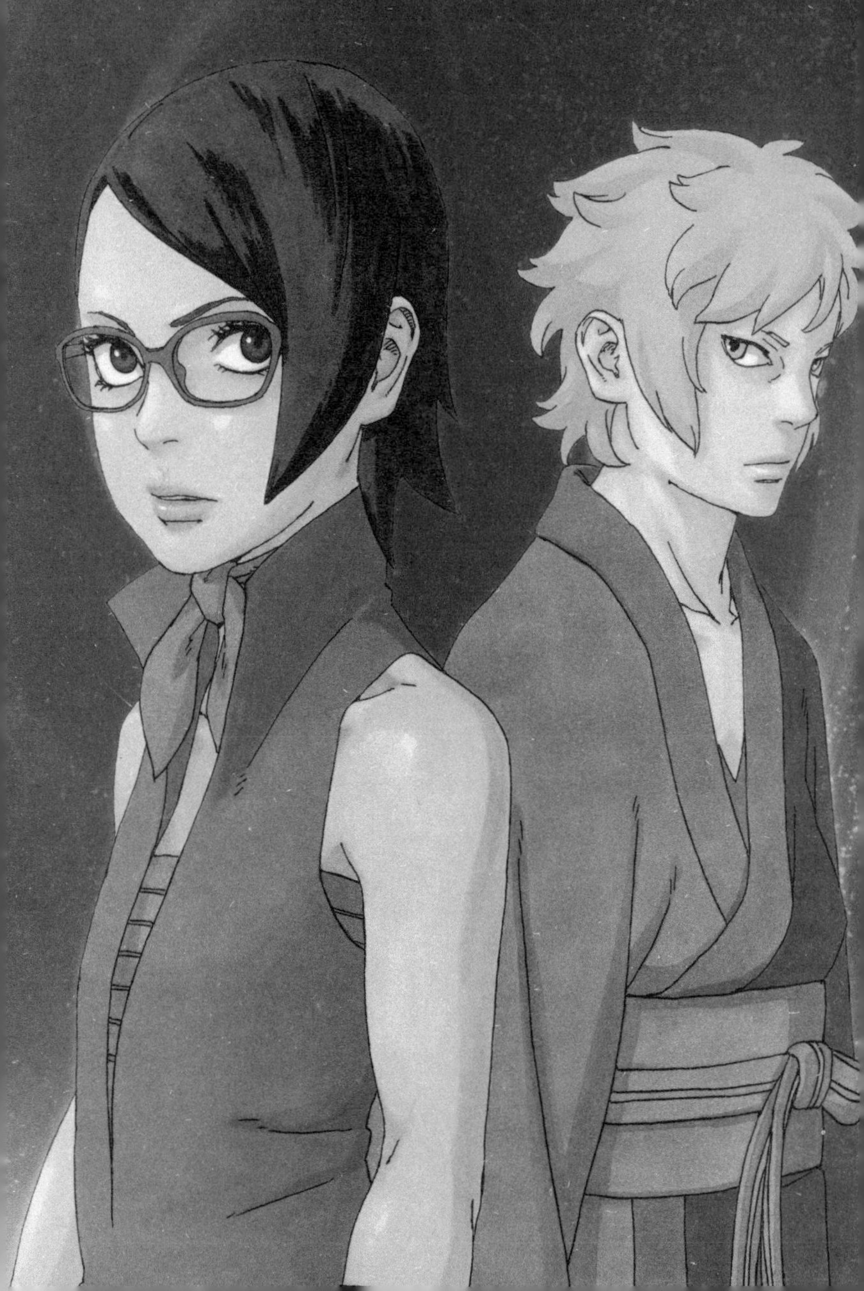

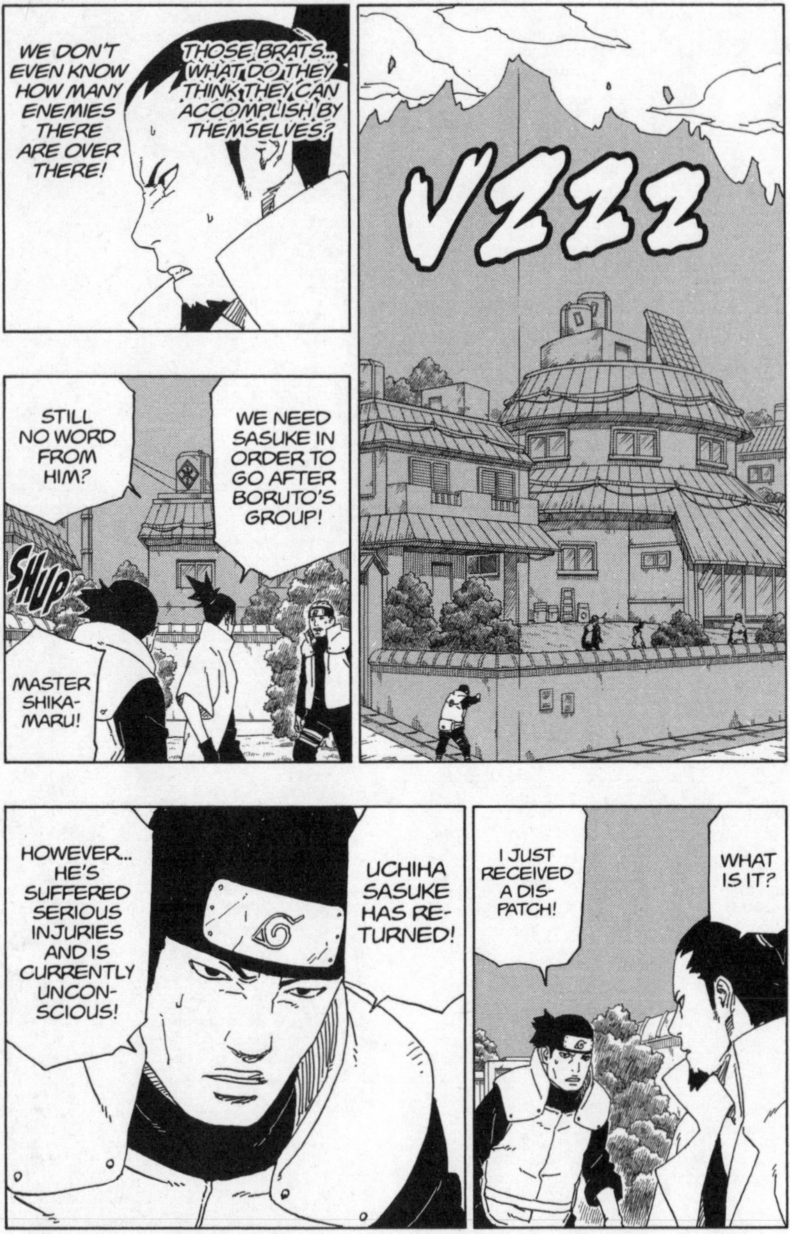
VZZZ
THOSE BRATS... WHAT DO THEY THINK THEY CAN ACCOMPLISH BY THEMSELVES?
WE DON'T EVEN KNOW HOW MANY ENEMIES THERE ARE OVER THERE!
WE NEED SASUKE IN ORDER TO GO AFTER BORUTO'S GROUP!
STILL NO WORD FROM HIM?
SHUP
MASTER SHIKAMARU!
WHAT IS IT?
I JUST RECEIVED A DISPATCH!
UCHIHA SASUKE HAS RETURNED!
HOWEVER... HE'S SUFFERED SERIOUS INJURIES AND IS CURRENTLY UNCONSCIOUS!

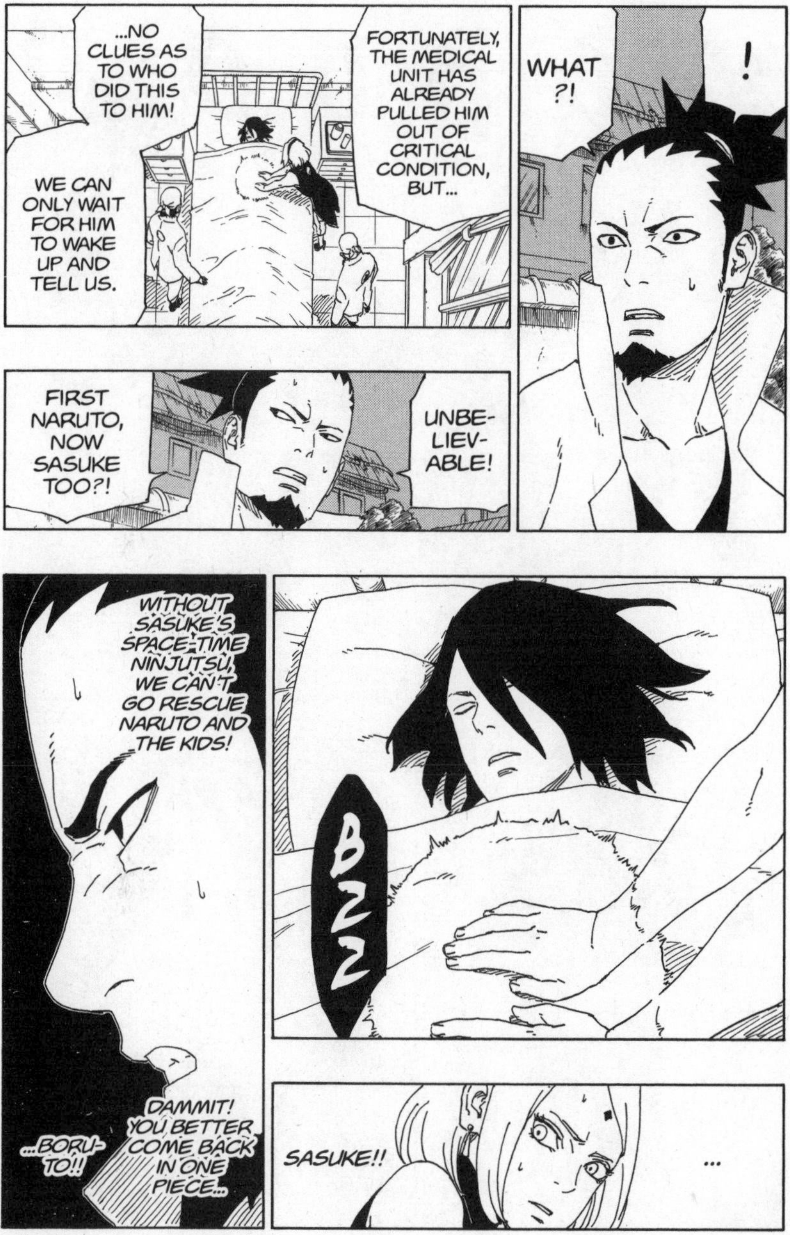
!
WHAT?!
FORTUNATELY, THE MEDICAL UNIT HAS ALREADY PULLED HIM OUT OF CRITICAL CONDITION, BUT...
...NO CLUES AS TO WHO DID THIS TO HIM!
WE CAN ONLY WAIT FOR HIM TO WAKE UP AND TELL US.
UNBE-LIEV-ABLE!
FIRST NARUTO, NOW SASUKE TOO?!
BZZ
...
SASUKE!!
WITHOUT SASUKE'S SPACE-TIME NINJUTSU, WE CAN'T GO RESCUE NARUTO AND THE KIDS!
DAMMIT! YOU BETTER COME BACK IN ONE PIECE...
...BORU-TO!!

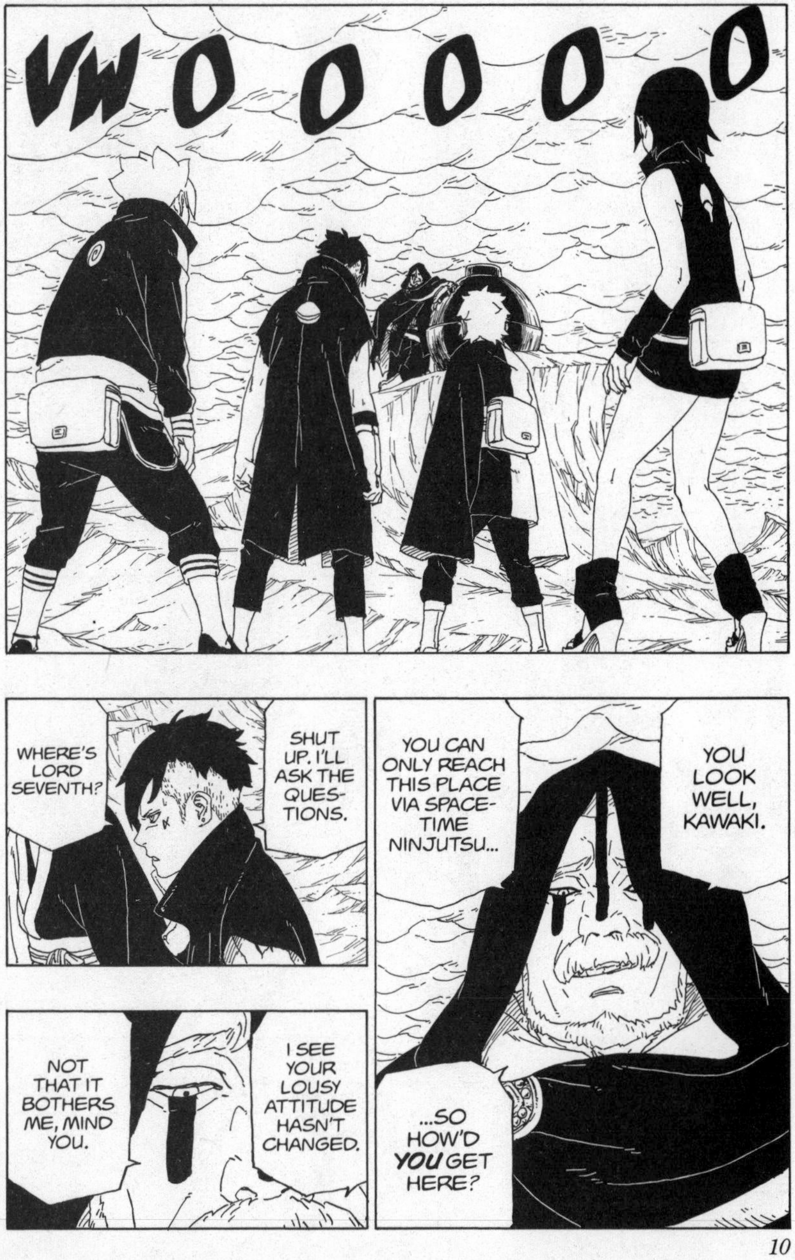
VWOOOOOO
YOU LOOK WELL, KAWAKI.
YOU CAN ONLY REACH THIS PLACE VIA SPACE-TIME NINJUTSU...
...SO HOW'D ***YOU*** GET HERE?
SHUT UP. I'LL ASK THE QUES-TIONS.
WHERE'S LORD SEVENTH?
I SEE YOUR LOUSY ATTITUDE HASN'T CHANGED.
NOT THAT IT BOTHERS ME, MIND YOU.

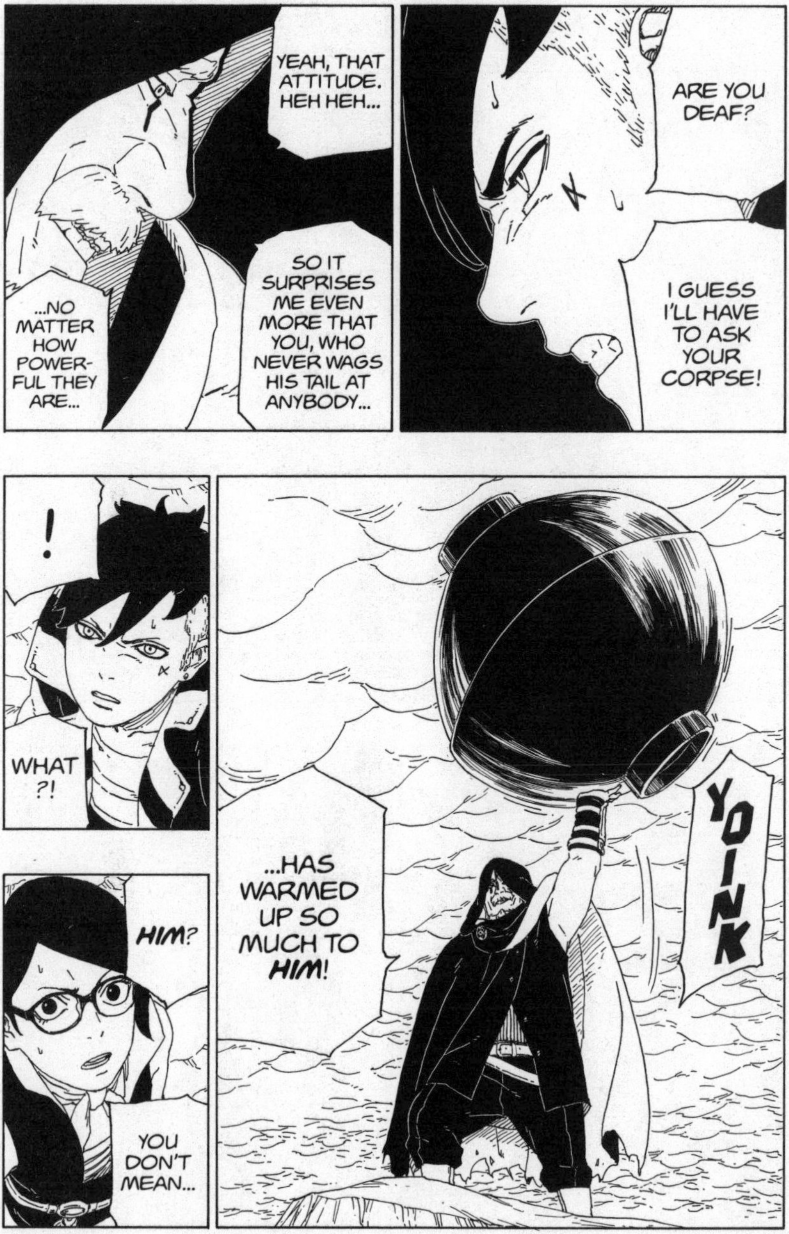
ARE YOU DEAF?
I GUESS I'LL HAVE TO ASK YOUR CORPSE!
YEAH, THAT ATTITUDE. HEH HEH...
...NO MATTER HOW POWER-FUL THEY ARE...
SO IT SURPRISES ME EVEN MORE THAT YOU, WHO NEVER WAGS HIS TAIL AT ANYBODY...
...HAS WARMED UP SO MUCH TO **HIM**!
YOINK
!
WHAT ?!
**HIM**?
YOU DON'T MEAN...

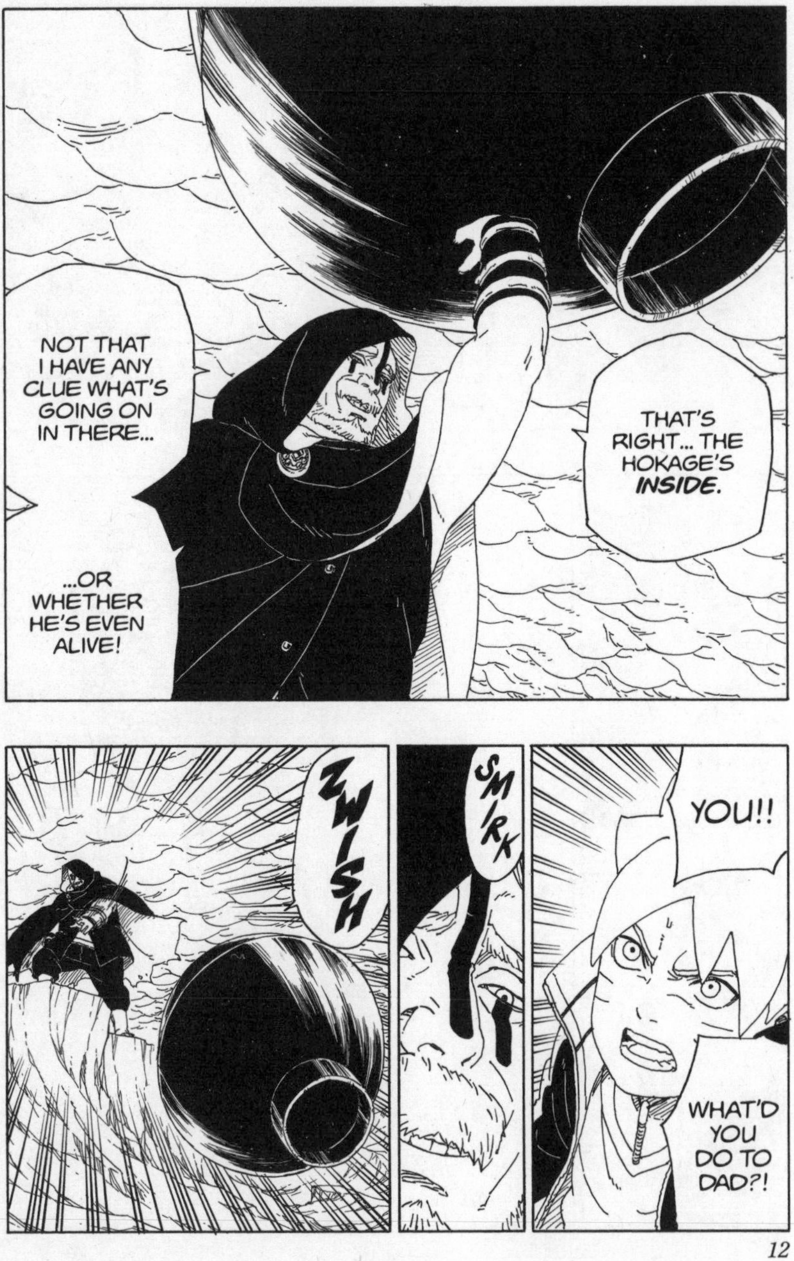
THAT'S RIGHT... THE HOKAGE'S ***INSIDE.***
NOT THAT I HAVE ANY CLUE WHAT'S GOING ON IN THERE...
...OR WHETHER HE'S EVEN ALIVE!
YOU!!
WHAT'D YOU DO TO DAD?!
SMIRK
ZWISH

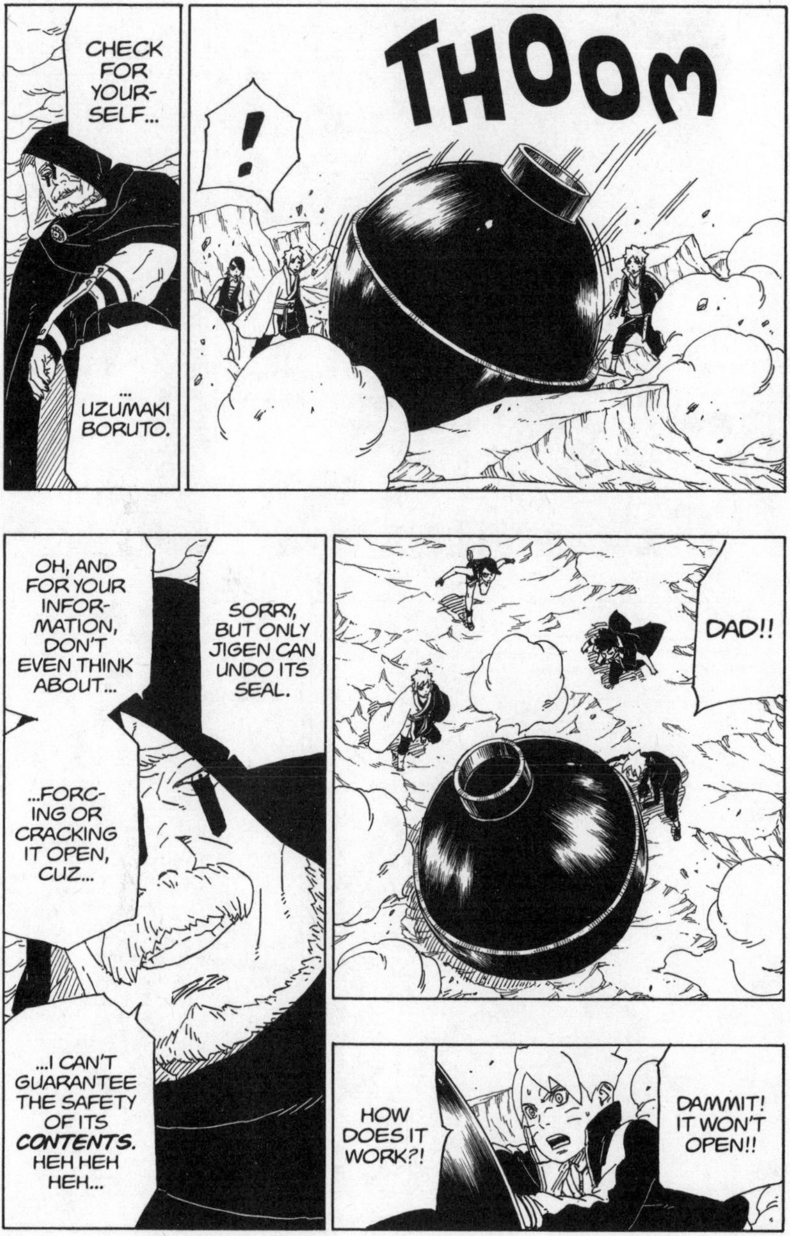
THOOM
!
CHECK FOR YOURSELF...
... UZUMAKI BORUTO.
DAD!!
DAMMIT! IT WON'T OPEN!!
HOW DOES IT WORK?!
SORRY, BUT ONLY JIGEN CAN UNDO ITS SEAL.
OH, AND FOR YOUR INFORMATION, DON'T EVEN THINK ABOUT...
...FORCING OR CRACKING IT OPEN, CUZ...
...I CAN'T GUARANTEE THE SAFETY OF ITS *CONTENTS*. HEH HEH HEH...

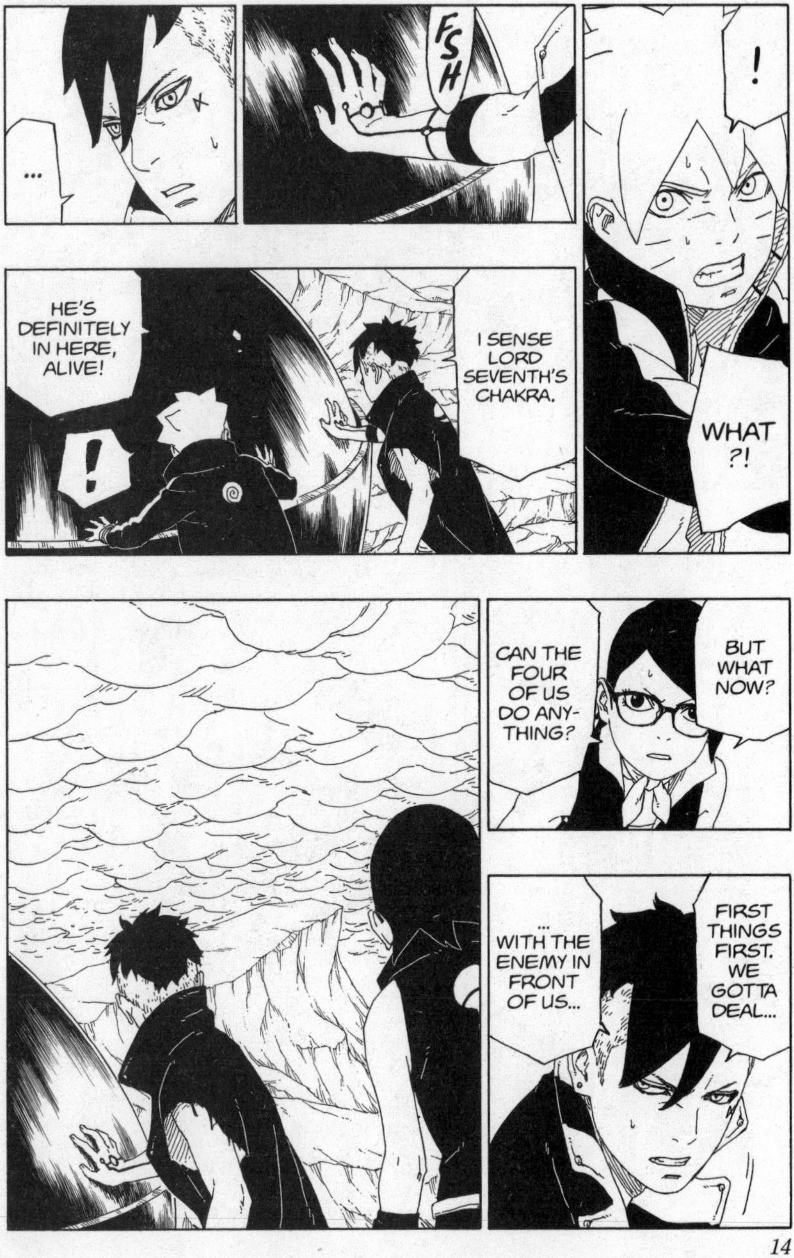
!
WHAT ?!
FSH
...
I SENSE LORD SEVENTH'S CHAKRA.
HE'S DEFINITELY IN HERE, ALIVE!
!
BUT WHAT NOW?
CAN THE FOUR OF US DO ANYTHING?
FIRST THINGS FIRST. WE GOTTA DEAL...
... WITH THE ENEMY IN FRONT OF US...

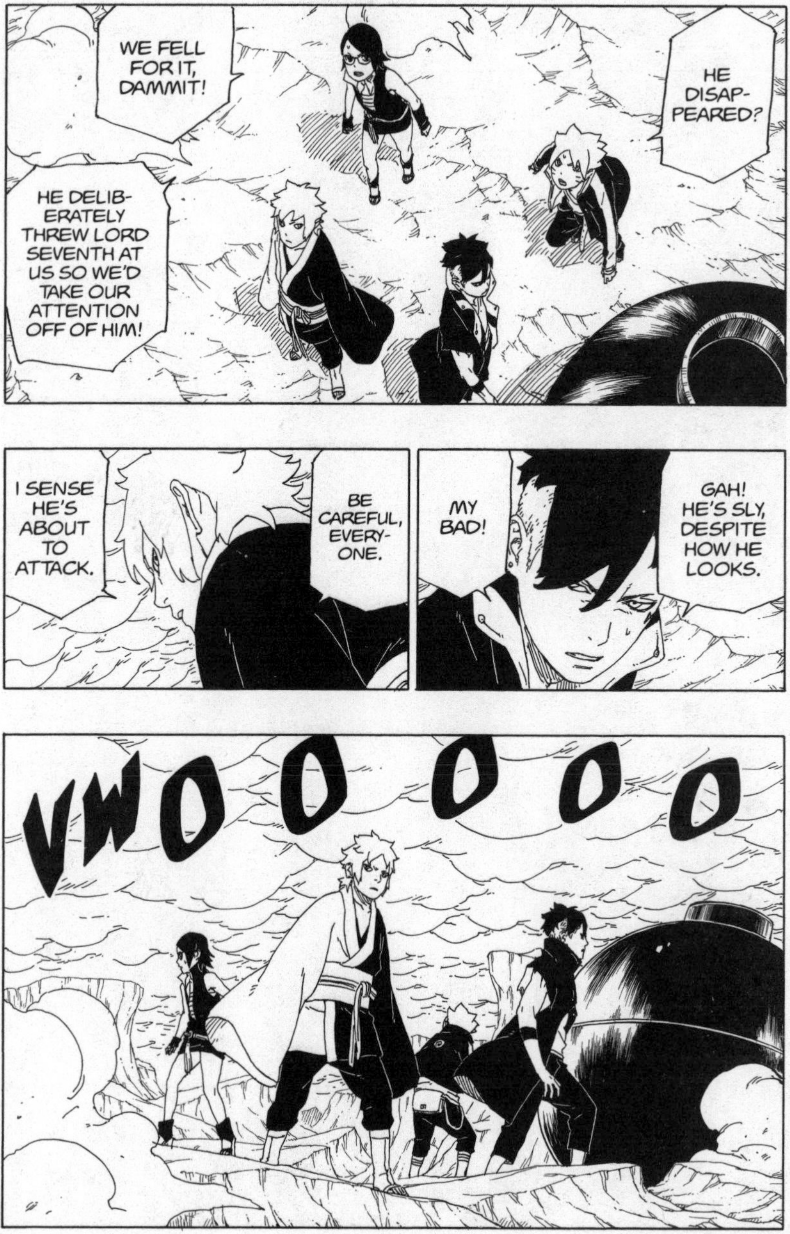
HE DISAPPEARED?
WE FELL FOR IT, DAMMIT!
HE DELIBERATELY THREW LORD SEVENTH AT US SO WE'D TAKE OUR ATTENTION OFF OF HIM!
GAH! HE'S SLY, DESPITE HOW HE LOOKS.
MY BAD!
BE CAREFUL, EVERYONE.
I SENSE HE'S ABOUT TO ATTACK.
VWOOOOO

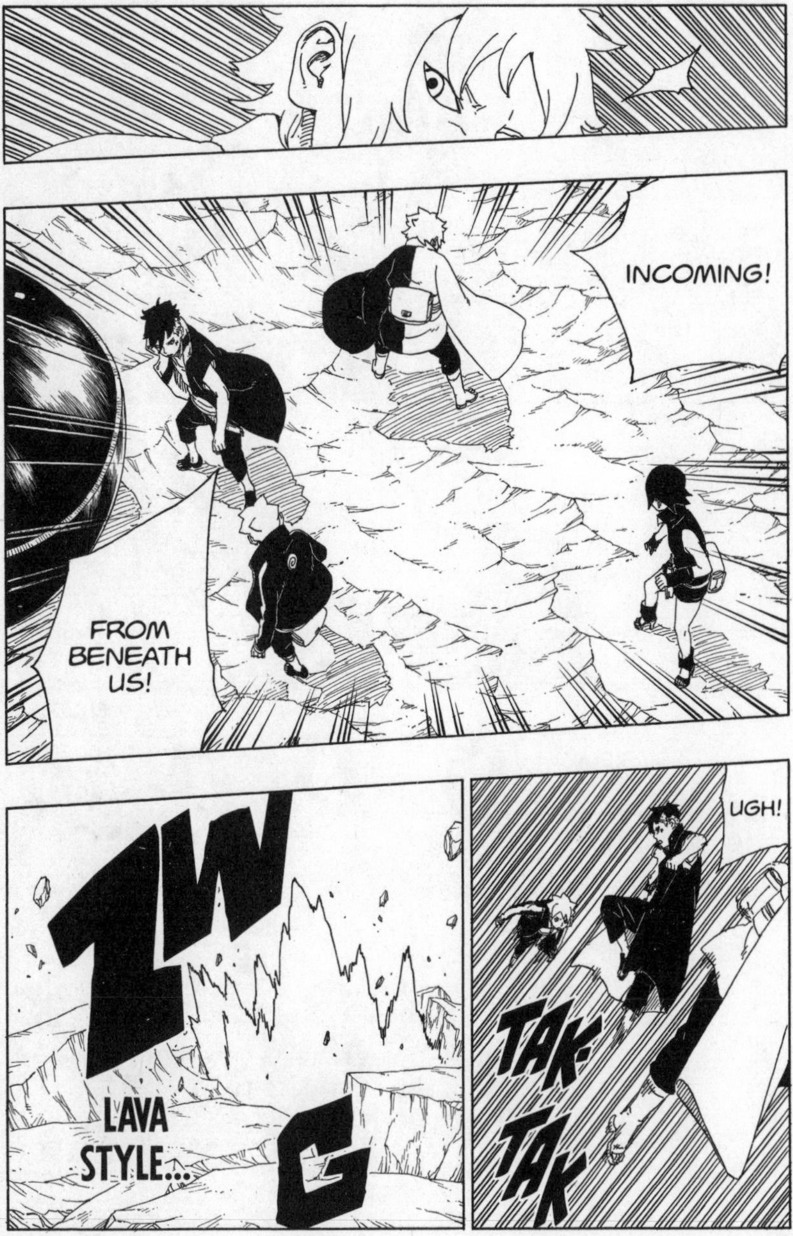
INCOMING!
FROM BENEATH US!
UGH!
TAK-TAK
ZWG
LAVA STYLE...

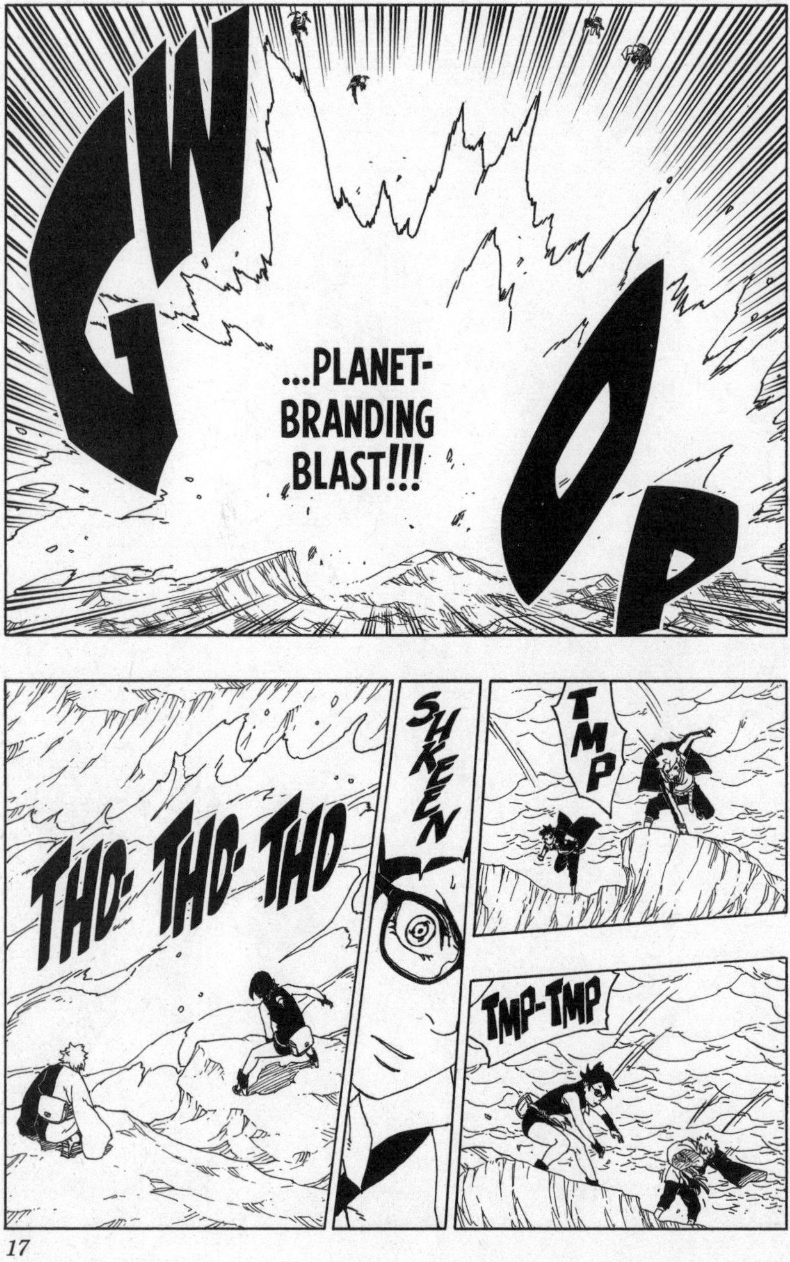
GWOP
...PLANET-BRANDING BLAST!!!
TMP
TMP-TMP
SHKEEN
THO- THO- THO

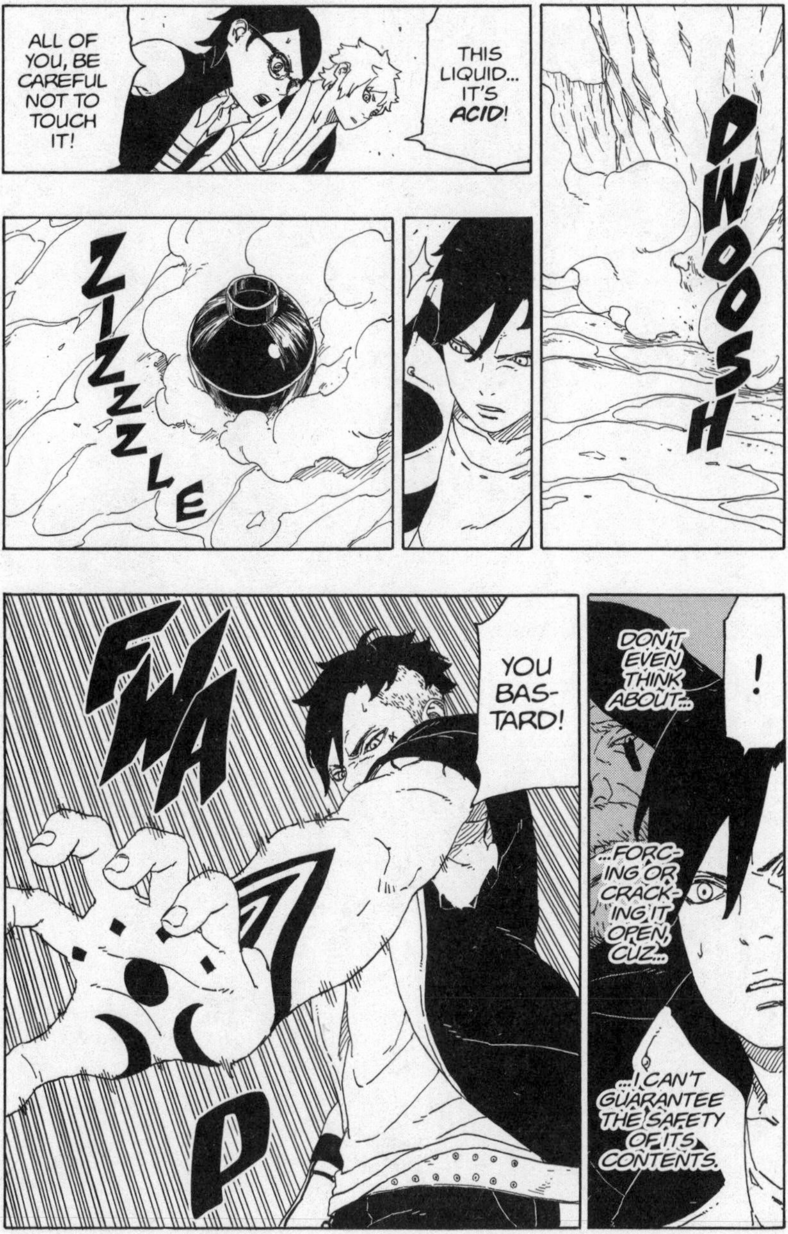
DWOOSH
THIS LIQUID... IT'S ACID!
ALL OF YOU, BE CAREFUL NOT TO TOUCH IT!
ZIZZZLE
!
DON'T EVEN THINK ABOUT...
...FORCING OR CRACKING IT OPEN, CUZ...
...I CAN'T GUARANTEE THE SAFETY OF ITS CONTENTS.
YOU BASTARD!
FWAP

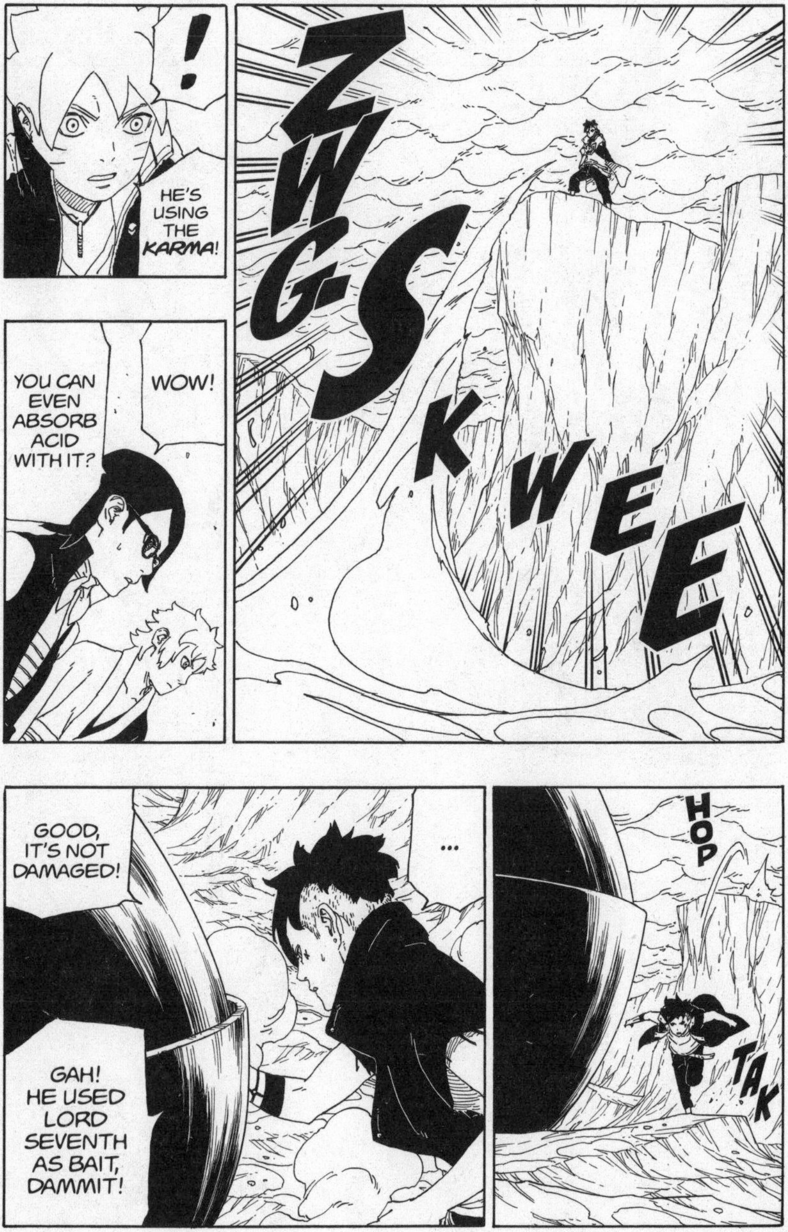
ZWG-S
KWEE
!
HE'S USING THE *KARMA*!
WOW!
YOU CAN EVEN ABSORB ACID WITH IT?
HOP
TAK
...
GOOD, IT'S NOT DAMAGED!
GAH! HE USED LORD SEVENTH AS BAIT, DAMMIT!

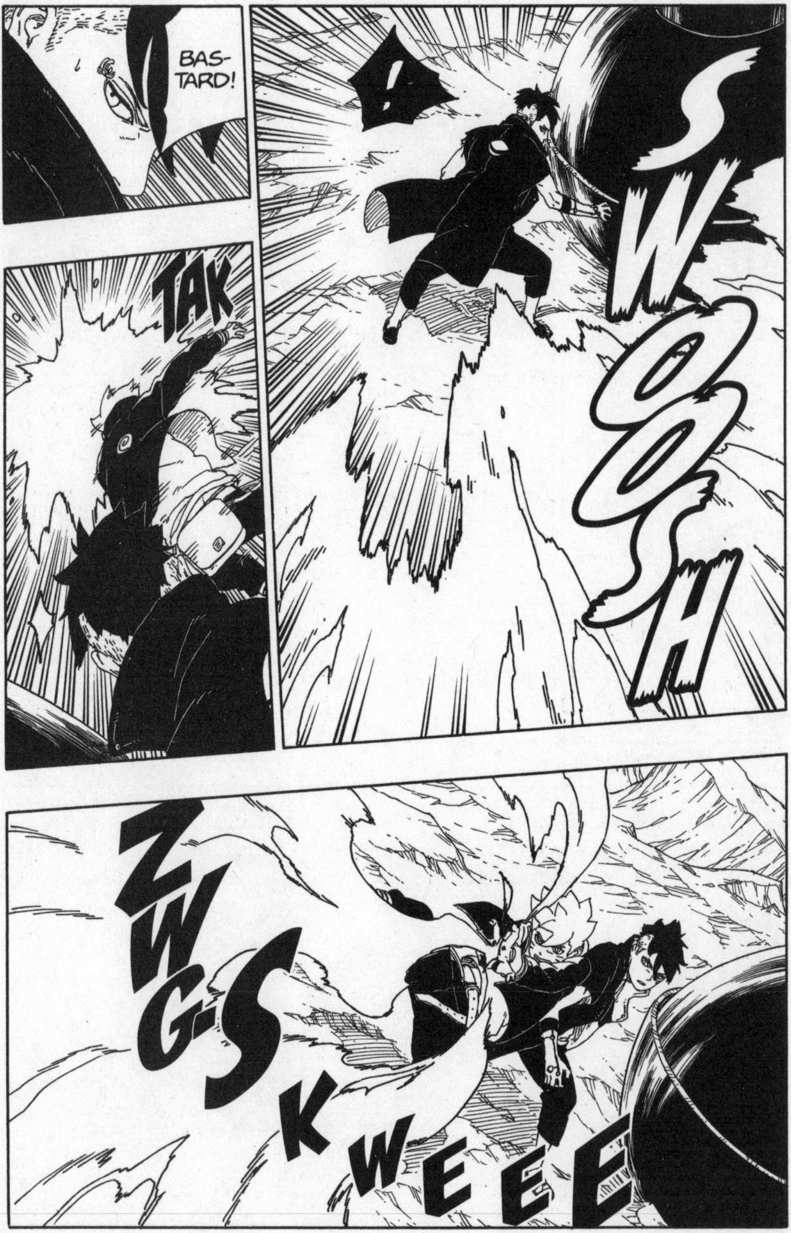
!
SWOOSH
BAS-TARD!
TAK
ZWG-SKWEEE

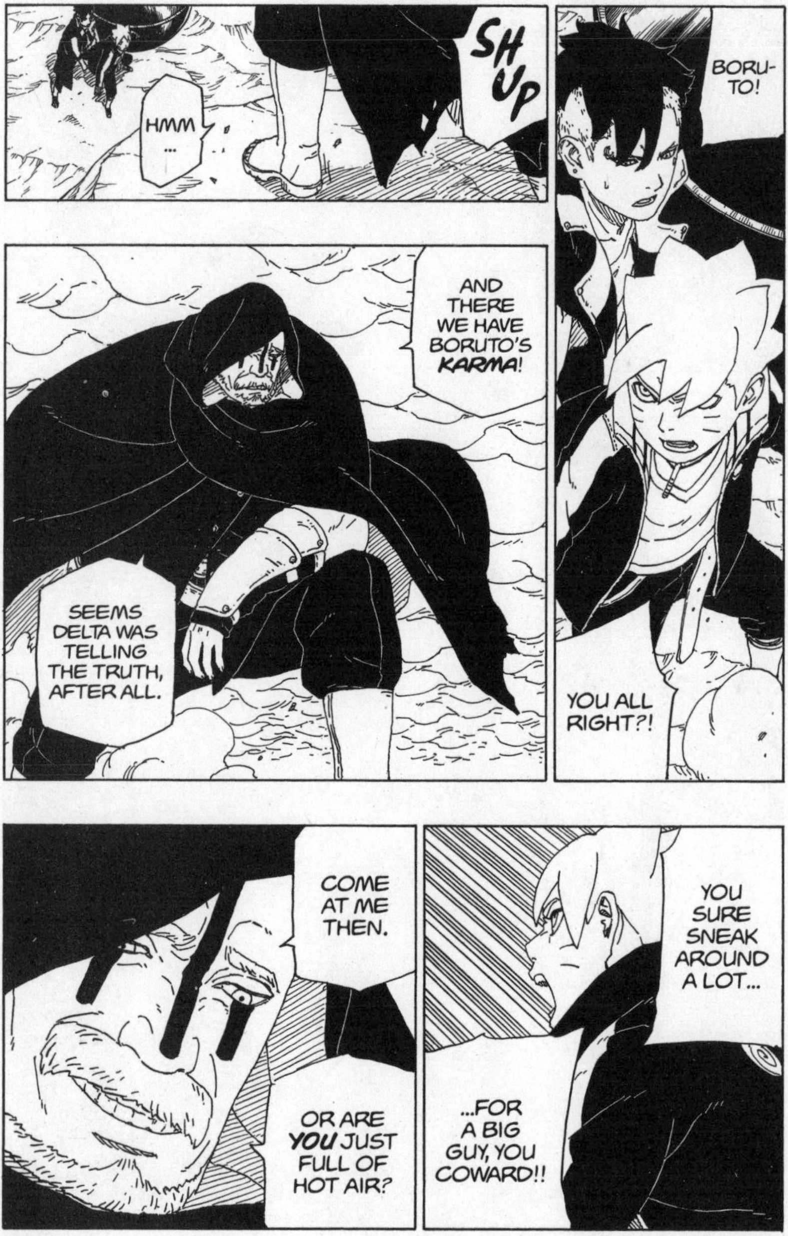
BORU-TO!
YOU ALL RIGHT?!
SHUP
HMM ...
AND THERE WE HAVE BORUTO'S *KARMA*!
SEEMS DELTA WAS TELLING THE TRUTH, AFTER ALL.
YOU SURE SNEAK AROUND A LOT...
...FOR A BIG GUY, YOU COWARD!!
COME AT ME THEN.
OR ARE ***YOU*** JUST FULL OF HOT AIR?

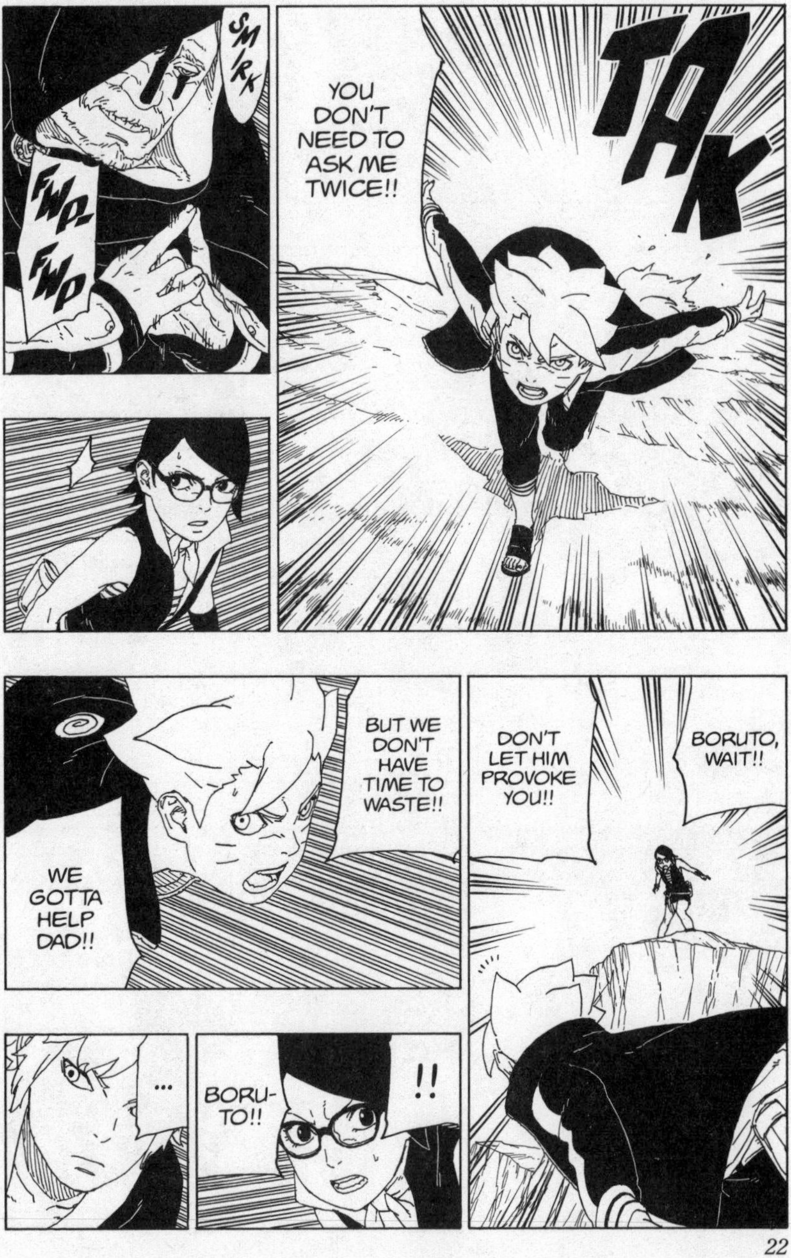
TAK
YOU DON'T NEED TO ASK ME TWICE!!
SMIRK
FWP-FWP
BORUTO, WAIT!!
DON'T LET HIM PROVOKE YOU!!
BUT WE DON'T HAVE TIME TO WASTE!!
WE GOTTA HELP DAD!!
!!
BORU-TO!!
...

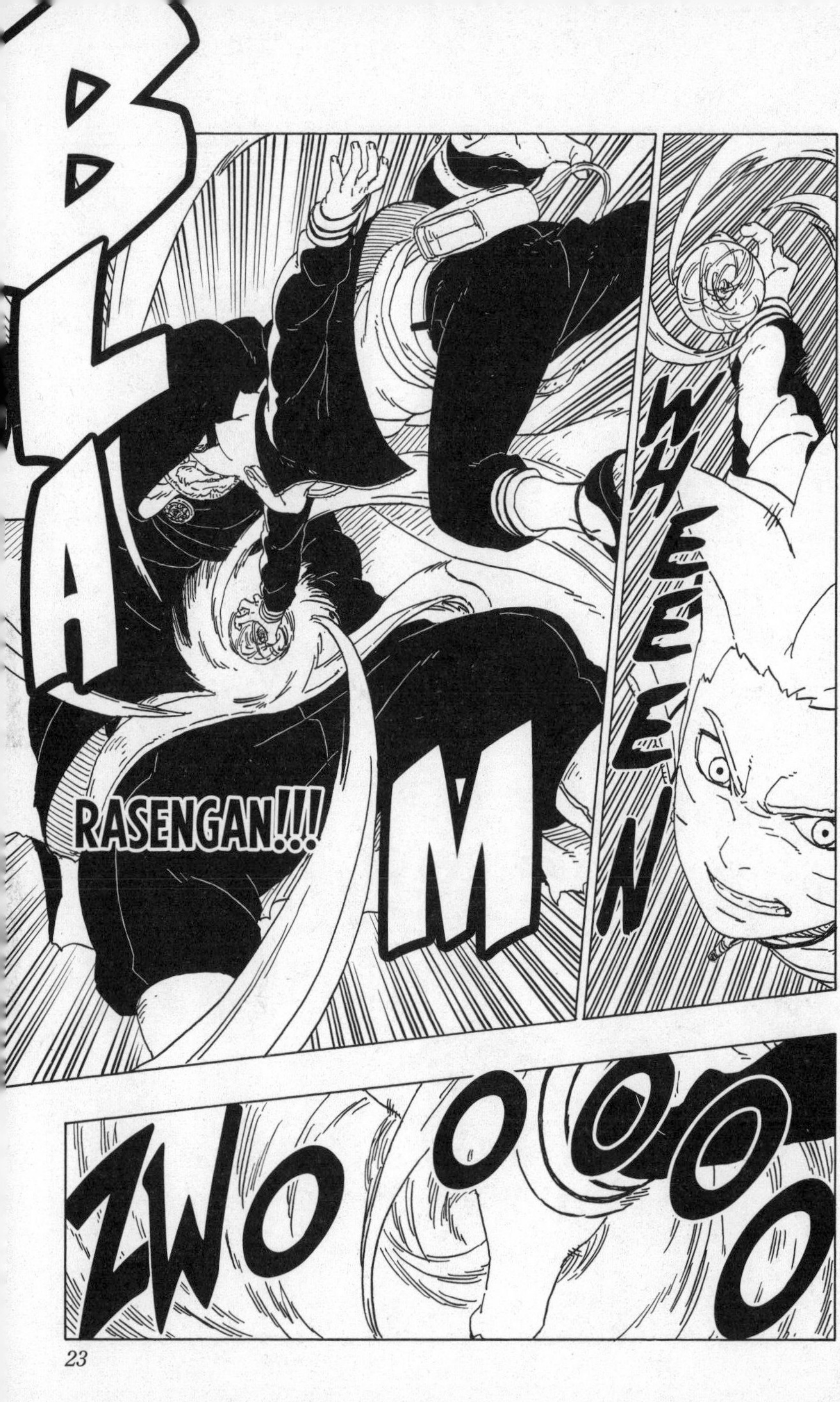
WHEEEEN
BLAM
RASENGAN!!!
ZWOOOOOO

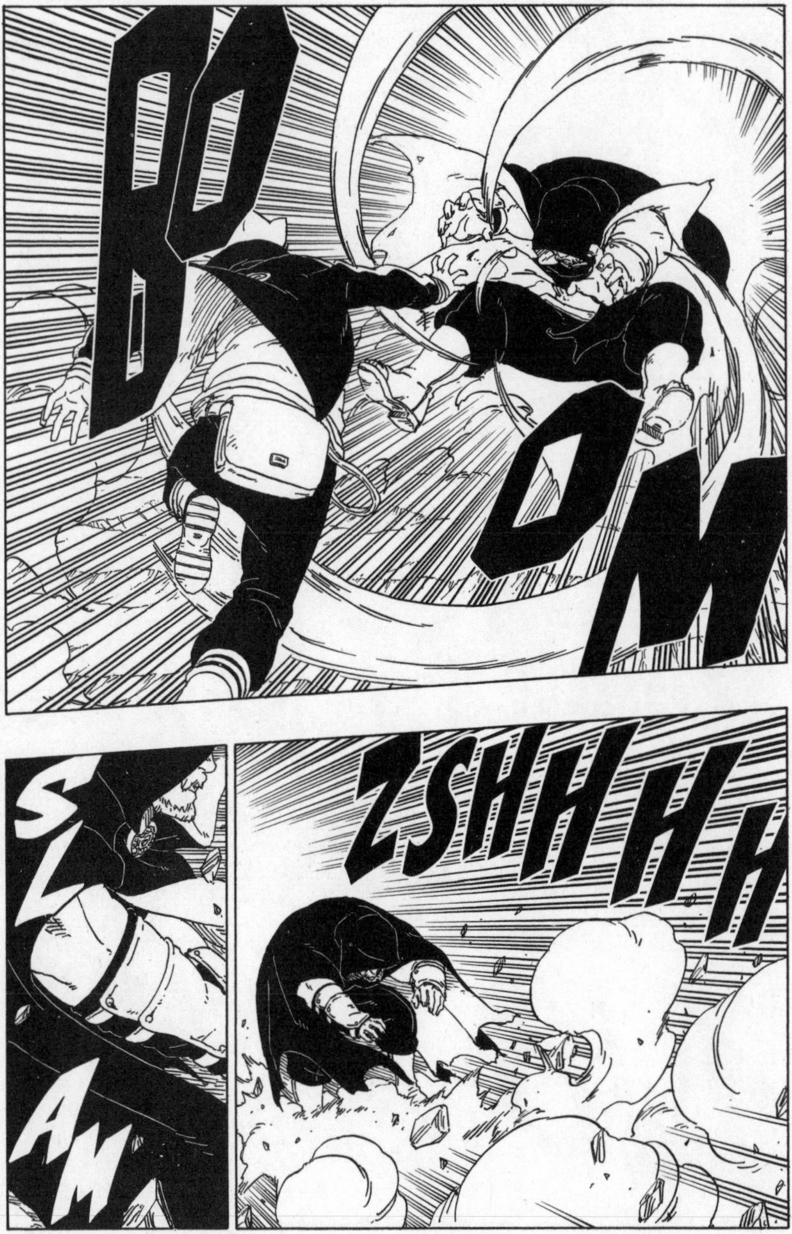
BOOM
ZSHHHH
SLAM

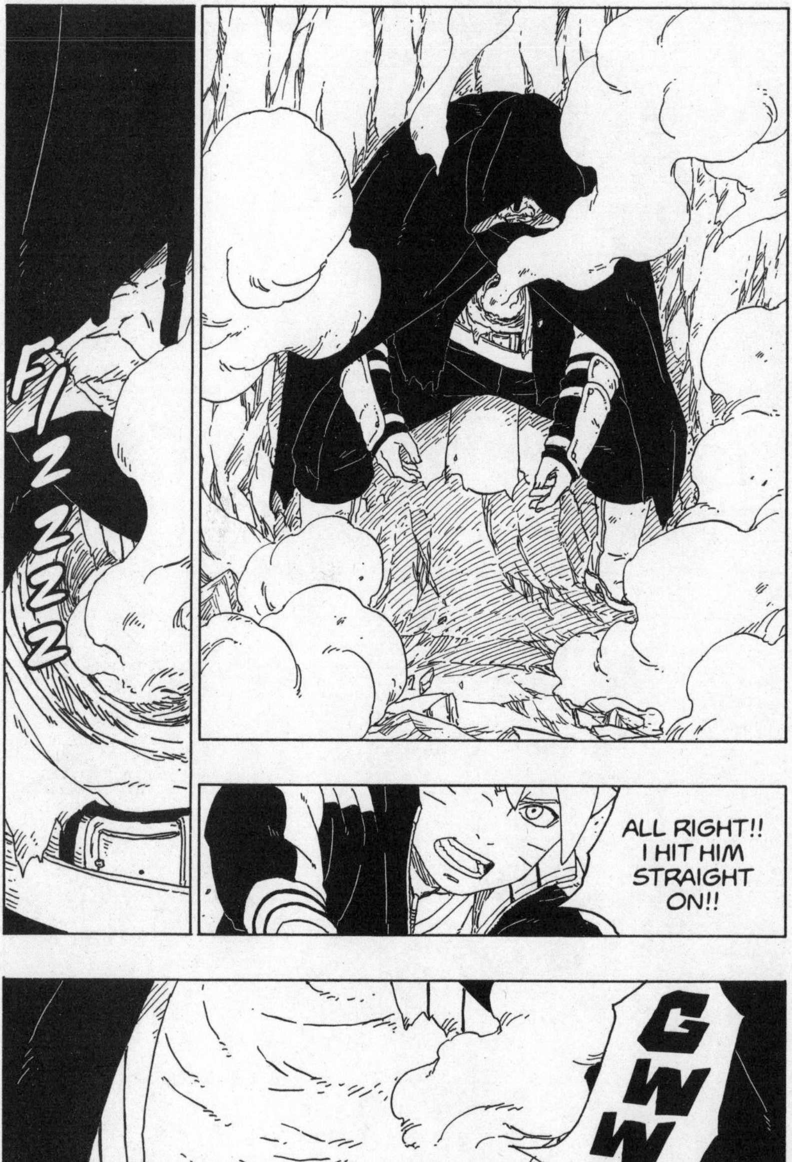
ALL RIGHT!! I HIT HIM STRAIGHT ON!!
FIZZZZ
GWWW

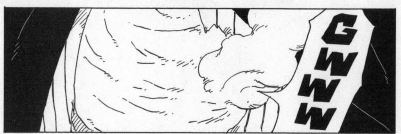

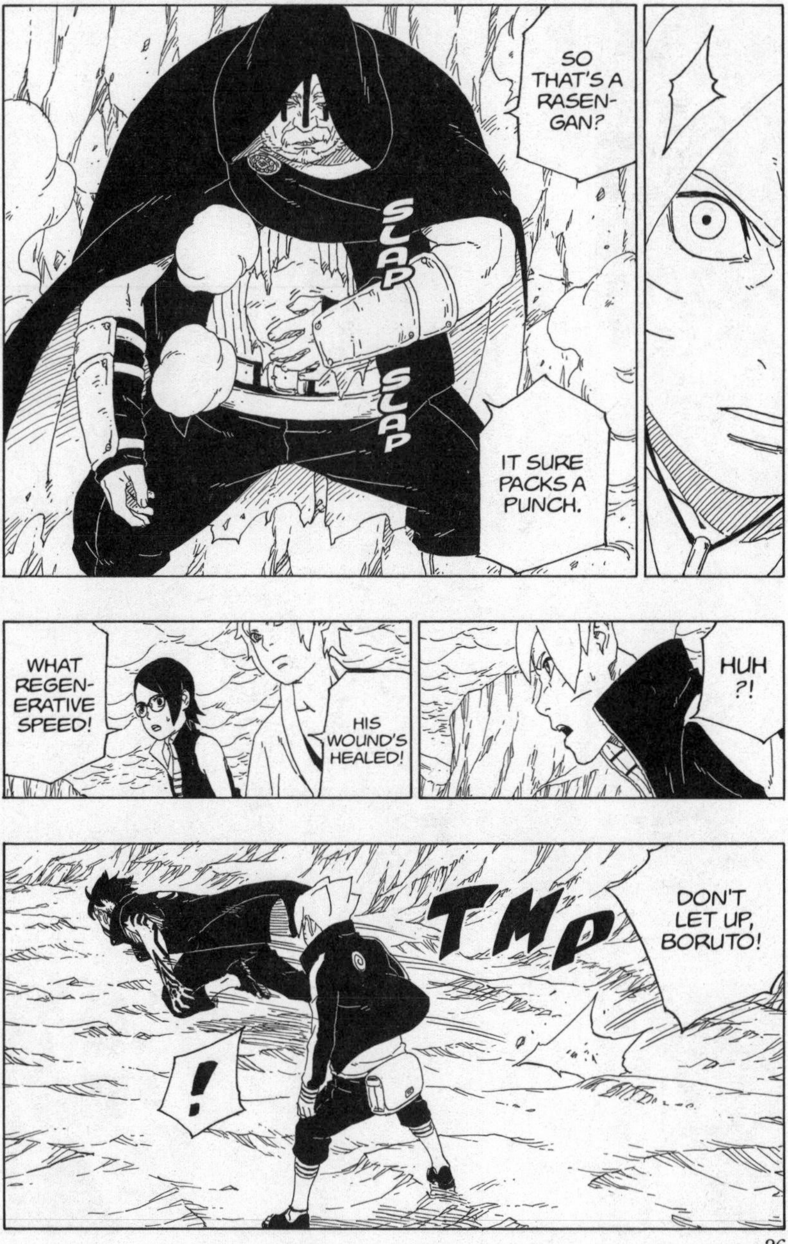

SO THAT'S A RASEN-GAN?
SLAP
SLAP
IT SURE PACKS A PUNCH.
HUH ?!
HIS WOUND'S HEALED!
WHAT REGEN-ERATIVE SPEED!
DON'T LET UP, BORUTO!
TMP
!

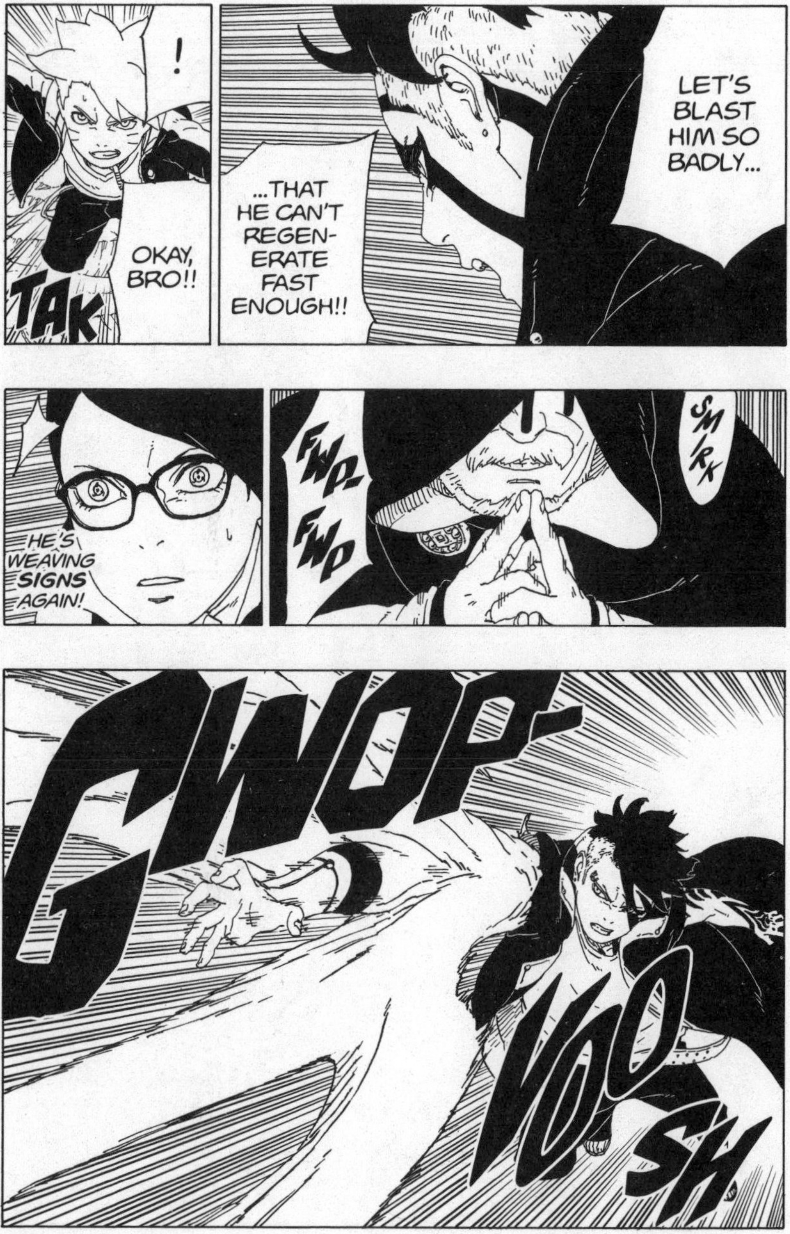
LET'S BLAST HIM SO BADLY...
...THAT HE CAN'T REGENERATE FAST ENOUGH!!
!
OKAY, BRO!!
TAK
SMIRK
FWP- FWP
HE'S WEAVING SIGNS AGAIN!
GWOP-
VOOOSH

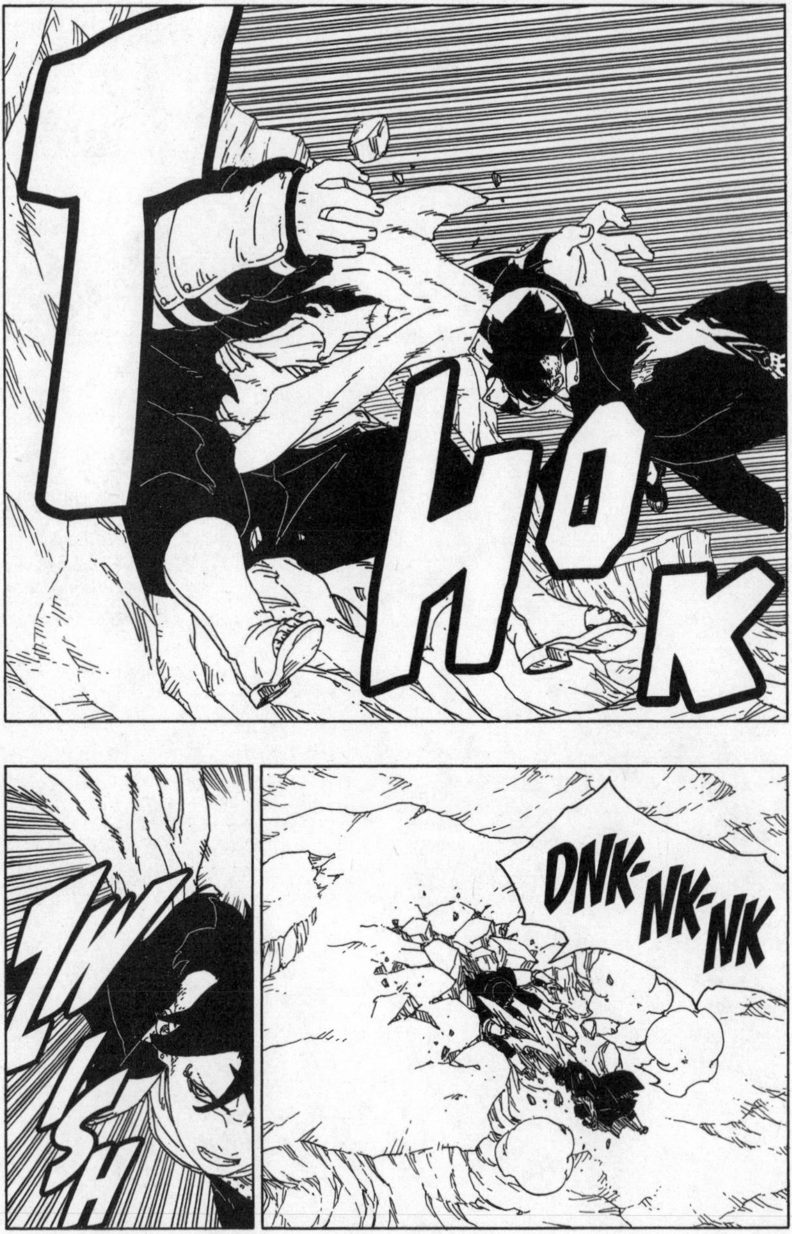
THOK
DNK-NK-NK
ZWISH

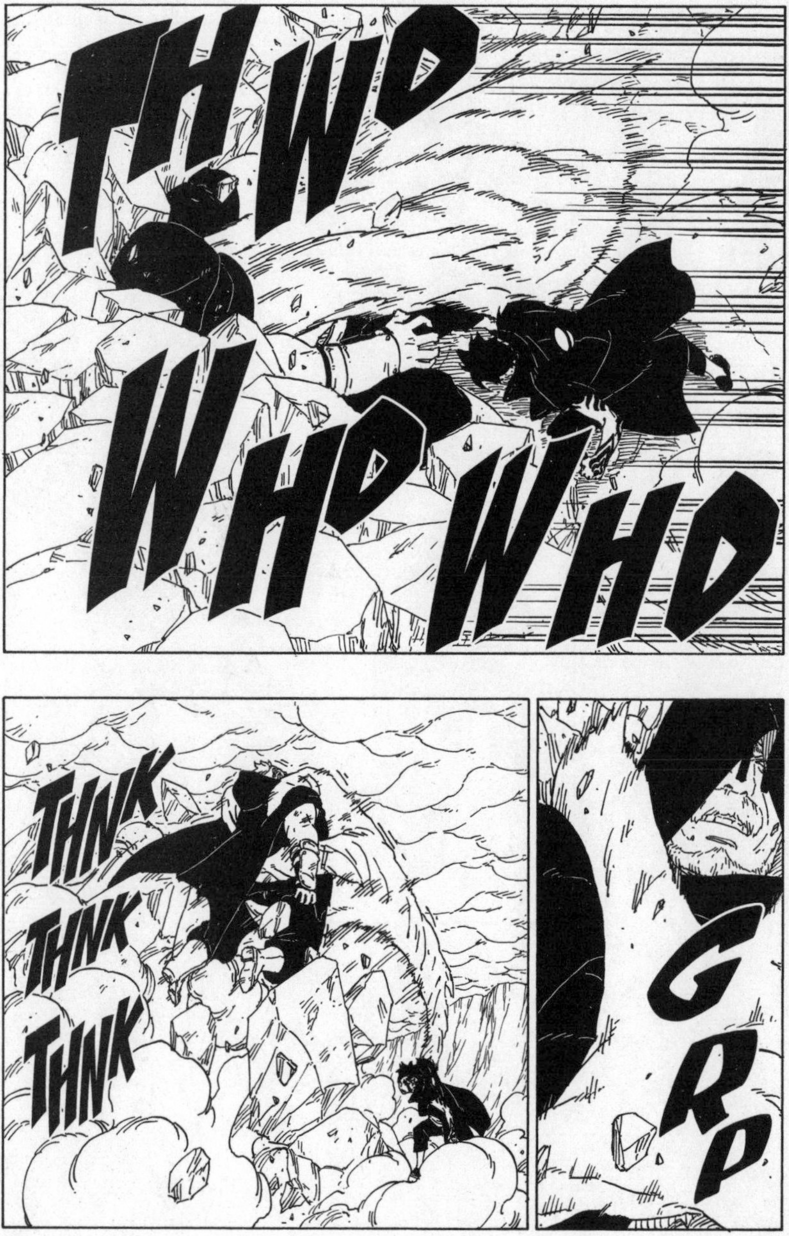
THWD
WHD WHD
GRP
THNK
THNK
THNK

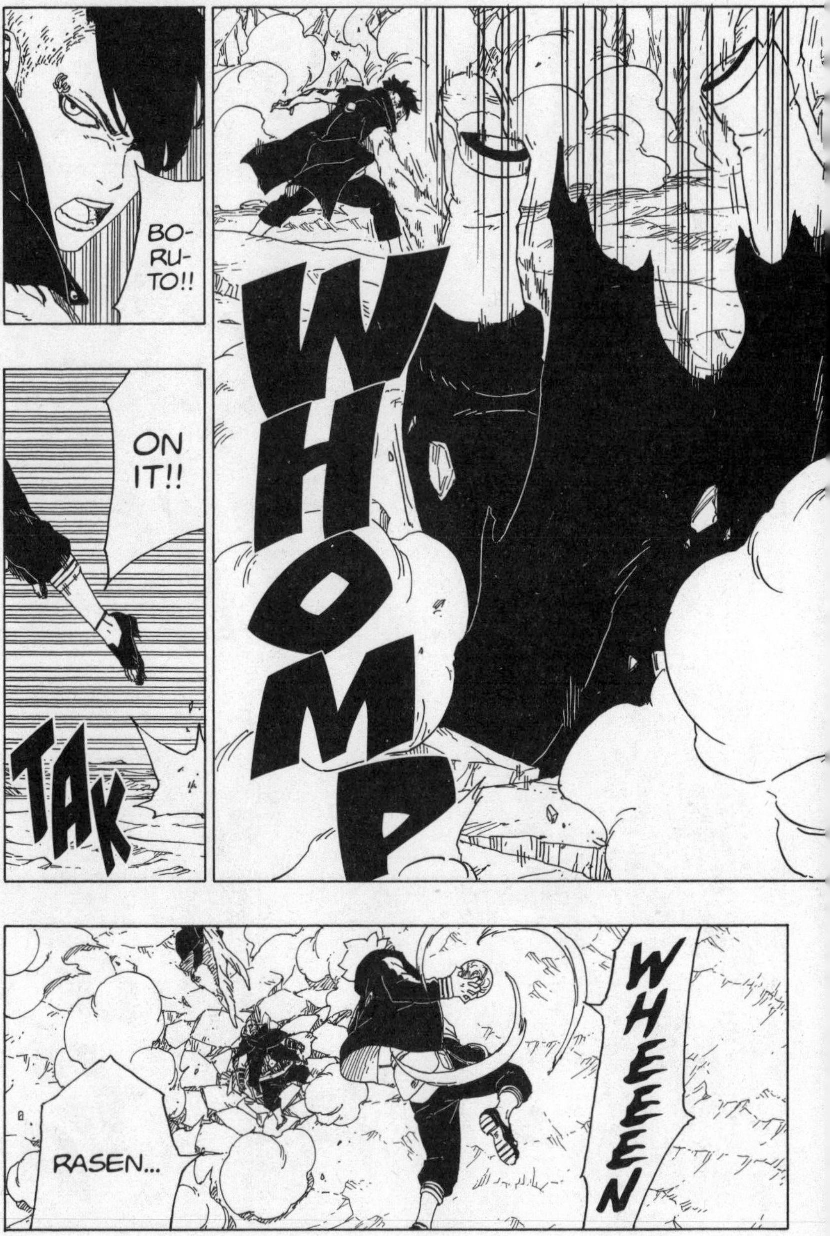
WHOMP
BO-RU-TO!!
ON IT!!
TAK
WHEEEN
RASEN...

...

HUH
?!

?!

GUH...

BORU...

HEY, WHAT HAP-PENED ?!

GWW

?!

DAM-MIT...!

D- D...

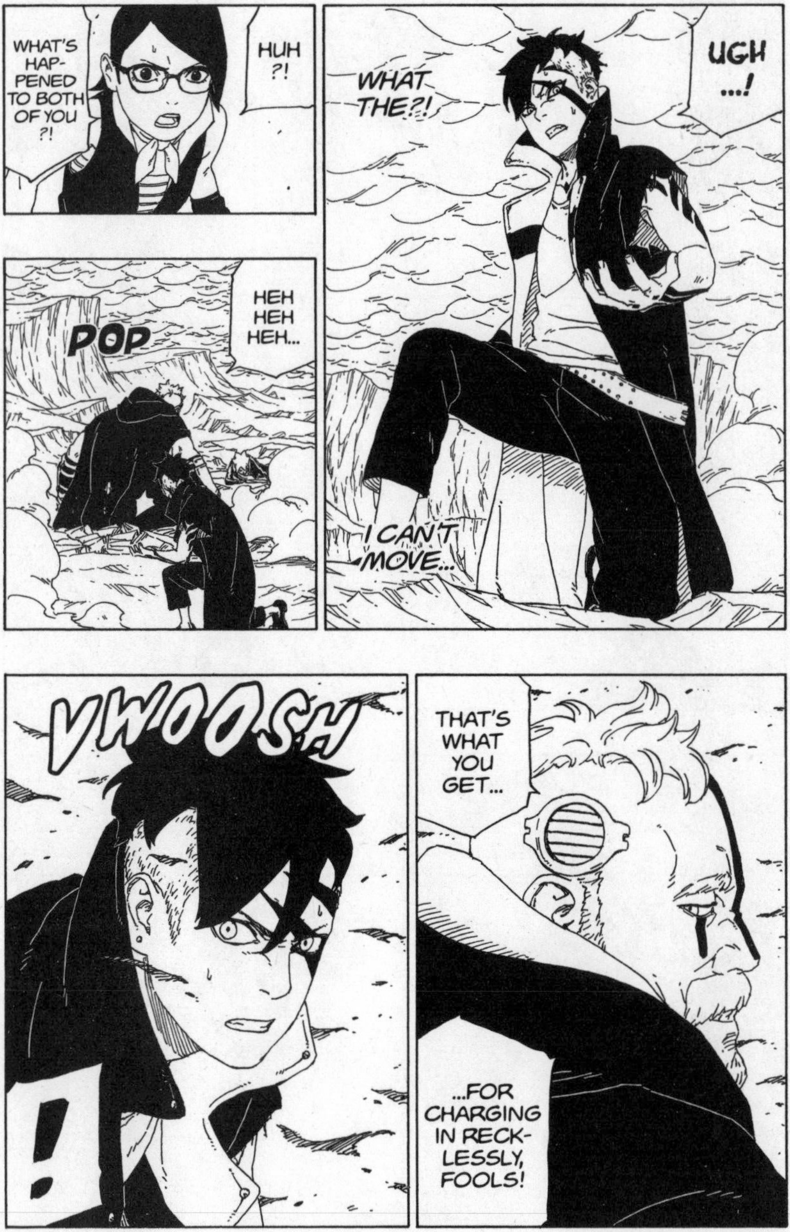
UGH ...!
WHAT THE?!
I CAN'T MOVE...
HUH ?!
WHAT'S HAP- PENED TO BOTH OF YOU ?!
HEH HEH HEH...
POP
THAT'S WHAT YOU GET...
...FOR CHARGING IN RECK- LESSLY, FOOLS!
VWOOSH
!

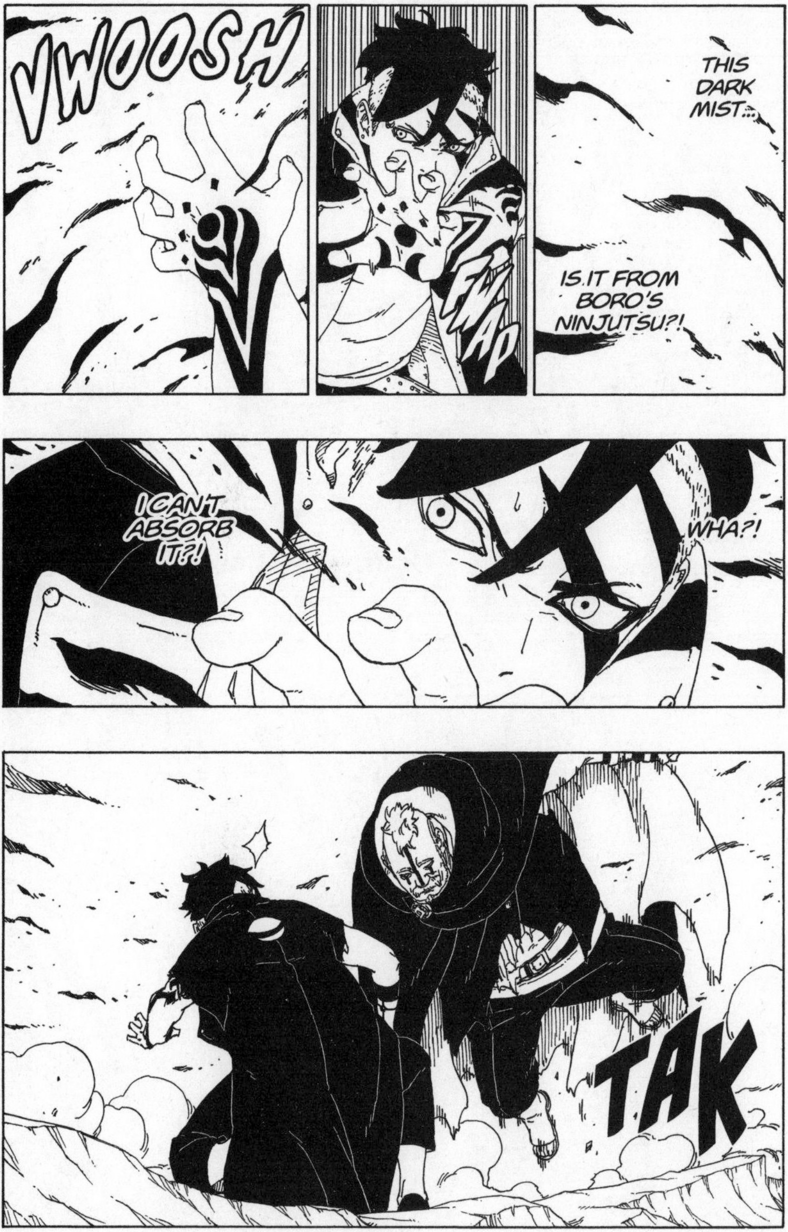
THIS DARK MIST...
IS IT FROM BORO'S NINJUTSU?!
FWAP
VWOOSH
WHA?!
I CAN'T ABSORB IT?!
TAK

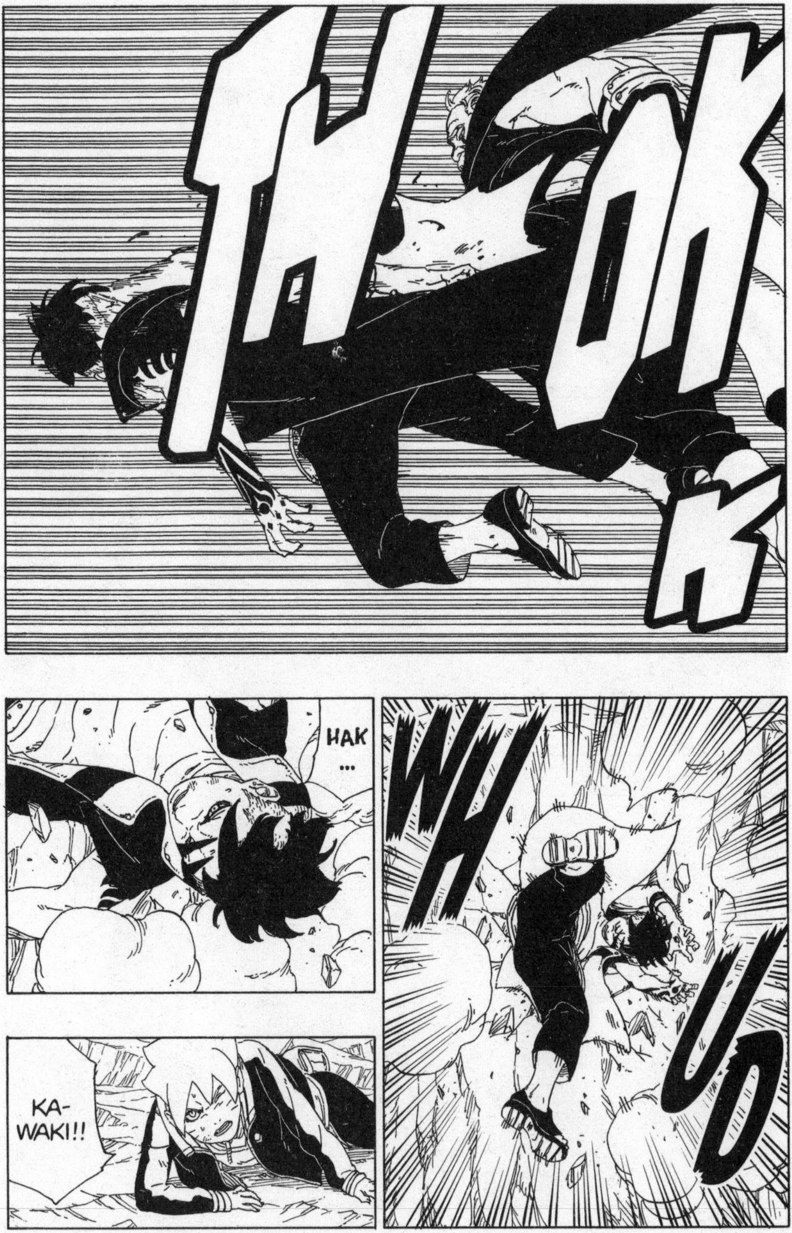
HAK ...
KA-WAKI!!

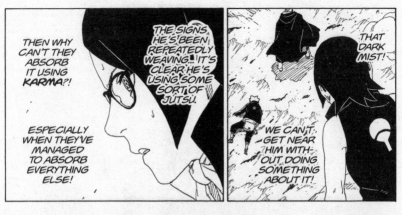

THAT DARK MIST!
WE CAN'T GET NEAR HIM WITHOUT DOING SOMETHING ABOUT IT!
THE SIGNS HE'S BEEN REPEATEDLY WEAVING... IT'S CLEAR HE'S USING SOME SORT OF JUTSU.
THEN WHY CAN'T THEY ABSORB IT USING **KARMA**?!
ESPECIALLY WHEN THEY'VE MANAGED TO ABSORB EVERYTHING ELSE!
VWOOOOO
NOW THEN ...
BORUTO, SON OF THE HOKAGE...
...AND OHTSUTSUKI MOMOSHIKI'S **VESSEL**.
I'M HAPPY I GOT TO MEET YOU...
I HAVEN'T BEEN THIS HAPPY SINCE KAWAKI FIRST SHOWED UP.

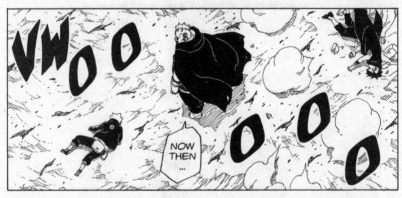

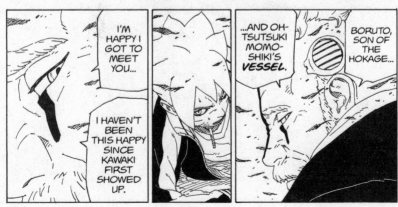

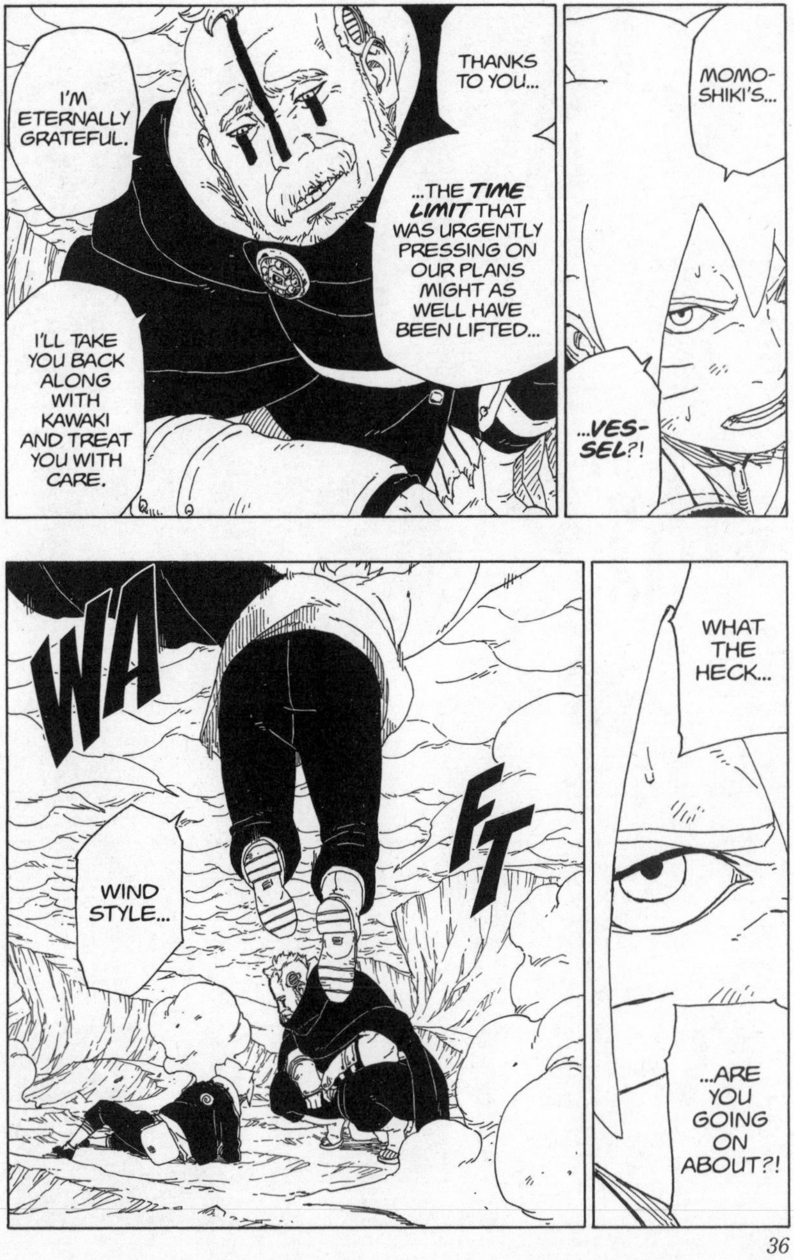
MOMO-SHIKI'S...
...VES-SEL?!
THANKS TO YOU...
...THE TIME LIMIT THAT WAS URGENTLY PRESSING ON OUR PLANS MIGHT AS WELL HAVE BEEN LIFTED...
I'M ETERNALLY GRATEFUL.
I'LL TAKE YOU BACK ALONG WITH KAWAKI AND TREAT YOU WITH CARE.
WHAT THE HECK...
...ARE YOU GOING ON ABOUT?!
WA
FT
WIND STYLE...

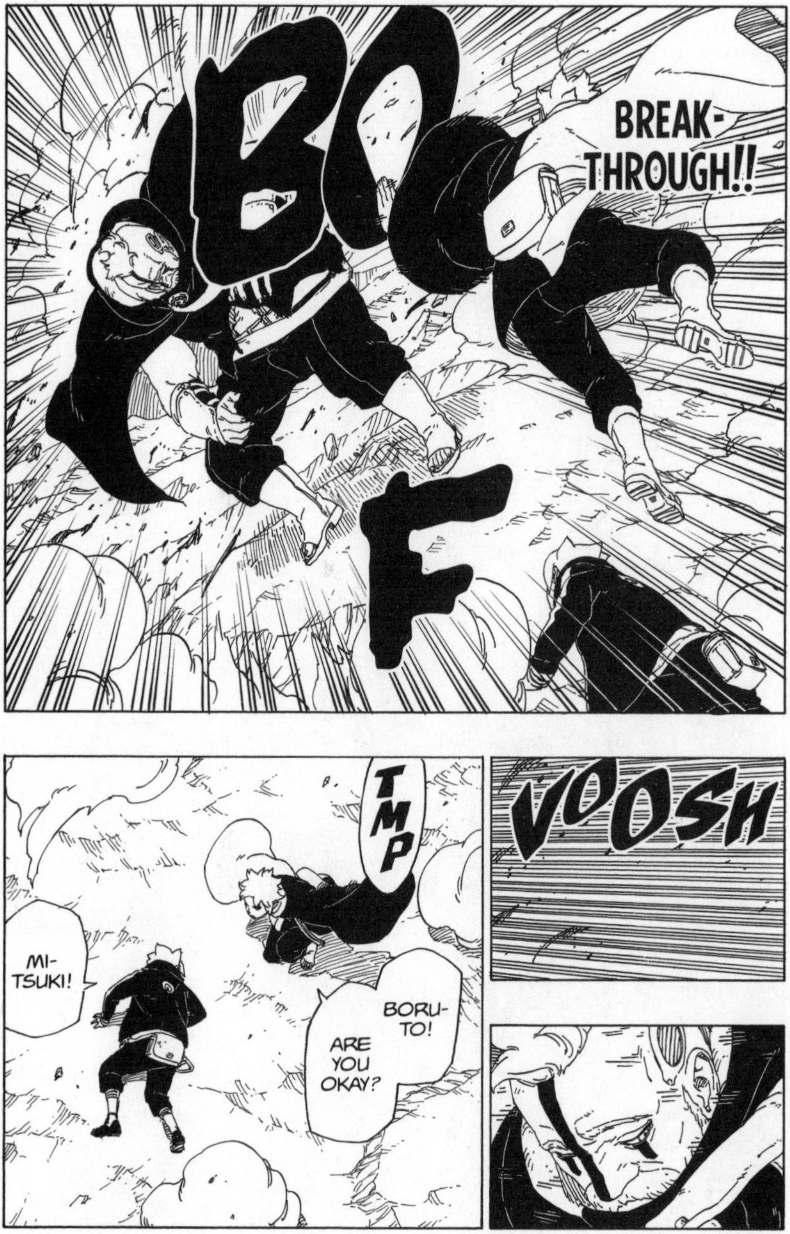
BOF
BREAK-THROUGH!!
VOOSH
TMP
BORU-TO!
ARE YOU OKAY?
MI-TSUKI!

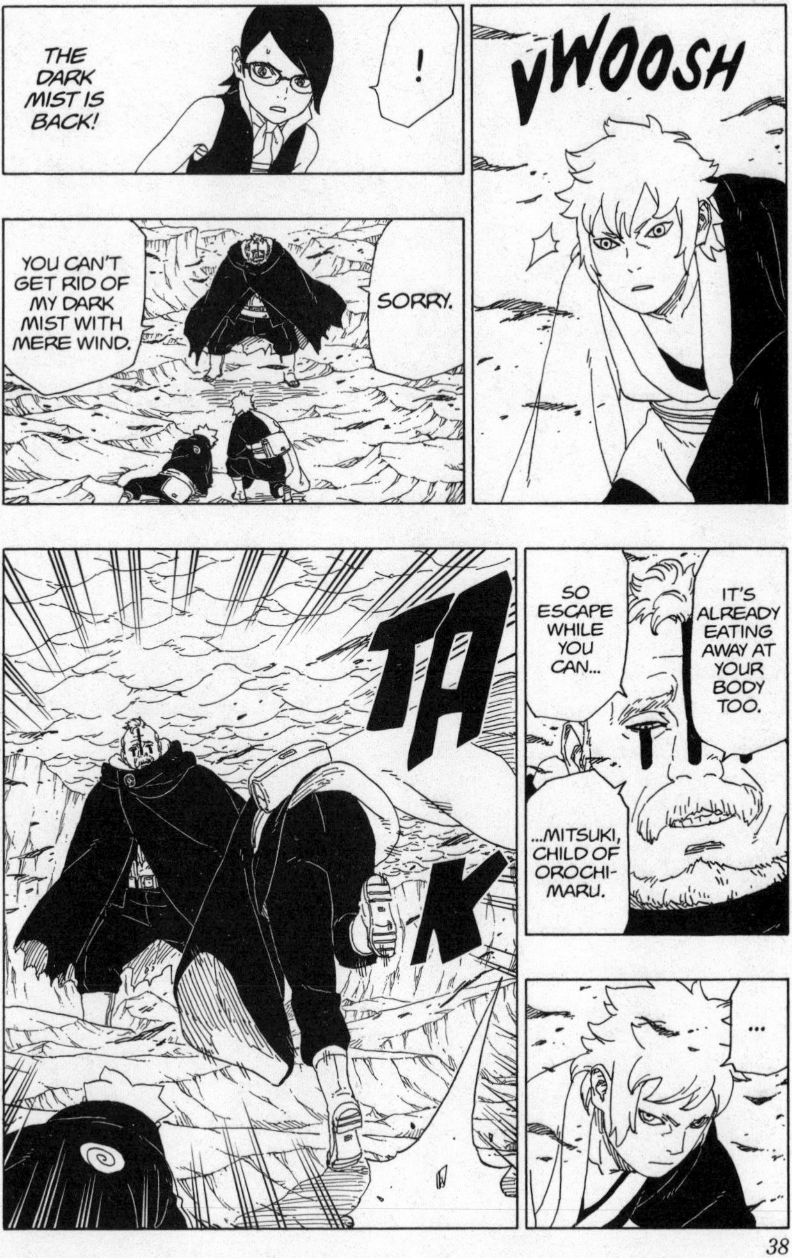
VWOOSH
!
THE DARK MIST IS BACK!
SORRY.
YOU CAN'T GET RID OF MY DARK MIST WITH MERE WIND.
IT'S ALREADY EATING AWAY AT YOUR BODY TOO.
SO ESCAPE WHILE YOU CAN...
...MITSUKI, CHILD OF OROCHI-MARU.
...
TA
K

LIGHTNING STYLE, SNAKE LIGHTNING!!
KRACKLE-KRACKLE
FWP-FWP
WATER STYLE, WALL OF WATER!!
WHAP
BZAP-ZP-ZP

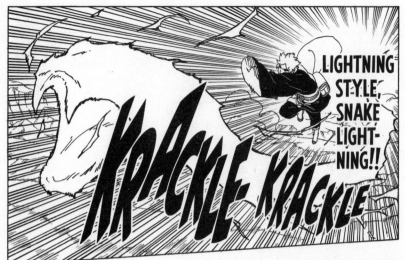

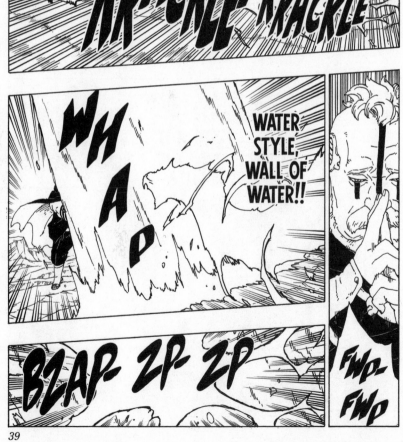

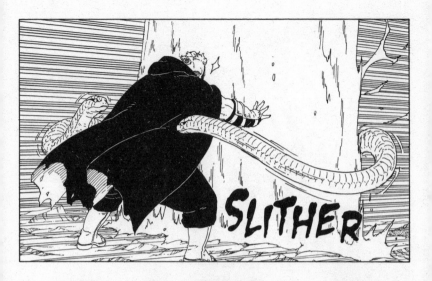

SLITHER
...
MY LIGHTNING ATTACK WAS JUST A DIVERSION.
NOT THAT I REALLY NEED TO EXPLAIN.
YEAH, YOU'RE RIGHT ABOUT THAT.
COMPLETELY IRRELEVANT.

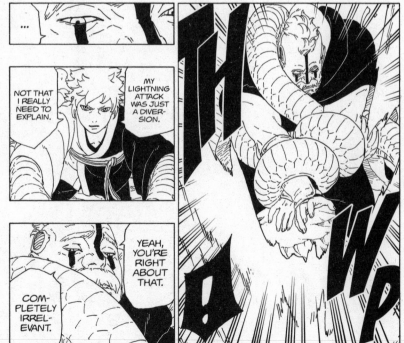

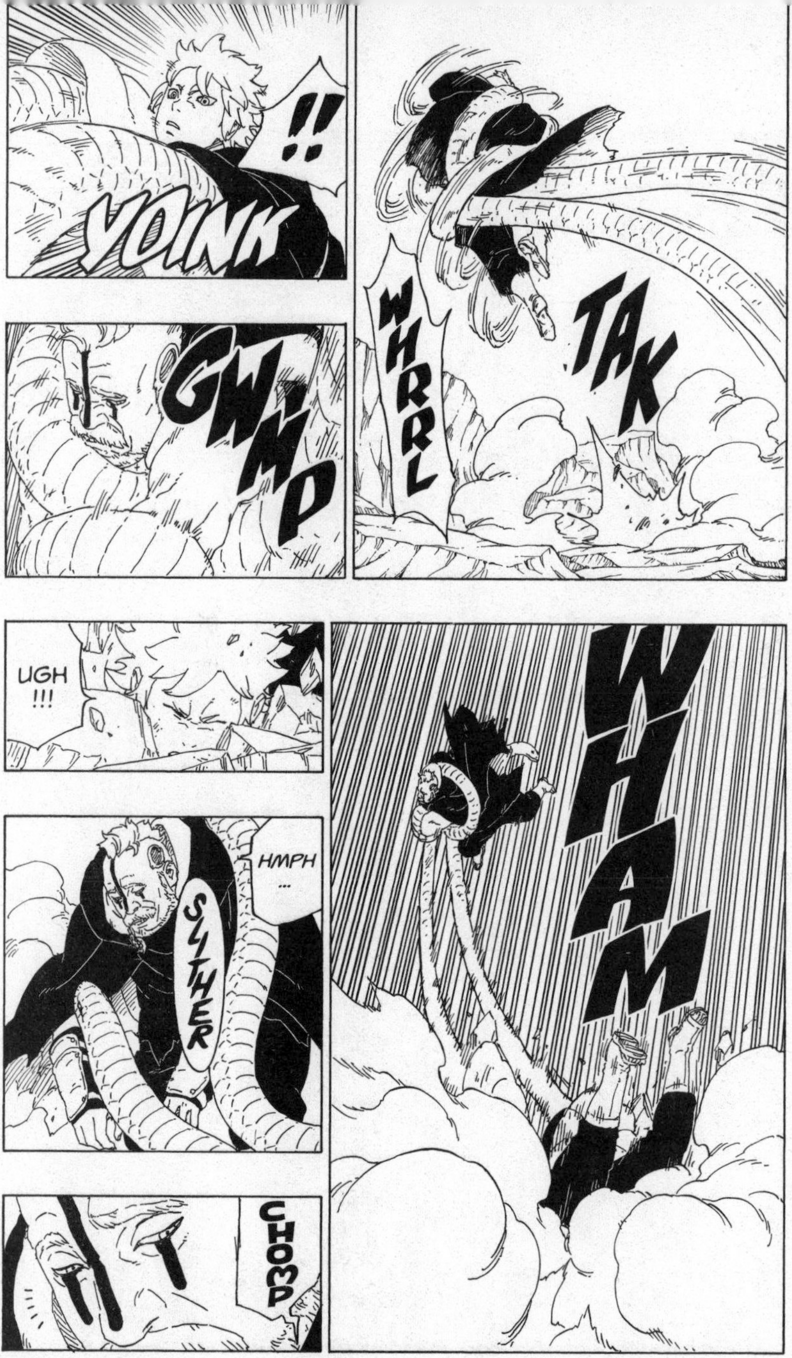
TAK
WHRRL
!!
YOINK
GWMP
WHAM
UGH !!!
HMPH ...
SLITHER
CHOMP

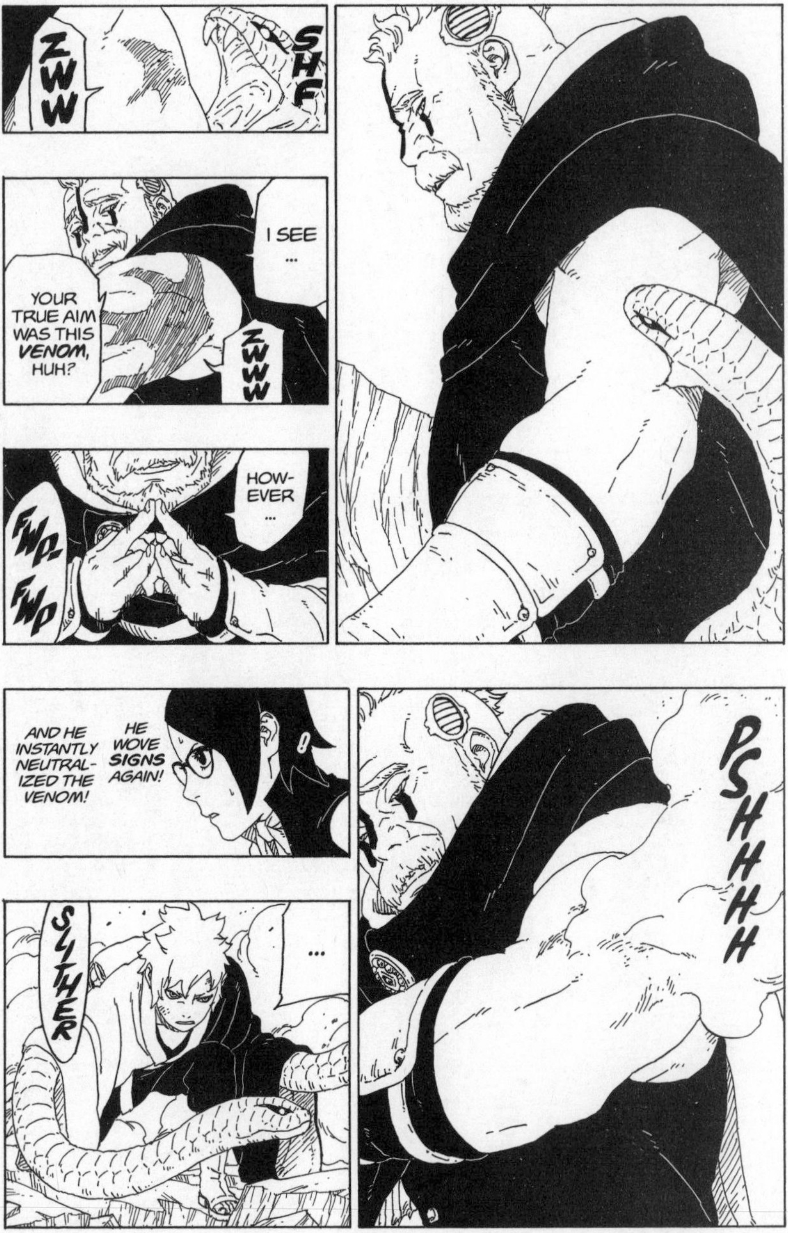
SHF
ZWW
I SEE ...
YOUR TRUE AIM WAS THIS VENOM, HUH?
ZWWW
HOW-EVER ...
FWP-FWP
PSHHHH
HE WOVE SIGNS AGAIN!
AND HE INSTANTLY NEUTRAL-IZED THE VENOM!
...
SLITHER

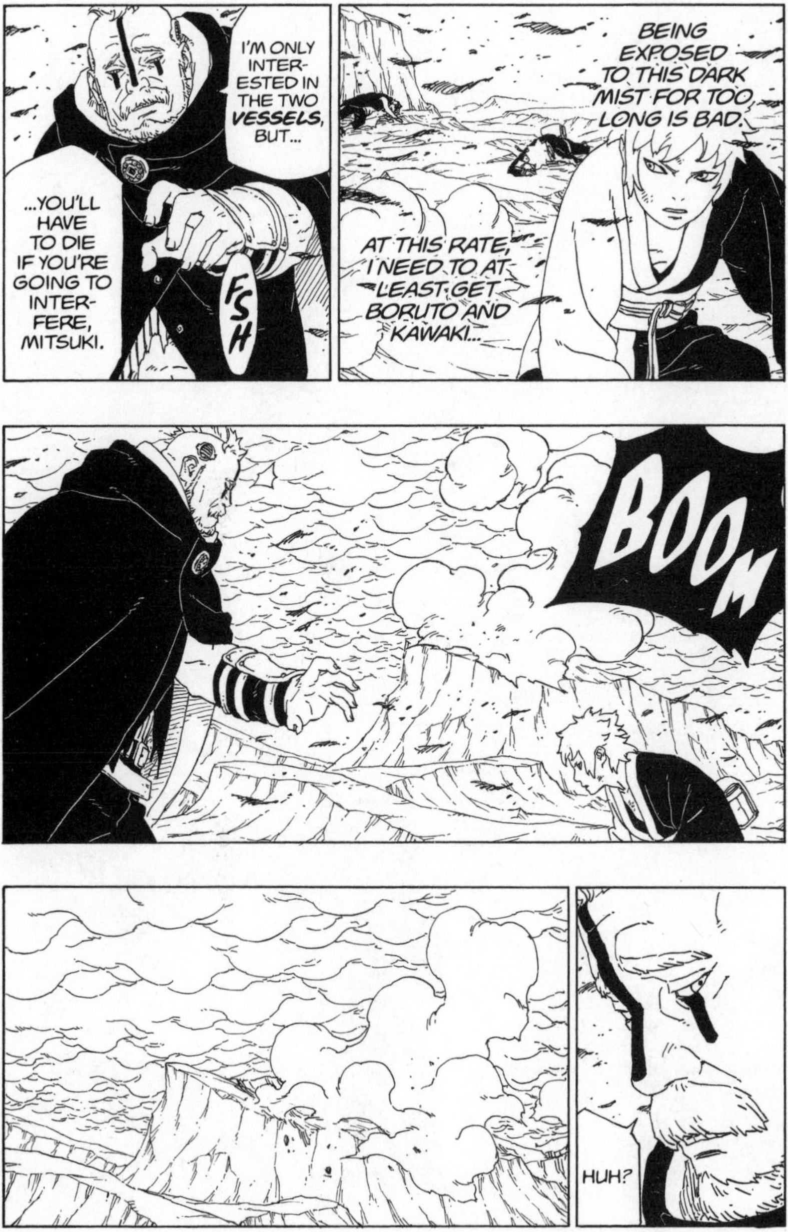
BEING EXPOSED TO THIS DARK MIST FOR TOO LONG IS BAD.
AT THIS RATE, I NEED TO AT LEAST GET BORUTO AND KAWAKI...
I'M ONLY INTERESTED IN THE TWO VESSELS, BUT...
FSH
...YOU'LL HAVE TO DIE IF YOU'RE GOING TO INTERFERE, MITSUKI.
BOOM
HUH?

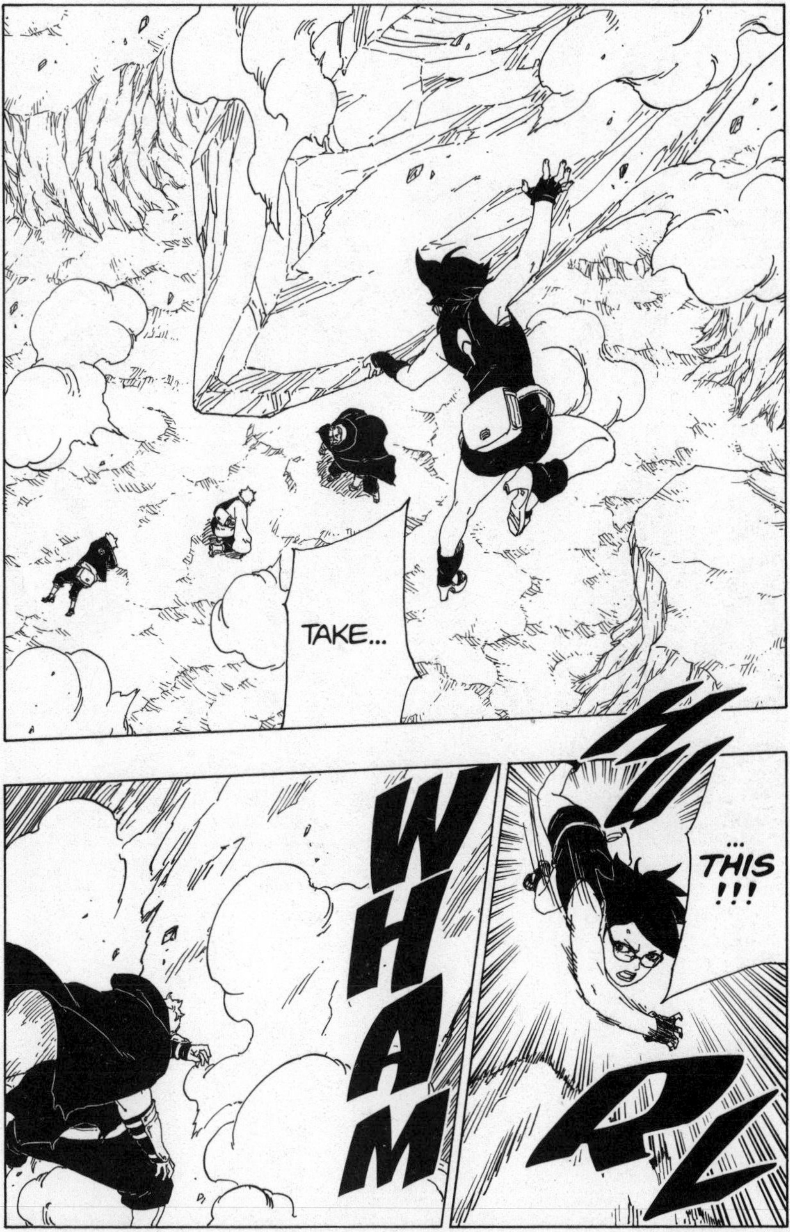
TAKE...
...THIS!!!
WHAM

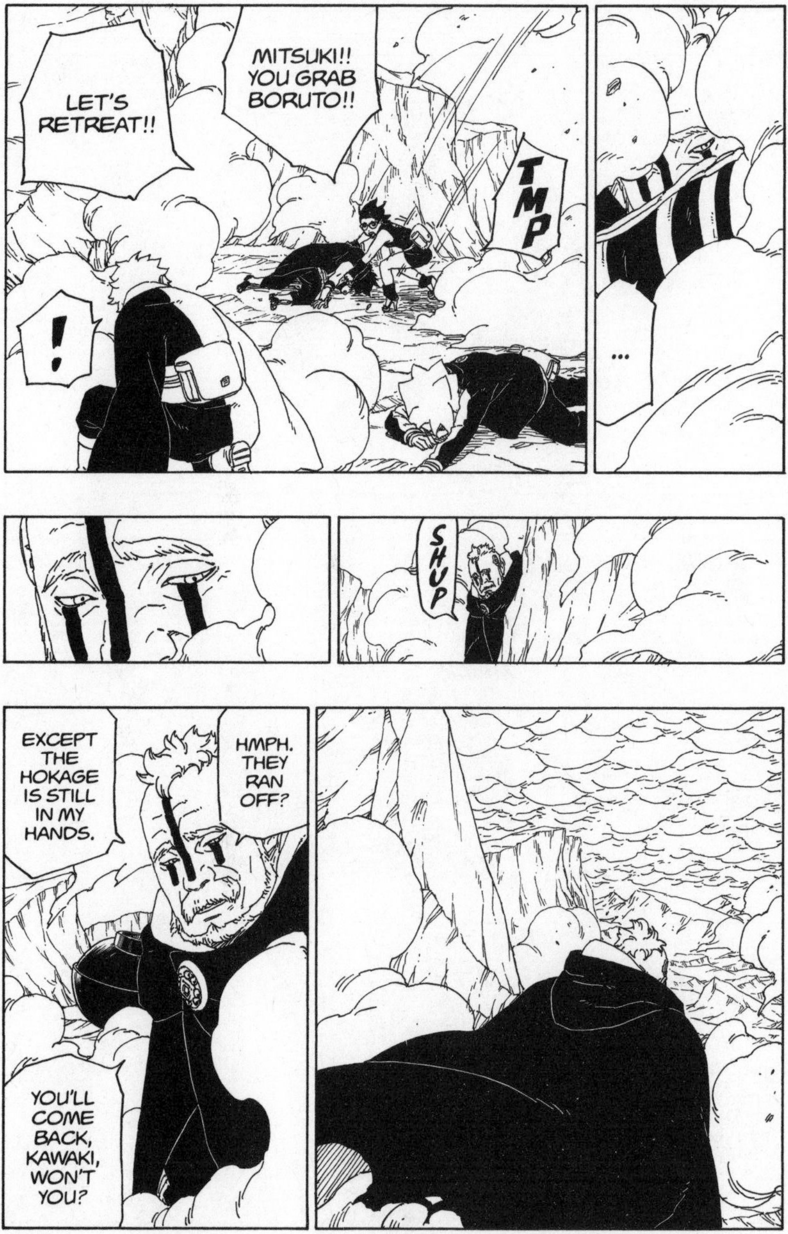

...
TMP
MITSUKI!! YOU GRAB BORUTO!!
LET'S RETREAT!!
!
SHUP
HMPH. THEY RAN OFF?
EXCEPT THE HOKAGE IS STILL IN MY HANDS.
YOU'LL COME BACK, KAWAKI, WON'T YOU?

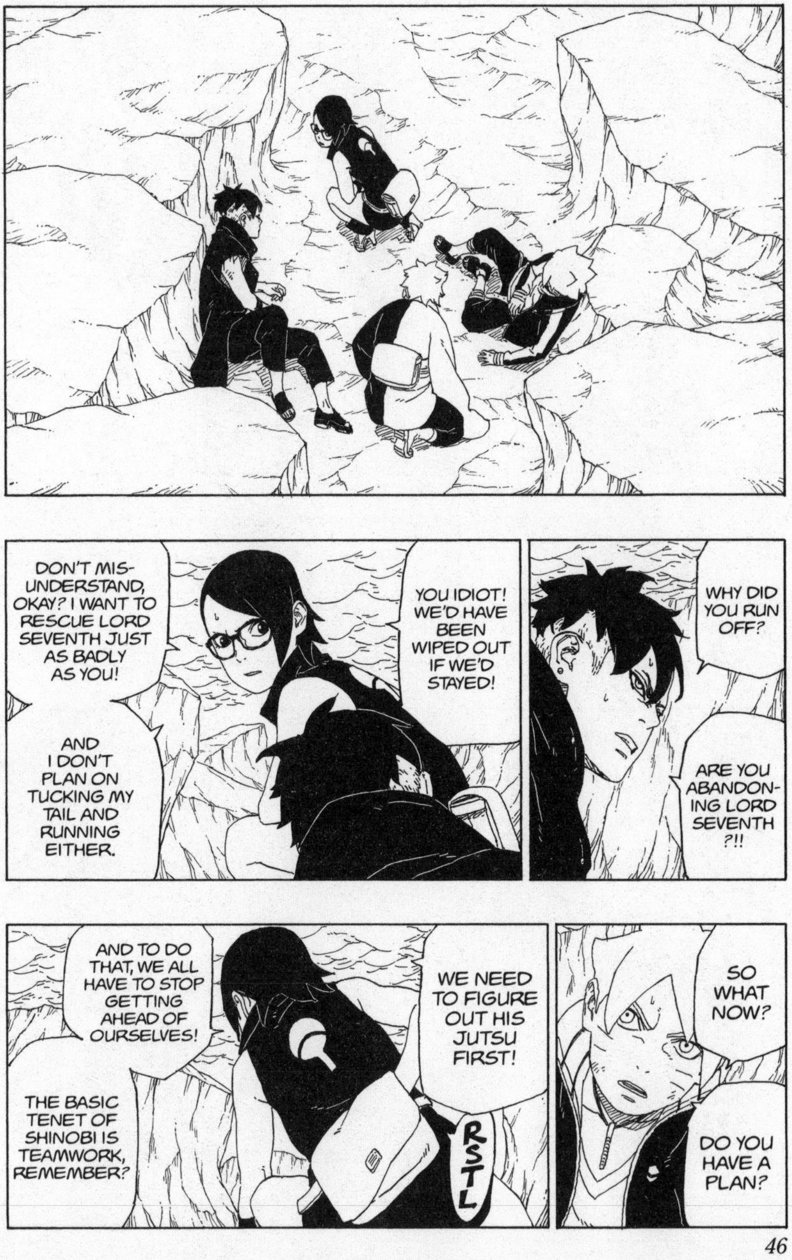
WHY DID YOU RUN OFF?
ARE YOU ABANDON-ING LORD SEVENTH ?!!
YOU IDIOT! WE'D HAVE BEEN WIPED OUT IF WE'D STAYED!
DON'T MIS-UNDERSTAND, OKAY? I WANT TO RESCUE LORD SEVENTH JUST AS BADLY AS YOU!
AND I DON'T PLAN ON TUCKING MY TAIL AND RUNNING EITHER.
SO WHAT NOW?
DO YOU HAVE A PLAN?
WE NEED TO FIGURE OUT HIS JUTSU FIRST!
AND TO DO THAT, WE ALL HAVE TO STOP GETTING AHEAD OF OURSELVES!
RSTL
THE BASIC TENET OF SHINOBI IS TEAMWORK, REMEMBER?

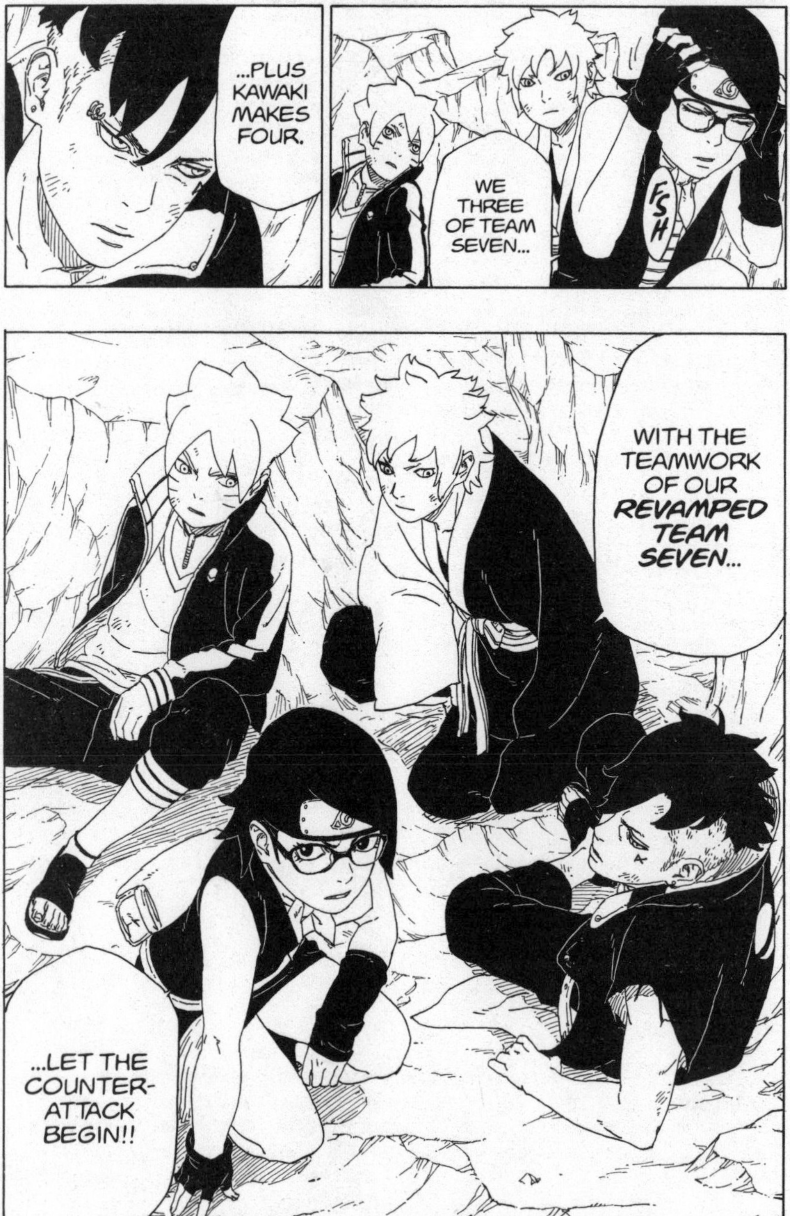

WE THREE OF TEAM SEVEN...
FSH
...PLUS KAWAKI MAKES FOUR.
WITH THE TEAMWORK OF OUR *REVAMPED TEAM SEVEN...*
...LET THE COUNTER-ATTACK BEGIN!!

## Shinobi Hiden Column 8: Scientific Ninja Tools

Scientific Ninja Tools

These are the Ninja Tools of the new era following the last Great Ninja War. They resulted from explosive development brought about by the postwar technology exchange between Villages and the release of private sector technology previously kept secret by the military sector.

The objects branded as Scientific Ninja Tools can be broadly divided into the following four categories:

① Capacitor Types

They operate by utilizing a chakra condenser to charge up the chakra necessary for using jutsu, then loading and activating jutsu sealed within miniaturized scrolls. As long as you know how to use the equipment, you can generate jutsu even if you don't have chakra or know how to weave jutsu. (There are, of course, limits to the condenser's capacity and the types of jutsu you can generate.)

The "shinobi gauntlet" Boruto inappropriately used during the Chunin Exams is representative.

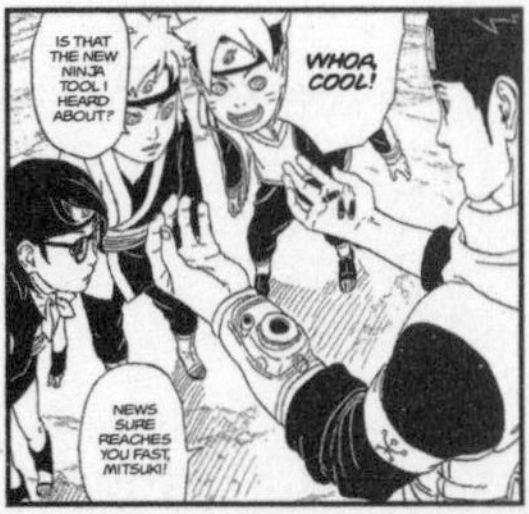
WHOA, COOL!
IS THAT THE NEW NINJA TOOL I HEARD ABOUT?
NEWS SURE REACHES YOU FAST, MITSUKI!

② Bionic Types

Extensions of the living body, such as prostheses and artificial organs, as exemplified by Naruto's prosthetic arm. Incorporating traditional puppet and Hashirama cell technology, it is possible to use ninjutsu and taijutsu just as with one's natural body, via synthetic meridians.

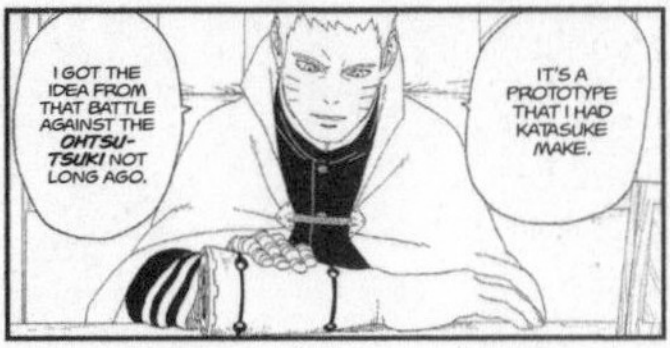
IT'S A PROTOTYPE THAT I HAD KATASUKE MAKE.
I GOT THE IDEA FROM THAT BATTLE AGAINST THE OHTSUTSUKI NOT LONG AGO.

Treatment technologies for ninja who lose parts of their body in fierce battle are seen as indispensable by all Villages, but after the Great Ninja War, they were also implemented in injured civilians.

Katasuke was originally a researcher in this field but has achieved success in the consumer sector as well.

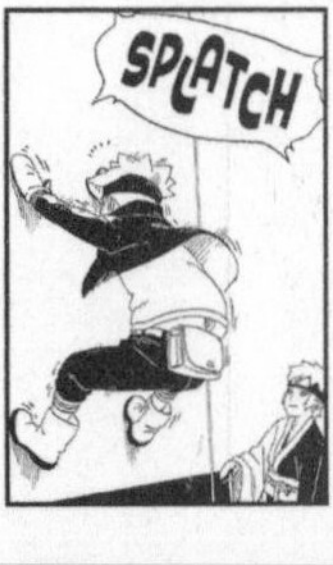
SPLATCH

③ Amplification Types

Scientific Ninja Tools that activate by amplifying the user's chakra and jutsu. The wall-adhering gloves that Inuzuka Akita developed correspond to this. While jutsu are used in their activation, the phenomena they manifest are purely physical (just like taijutsu), so they often are not affected by ninjutsu that absorb or neutralize jutsu.

Continued on page 130!!

Text: Ukyo Kodachi

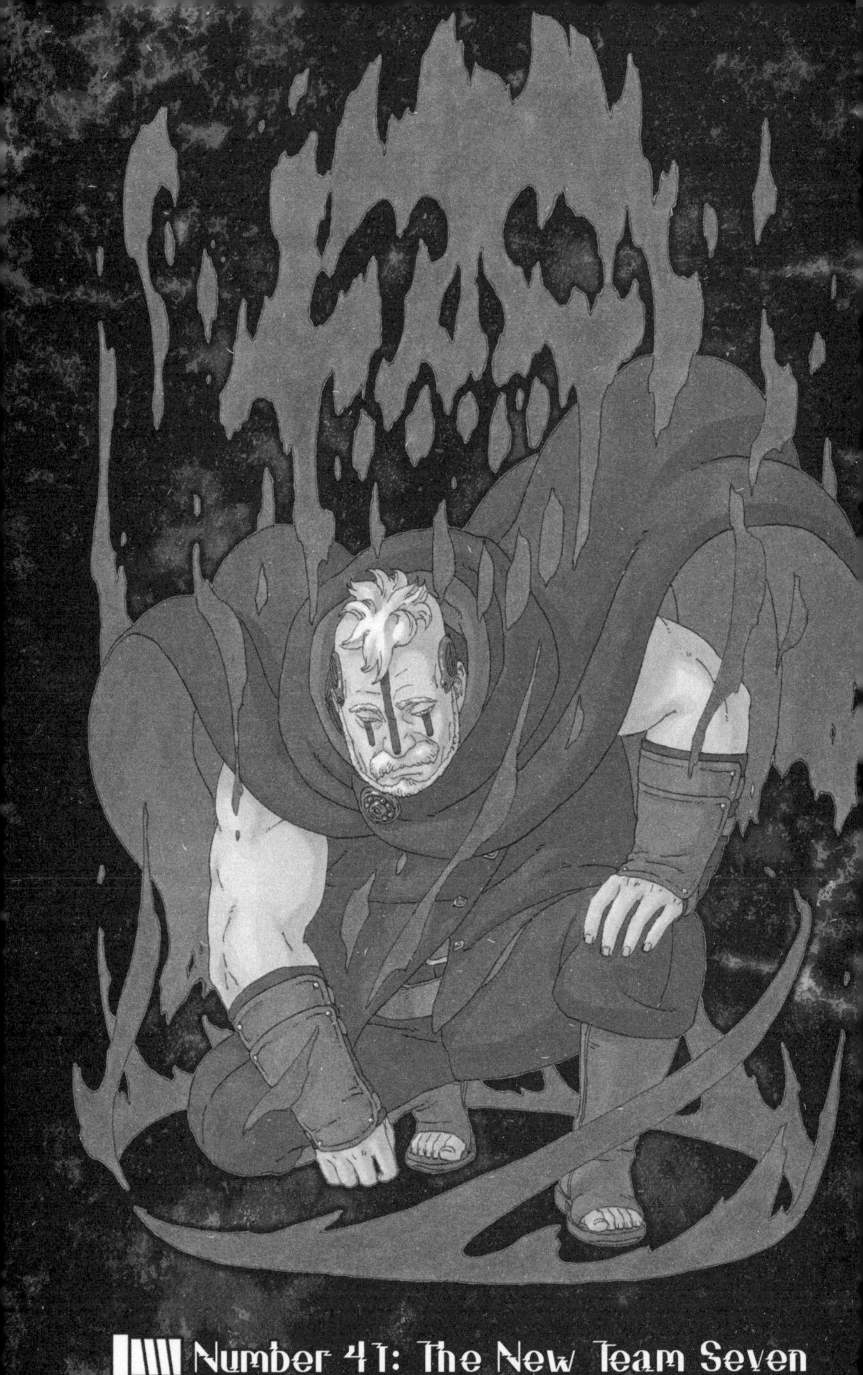

# Number 41: The New Team Seven

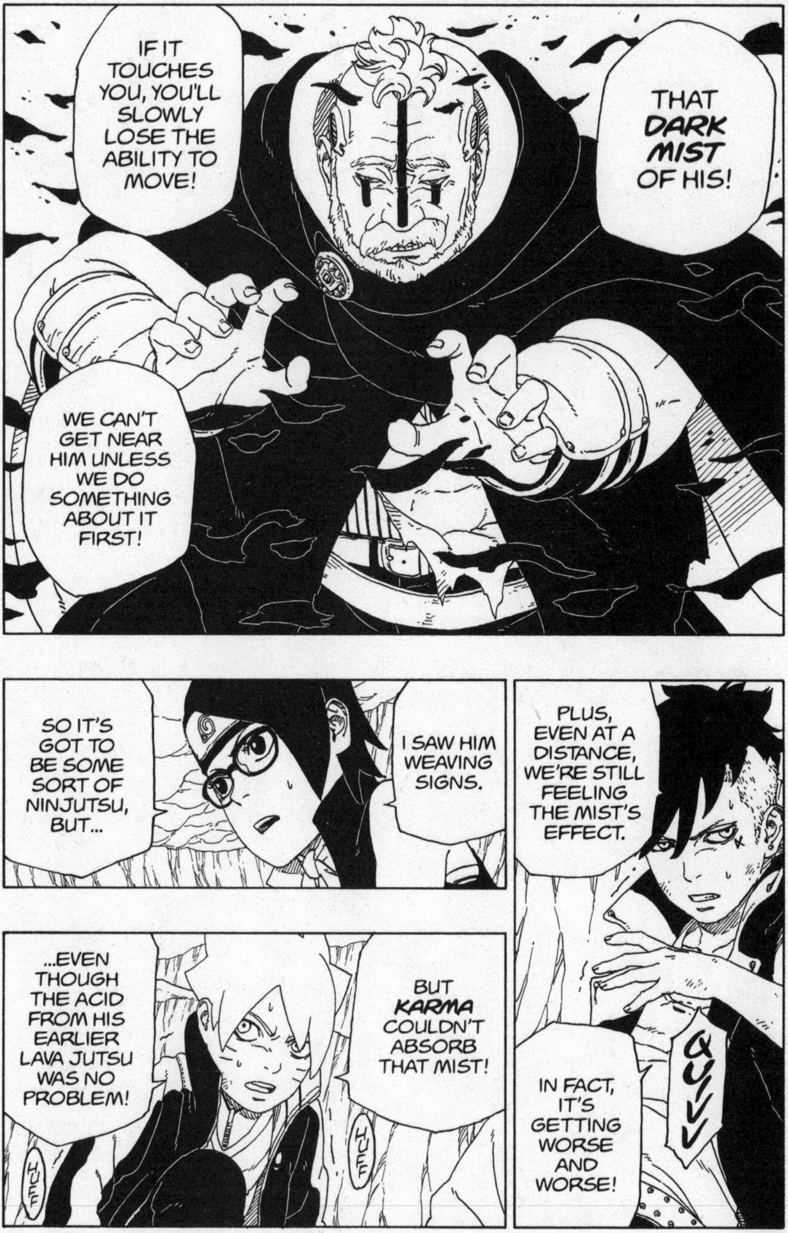
THAT DARK MIST OF HIS!
IF IT TOUCHES YOU, YOU'LL SLOWLY LOSE THE ABILITY TO MOVE!
WE CAN'T GET NEAR HIM UNLESS WE DO SOMETHING ABOUT IT FIRST!
PLUS, EVEN AT A DISTANCE, WE'RE STILL FEELING THE MIST'S EFFECT.
QUIVVV
IN FACT, IT'S GETTING WORSE AND WORSE!
I SAW HIM WEAVING SIGNS.
SO IT'S GOT TO BE SOME SORT OF NINJUTSU, BUT...
BUT KARMA COULDN'T ABSORB THAT MIST!
...EVEN THOUGH THE ACID FROM HIS EARLIER LAVA JUTSU WAS NO PROBLEM!
HUFF
HUFF

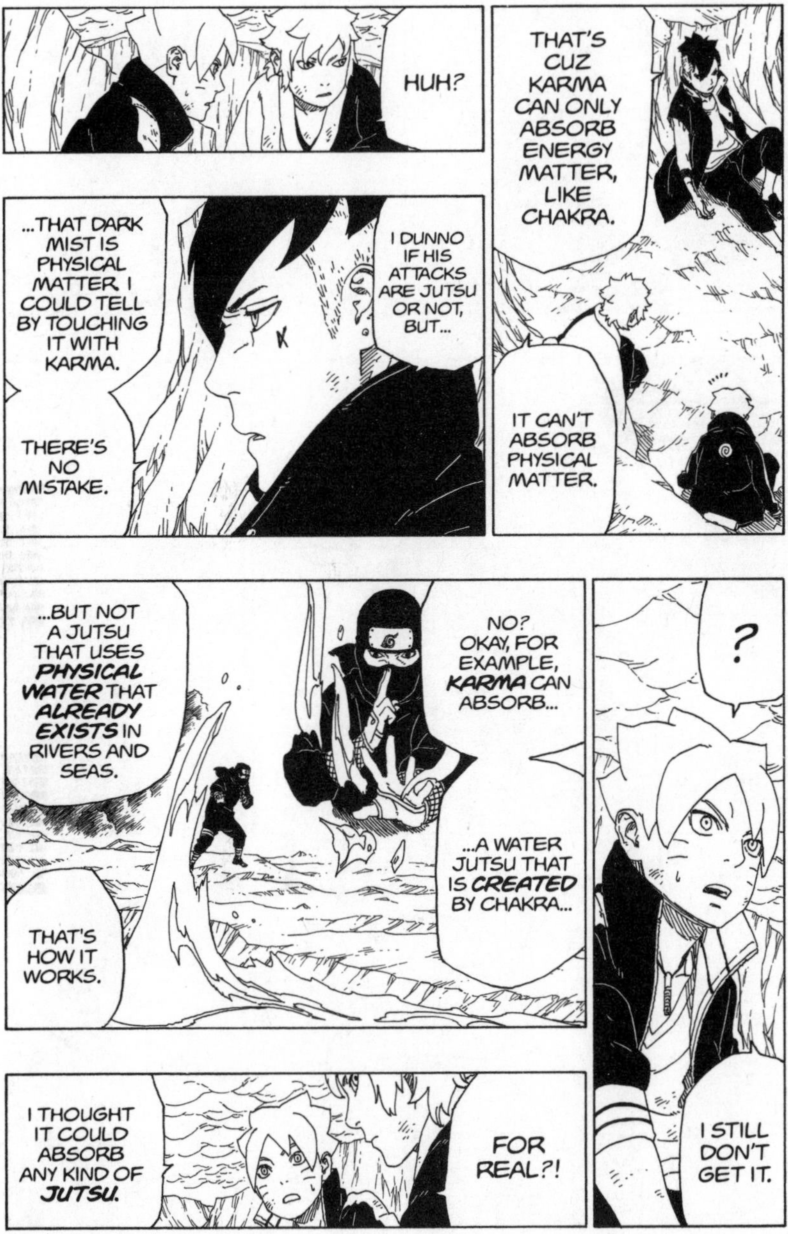
THAT'S CUZ KARMA CAN ONLY ABSORB ENERGY MATTER, LIKE CHAKRA.
IT CAN'T ABSORB PHYSICAL MATTER.
HUH?
I DUNNO IF HIS ATTACKS ARE JUTSU OR NOT, BUT...
...THAT DARK MIST IS PHYSICAL MATTER. I COULD TELL BY TOUCHING IT WITH KARMA.
THERE'S NO MISTAKE.
?
I STILL DON'T GET IT.
NO? OKAY, FOR EXAMPLE, **KARMA** CAN ABSORB...
...A WATER JUTSU THAT IS **CREATED** BY CHAKRA...
...BUT NOT A JUTSU THAT USES **PHYSICAL WATER** THAT **ALREADY EXISTS** IN RIVERS AND SEAS.
THAT'S HOW IT WORKS.
FOR REAL?!
I THOUGHT IT COULD ABSORB ANY KIND OF **JUTSU.**

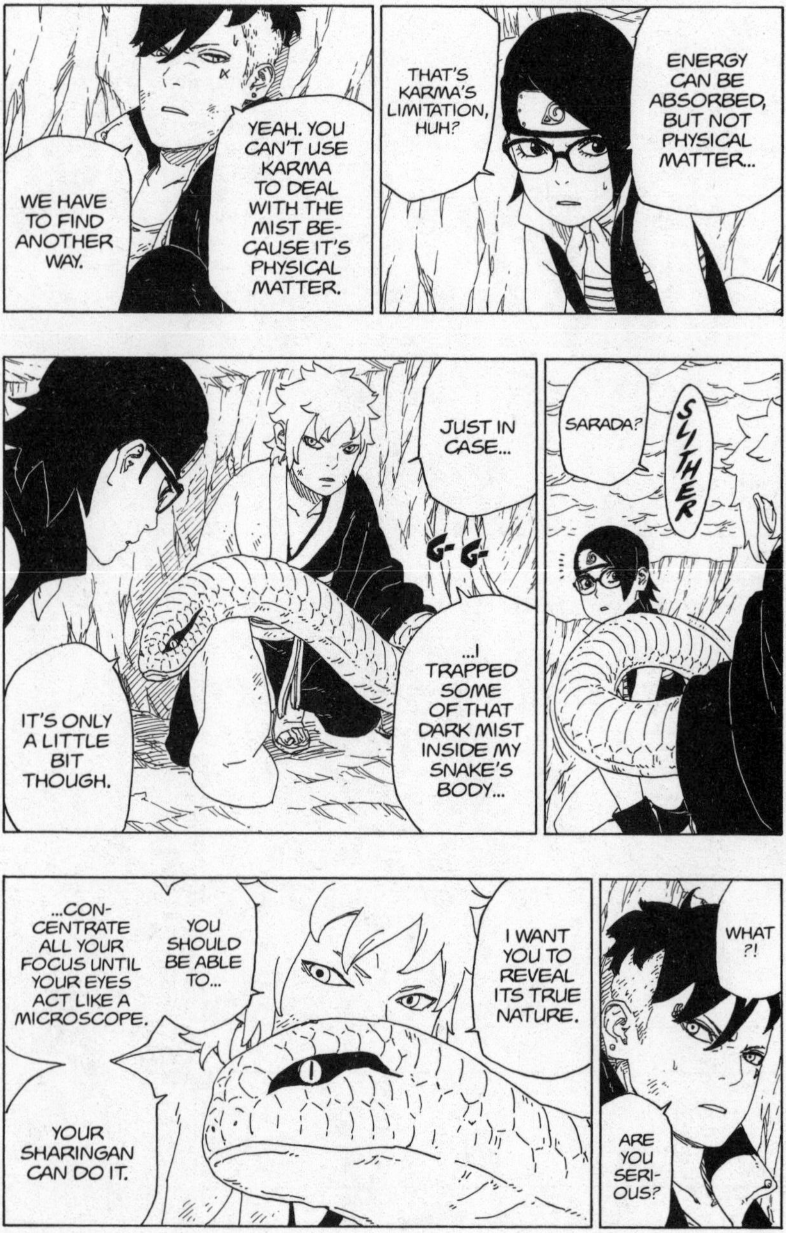
ENERGY CAN BE ABSORBED, BUT NOT PHYSICAL MATTER...
THAT'S KARMA'S LIMITATION, HUH?
YEAH. YOU CAN'T USE KARMA TO DEAL WITH THE MIST BECAUSE IT'S PHYSICAL MATTER.
WE HAVE TO FIND ANOTHER WAY.
SLITHER
SARADA?
JUST IN CASE...
G- G-
...I TRAPPED SOME OF THAT DARK MIST INSIDE MY SNAKE'S BODY...
IT'S ONLY A LITTLE BIT THOUGH.
WHAT?!
ARE YOU SERIOUS?
I WANT YOU TO REVEAL ITS TRUE NATURE.
YOU SHOULD BE ABLE TO...
...CONCENTRATE ALL YOUR FOCUS UNTIL YOUR EYES ACT LIKE A MICROSCOPE.
YOUR SHARINGAN CAN DO IT.

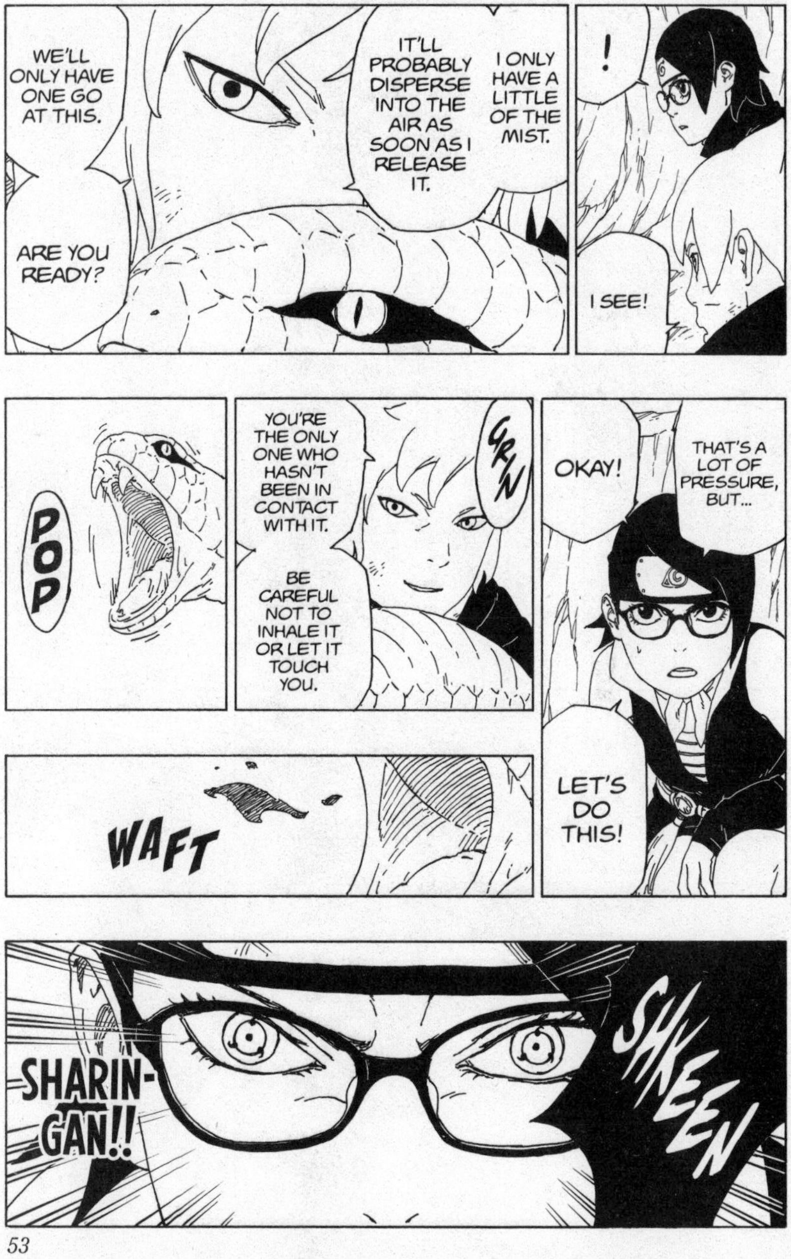
!
I SEE!
I ONLY HAVE A LITTLE OF THE MIST.
IT'LL PROBABLY DISPERSE INTO THE AIR AS SOON AS I RELEASE IT.
WE'LL ONLY HAVE ONE GO AT THIS.
ARE YOU READY?
THAT'S A LOT OF PRESSURE, BUT...
OKAY!
LET'S DO THIS!
GRIN
YOU'RE THE ONLY ONE WHO HASN'T BEEN IN CONTACT WITH IT.
BE CAREFUL NOT TO INHALE IT OR LET IT TOUCH YOU.
POP
WAFT
SHEEN
SHARIN-GAN!!

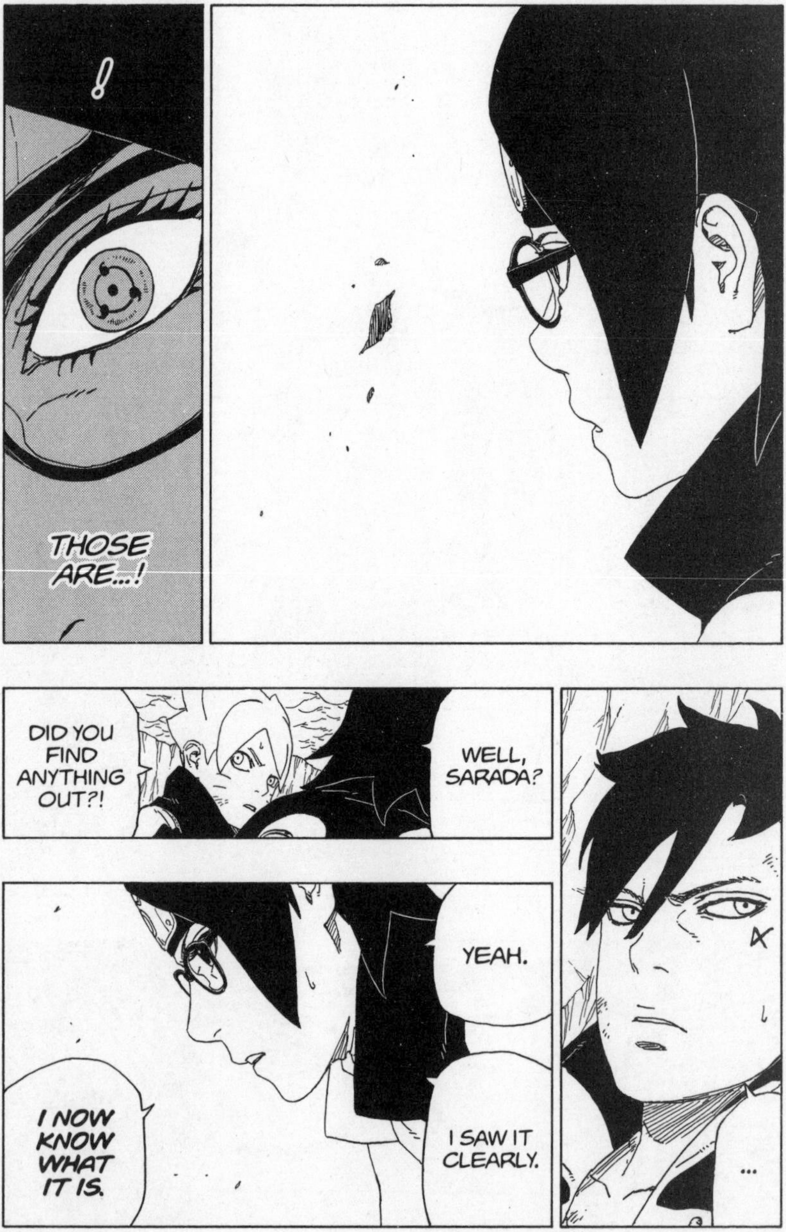
!
THOSE ARE...!
...
WELL, SARADA?
DID YOU FIND ANYTHING OUT?!
YEAH.
I SAW IT CLEARLY.
I NOW KNOW WHAT IT IS.

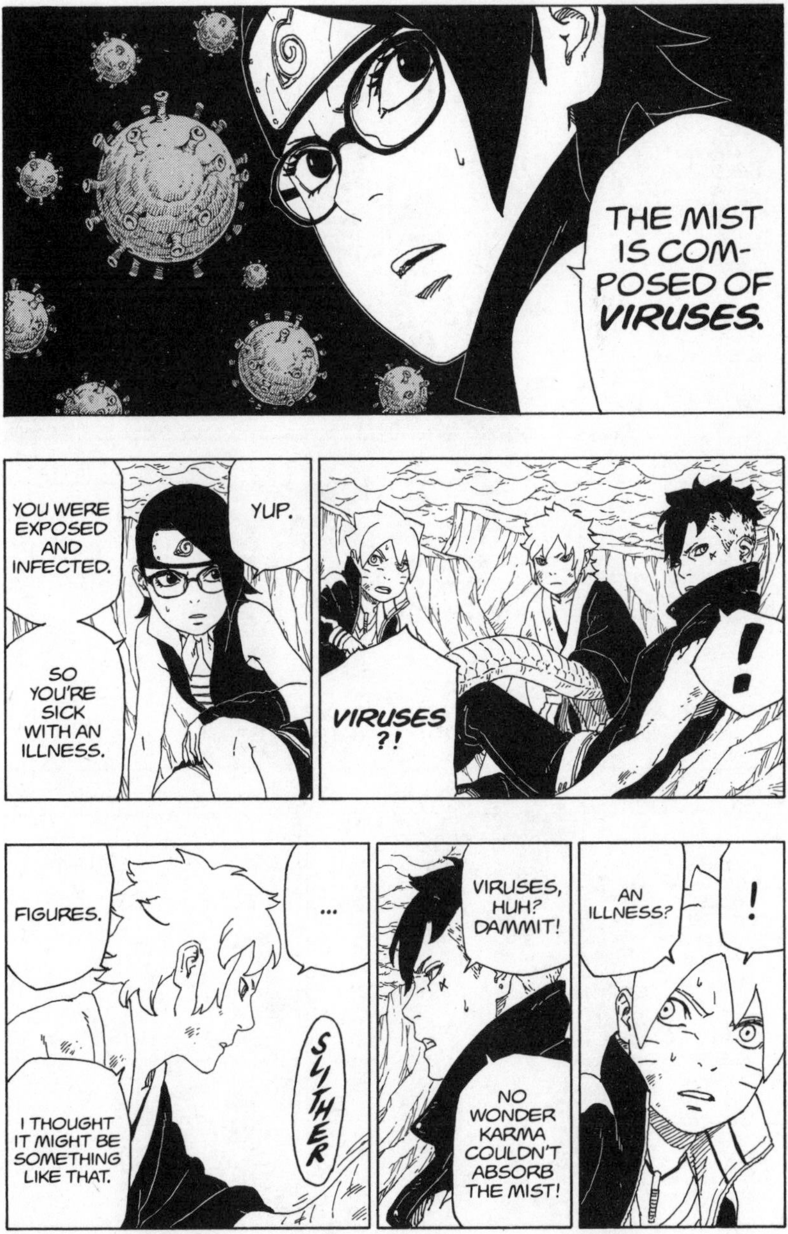
THE MIST IS COMPOSED OF VIRUSES.
!
VIRUSES ?!
YUP.
YOU WERE EXPOSED AND INFECTED.
SO YOU'RE SICK WITH AN ILLNESS.
!
AN ILLNESS?
VIRUSES, HUH? DAMMIT!
NO WONDER KARMA COULDN'T ABSORB THE MIST!
...
FIGURES.
SLITHER
I THOUGHT IT MIGHT BE SOMETHING LIKE THAT.

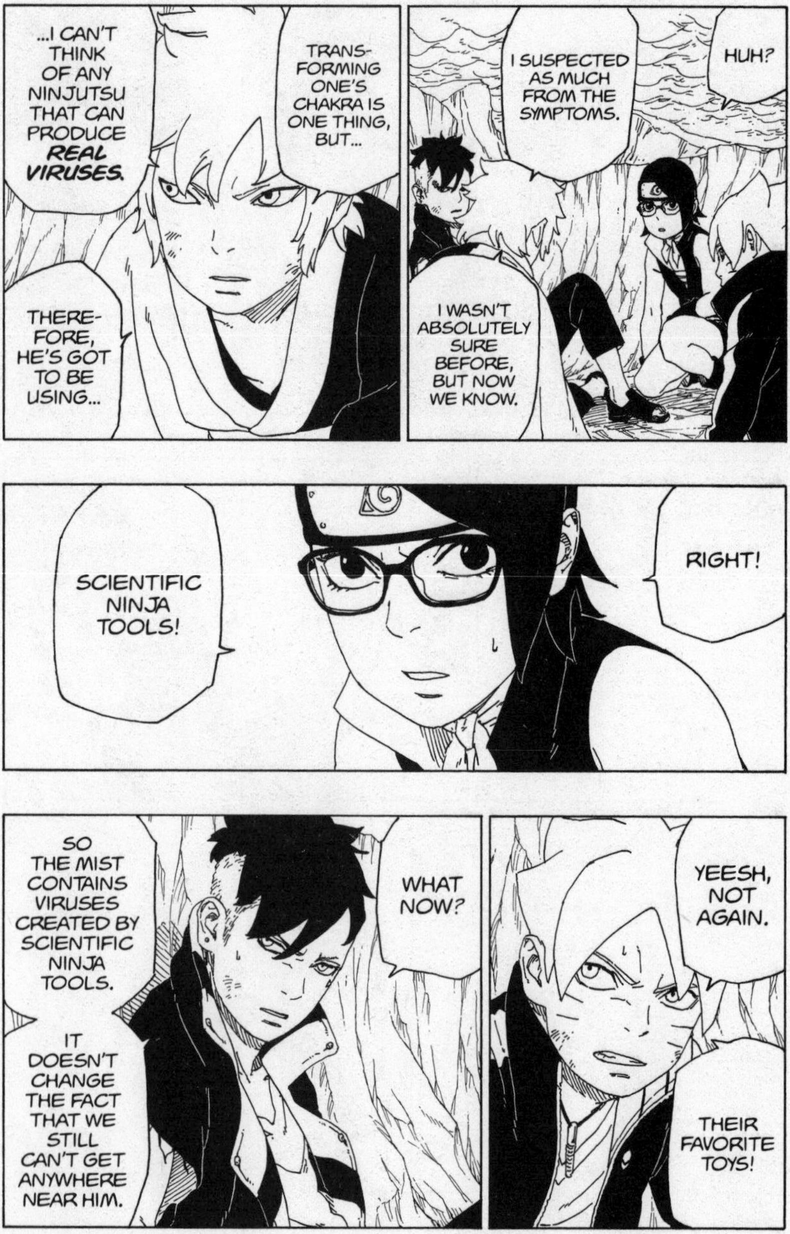
HUH?
I SUSPECTED AS MUCH FROM THE SYMPTOMS.
I WASN'T ABSOLUTELY SURE BEFORE, BUT NOW WE KNOW.
TRANS-FORMING ONE'S CHAKRA IS ONE THING, BUT...
...I CAN'T THINK OF ANY NINJUTSU THAT CAN PRODUCE ***REAL VIRUSES.***
THERE-FORE, HE'S GOT TO BE USING...
RIGHT!
SCIENTIFIC NINJA TOOLS!
YEESH, NOT AGAIN.
THEIR FAVORITE TOYS!
WHAT NOW?
SO THE MIST CONTAINS VIRUSES CREATED BY SCIENTIFIC NINJA TOOLS.
IT DOESN'T CHANGE THE FACT THAT WE STILL CAN'T GET ANYWHERE NEAR HIM.

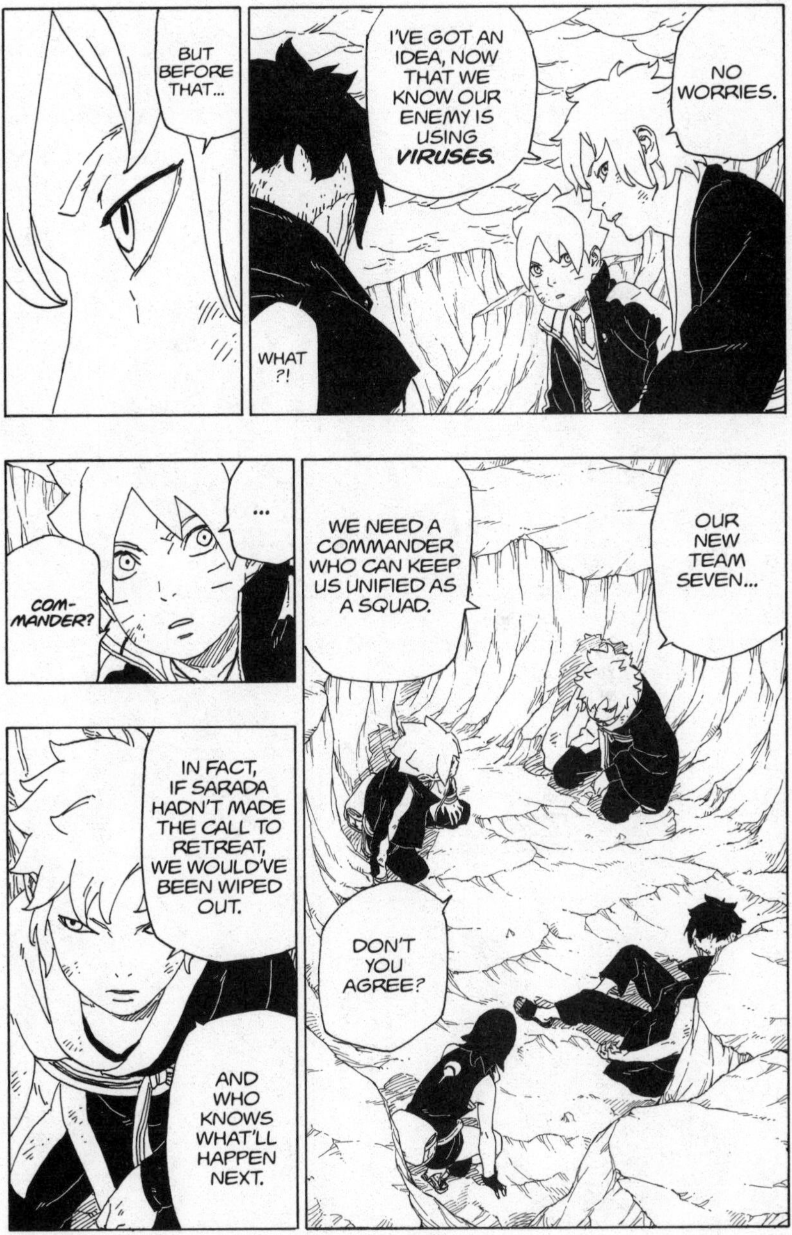
NO WORRIES.
I'VE GOT AN IDEA, NOW THAT WE KNOW OUR ENEMY IS USING ***VIRUSES.***
WHAT ?!
BUT BEFORE THAT...
OUR NEW TEAM SEVEN...
WE NEED A COMMANDER WHO CAN KEEP US UNIFIED AS A SQUAD.
DON'T YOU AGREE?
...
COM-MANDER?
IN FACT, IF SARADA HADN'T MADE THE CALL TO RETREAT, WE WOULD'VE BEEN WIPED OUT.
AND WHO KNOWS WHAT'LL HAPPEN NEXT.

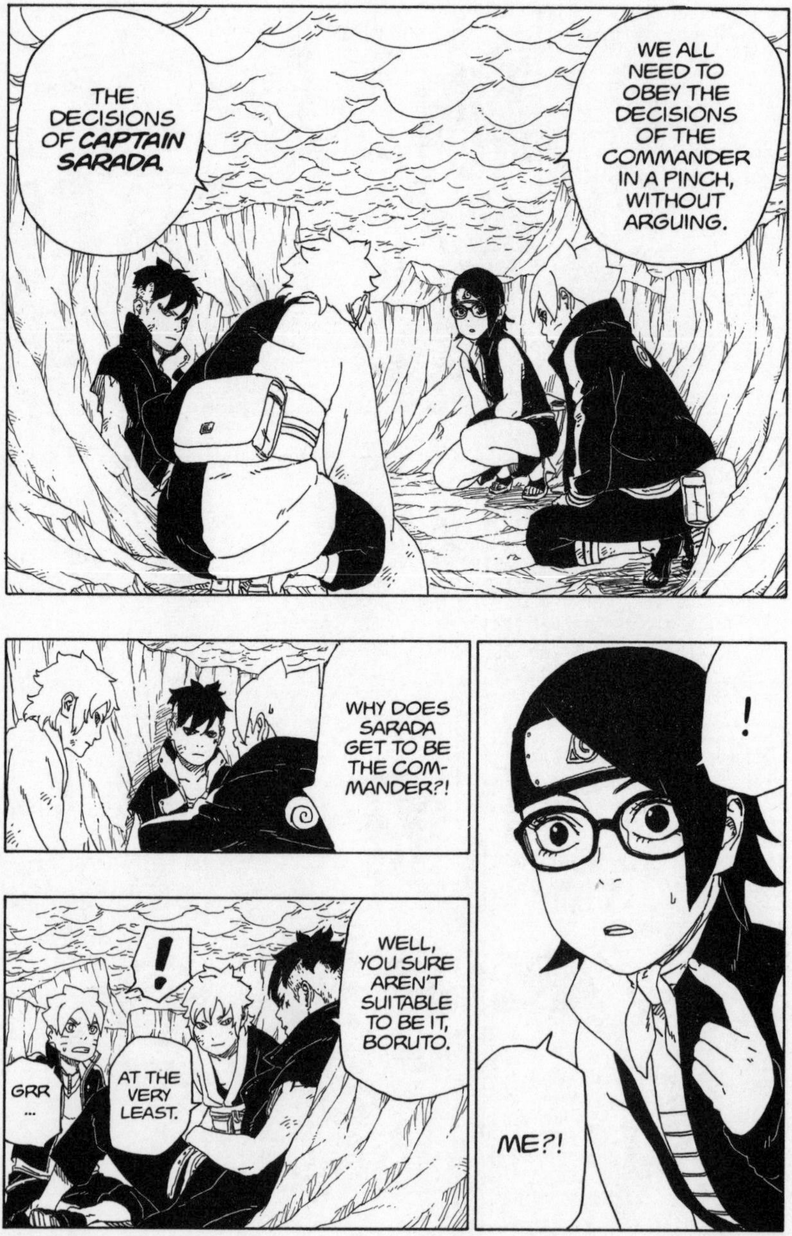
WE ALL NEED TO OBEY THE DECISIONS OF THE COMMANDER IN A PINCH, WITHOUT ARGUING.
THE DECISIONS OF **CAPTAIN SARADA.**
!
ME?!
WHY DOES SARADA GET TO BE THE COMMANDER?!
WELL, YOU SURE AREN'T SUITABLE TO BE IT, BORUTO.
!
AT THE VERY LEAST.
GRR ...

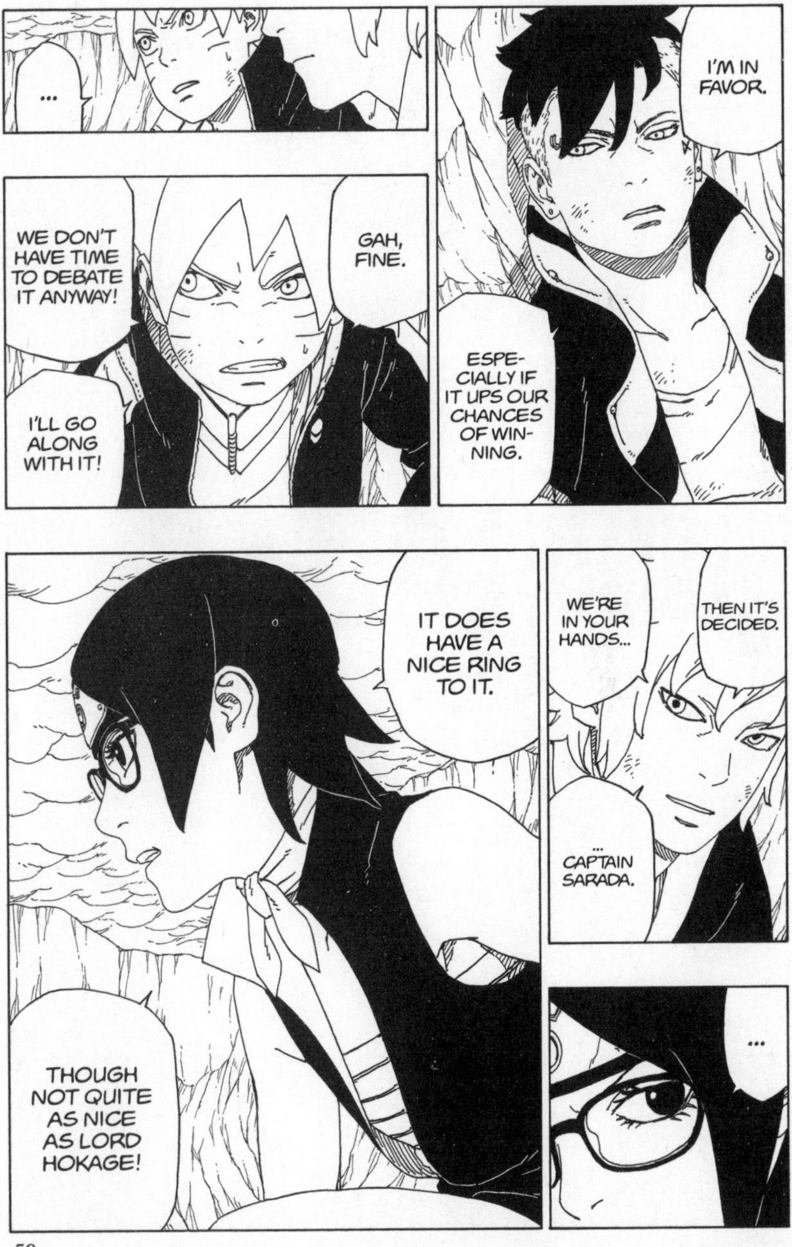
I'M IN FAVOR.
ESPECIALLY IF IT UPS OUR CHANCES OF WINNING.
...
GAH, FINE.
WE DON'T HAVE TIME TO DEBATE IT ANYWAY!
I'LL GO ALONG WITH IT!
THEN IT'S DECIDED.
WE'RE IN YOUR HANDS...
... CAPTAIN SARADA.
...
IT DOES HAVE A NICE RING TO IT.
THOUGH NOT QUITE AS NICE AS LORD HOKAGE!

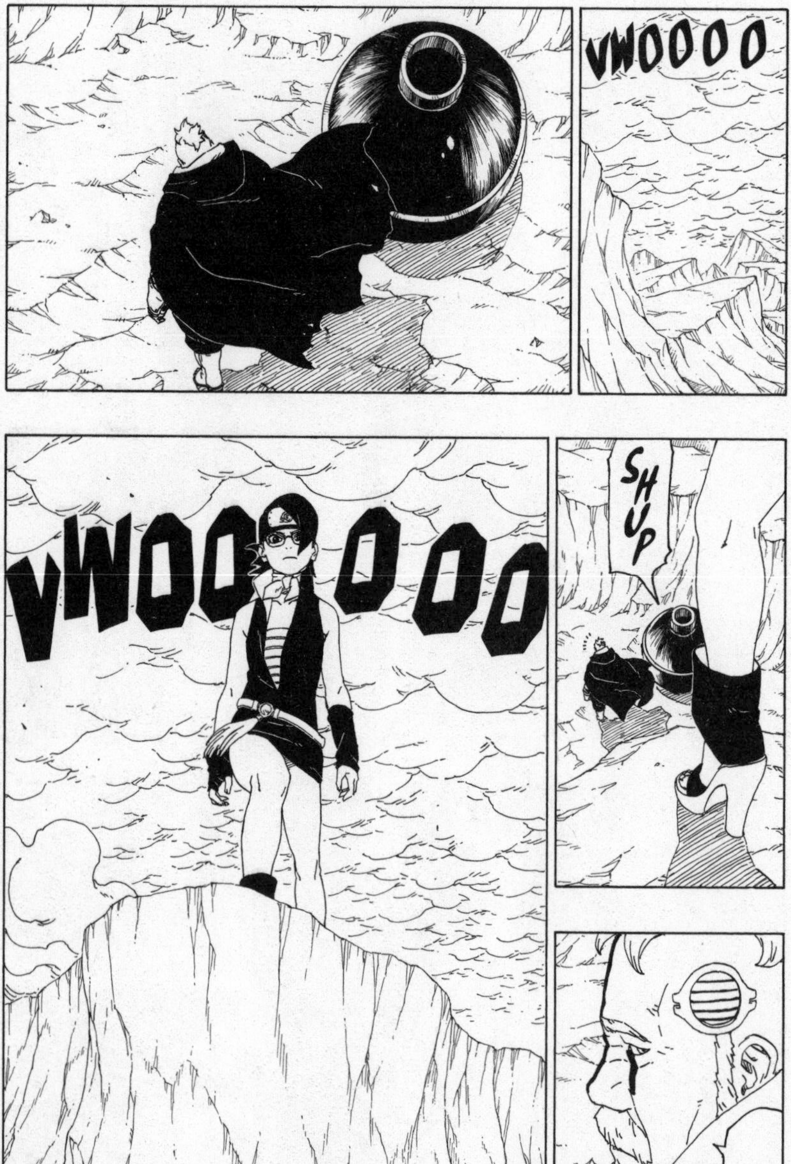
VWOOOO
SHUP
...
VWOOOOOO

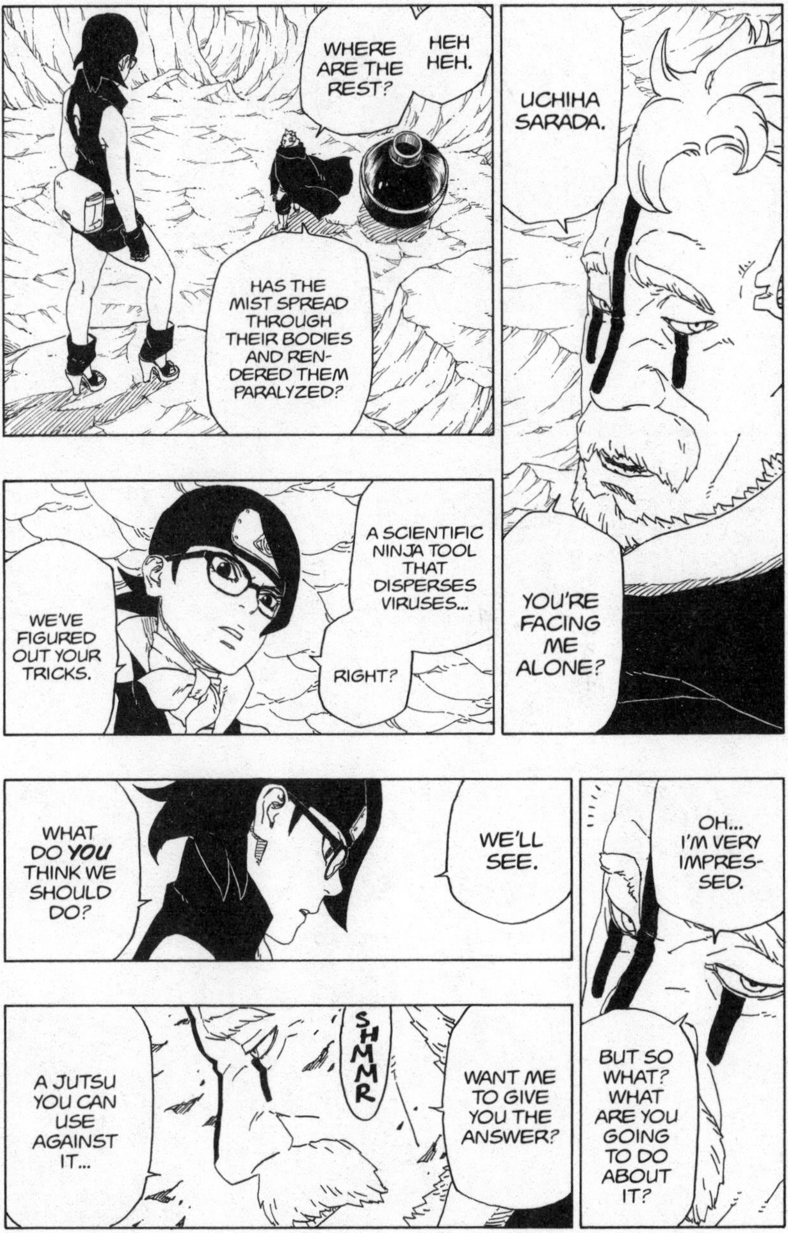
UCHIHA SARADA.
YOU'RE FACING ME ALONE?
HEH HEH.
WHERE ARE THE REST?
HAS THE MIST SPREAD THROUGH THEIR BODIES AND RENDERED THEM PARALYZED?
A SCIENTIFIC NINJA TOOL THAT DISPERSES VIRUSES...
RIGHT?
WE'VE FIGURED OUT YOUR TRICKS.
OH... I'M VERY IMPRESSED.
BUT SO WHAT? WHAT ARE YOU GOING TO DO ABOUT IT?
WE'LL SEE.
WHAT DO *YOU* THINK WE SHOULD DO?
SHMMR
WANT ME TO GIVE YOU THE ANSWER?
A JUTSU YOU CAN USE AGAINST IT...

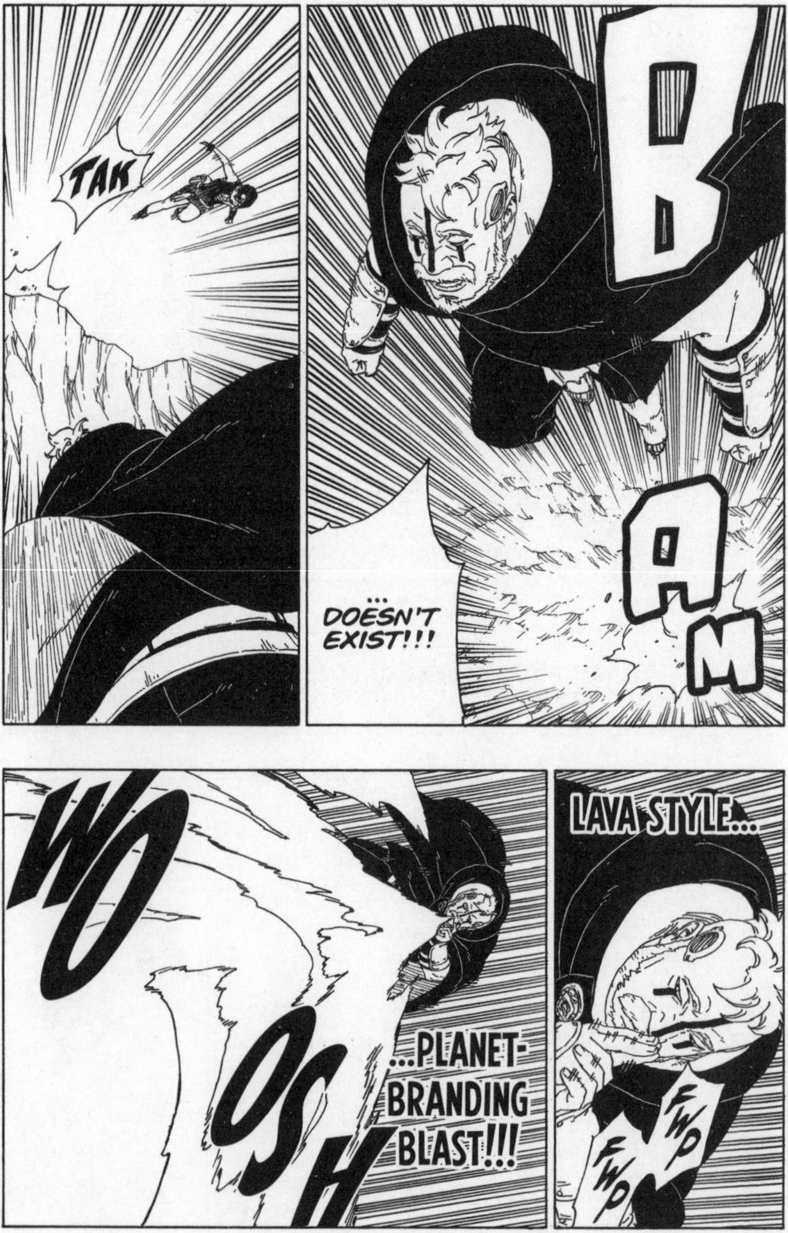
BAM
...DOESN'T EXIST!!!
TAK
LAVA STYLE...
FWP FWP
WHOOSH
...PLANET-BRANDING BLAST!!!

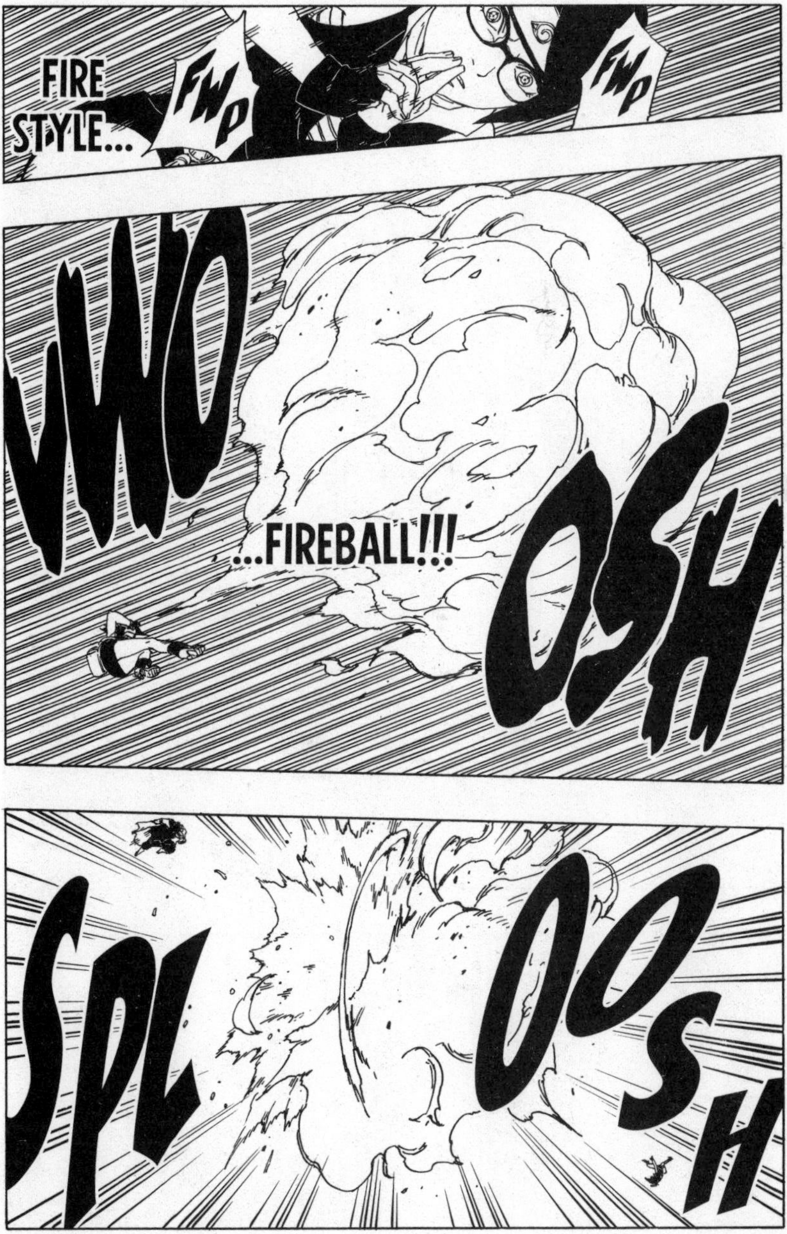
FWP
FWP
FIRE STYLE...
OOSH
...FIREBALL!!!
WHO
OOSH
SPL

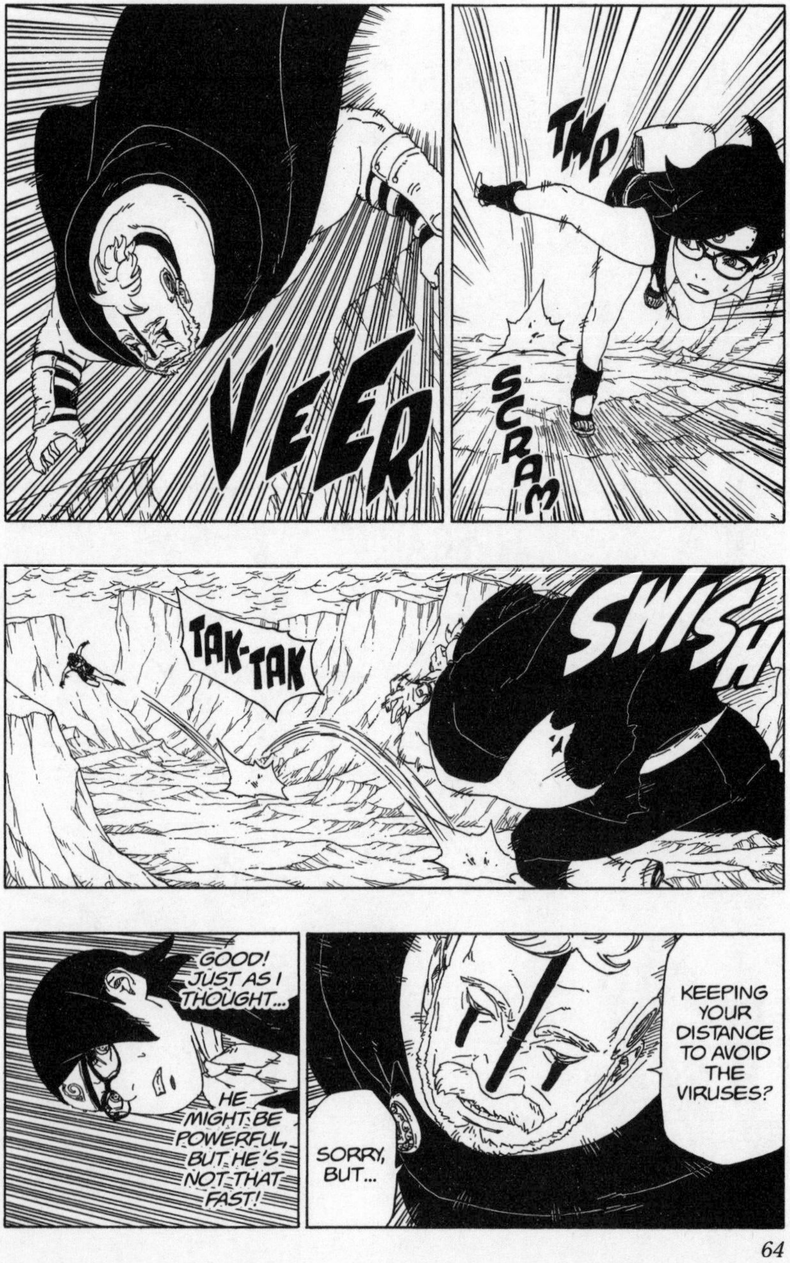
TMP
SCRAM
VEER
SWISH
TAK-TAK
KEEPING YOUR DISTANCE TO AVOID THE VIRUSES?
SORRY, BUT...
GOOD! JUST AS I THOUGHT...
HE MIGHT BE POWERFUL, BUT HE'S NOT THAT FAST!

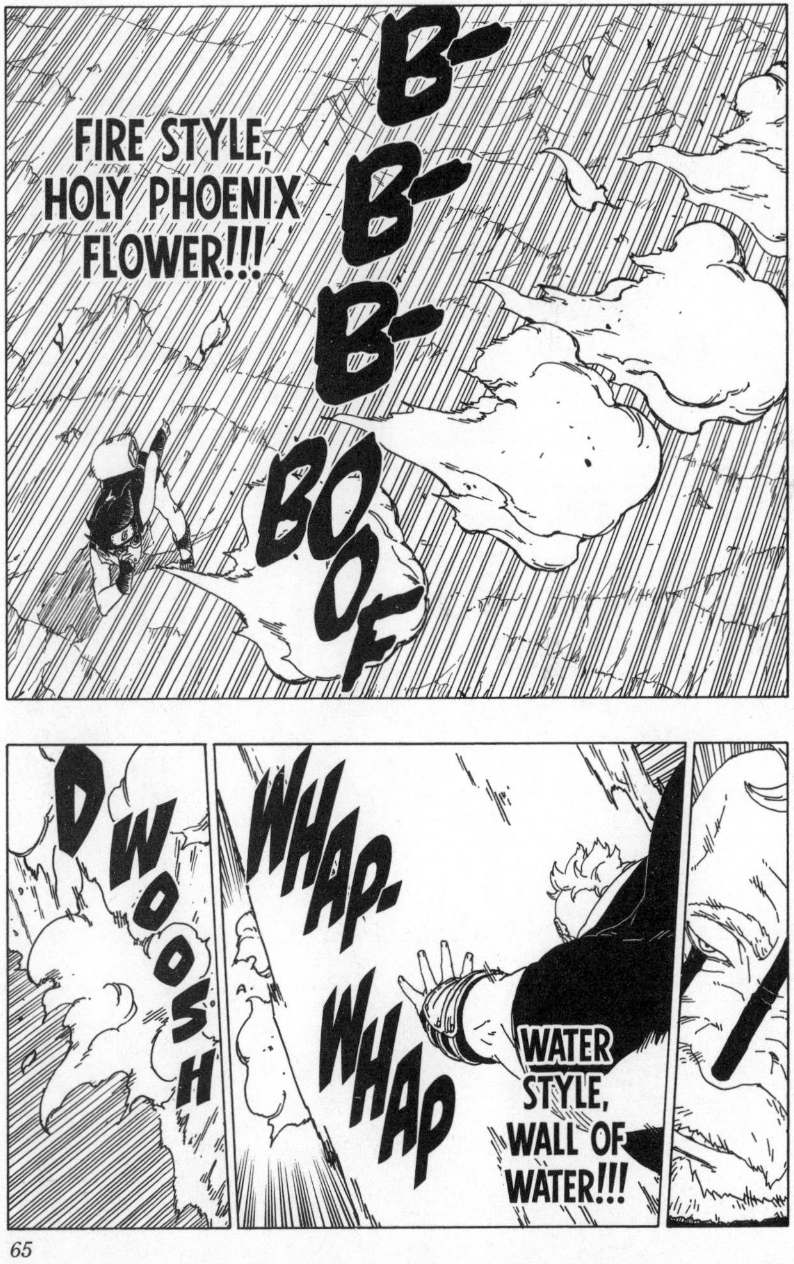
B-B-B-BOOF
FIRE STYLE, HOLY PHOENIX FLOWER!!!
WHAP-WHAP
WATER STYLE, WALL OF WATER!!!
DWOOSH

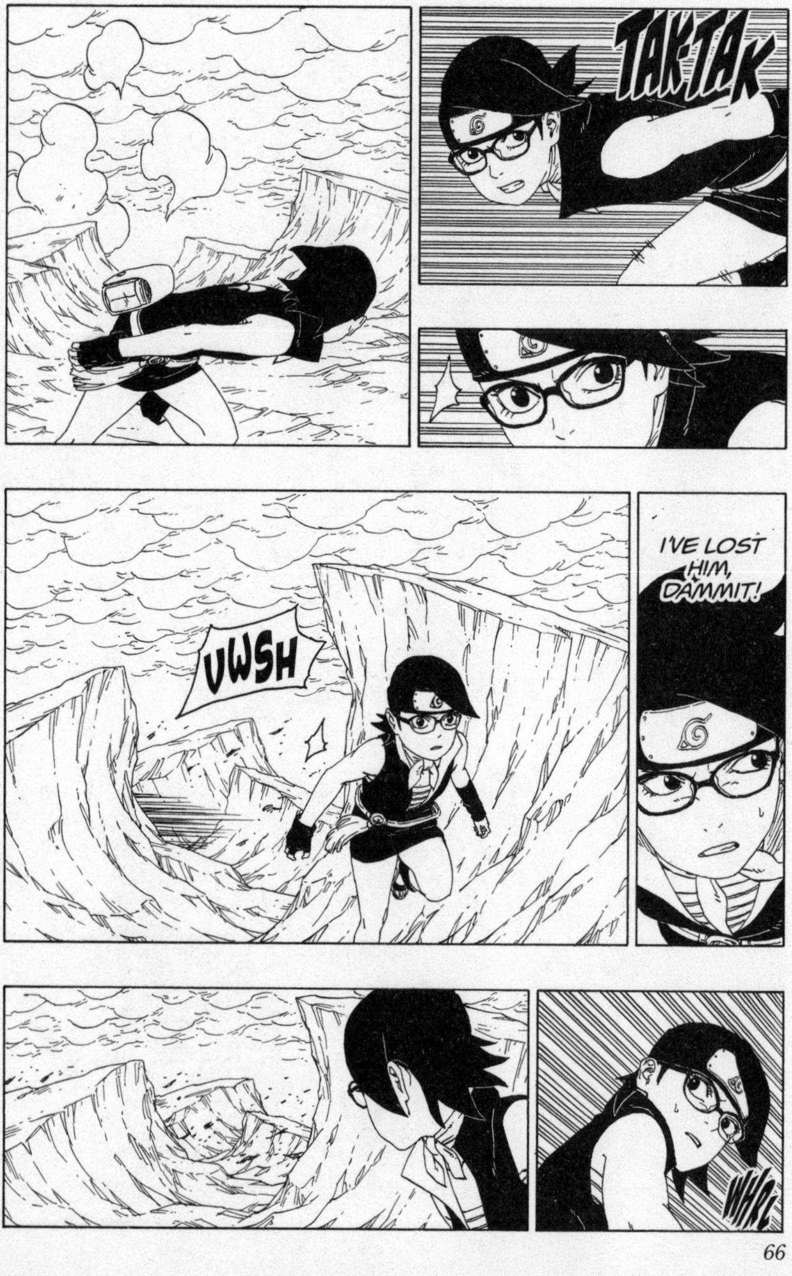
TAK TAK
I'VE LOST HIM, DAMMIT!
VWSH
WHRL

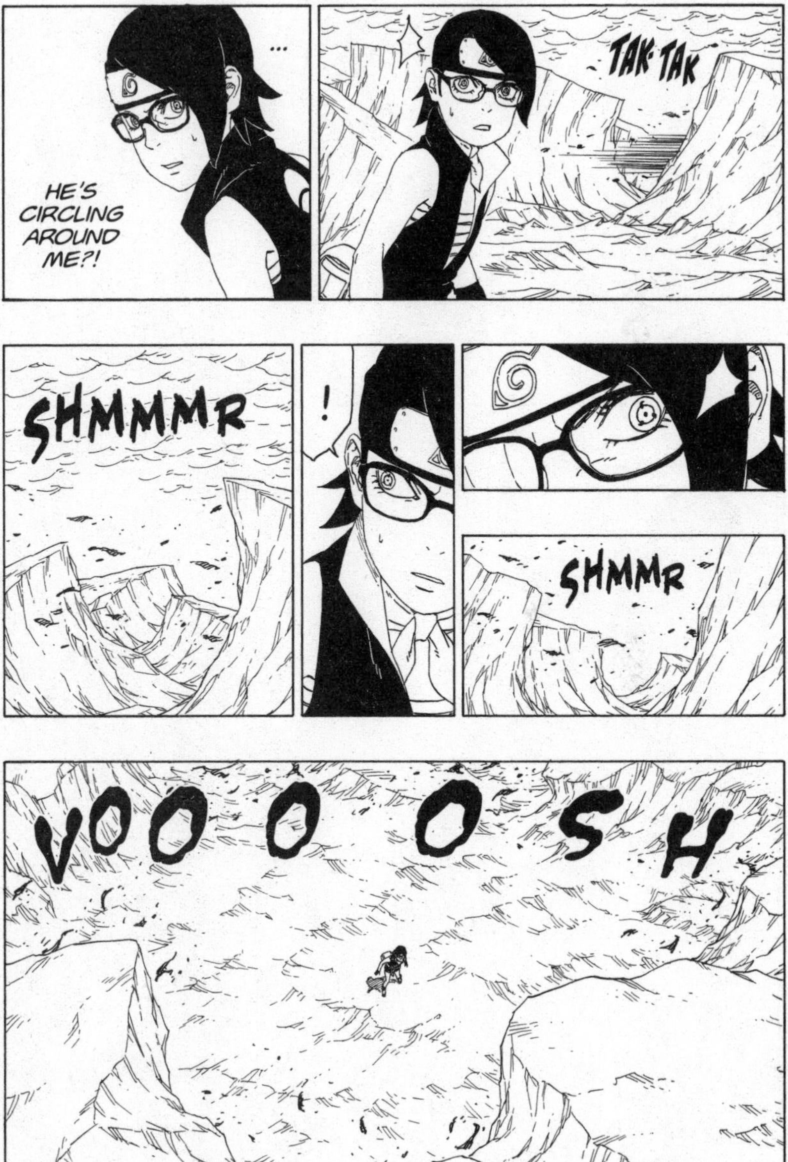
TAK TAK
...
HE'S CIRCLING AROUND ME?!
SHMMR
!
SHMMMR
VOOOOSH

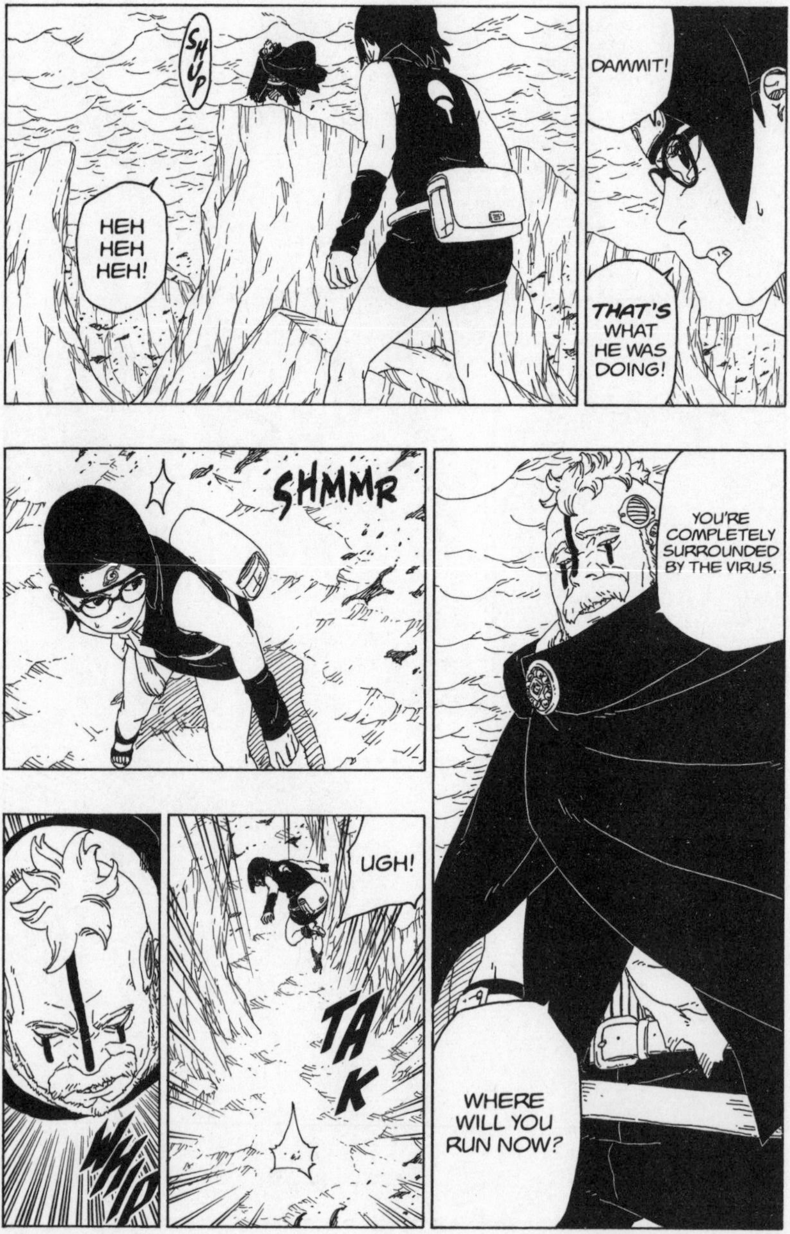
DAMMIT!
THAT'S WHAT HE WAS DOING!
SHUP
HEH HEH HEH!
YOU'RE COMPLETELY SURROUNDED BY THE VIRUS.
WHERE WILL YOU RUN NOW?
SHMMR
UGH!
TAK
WHIP

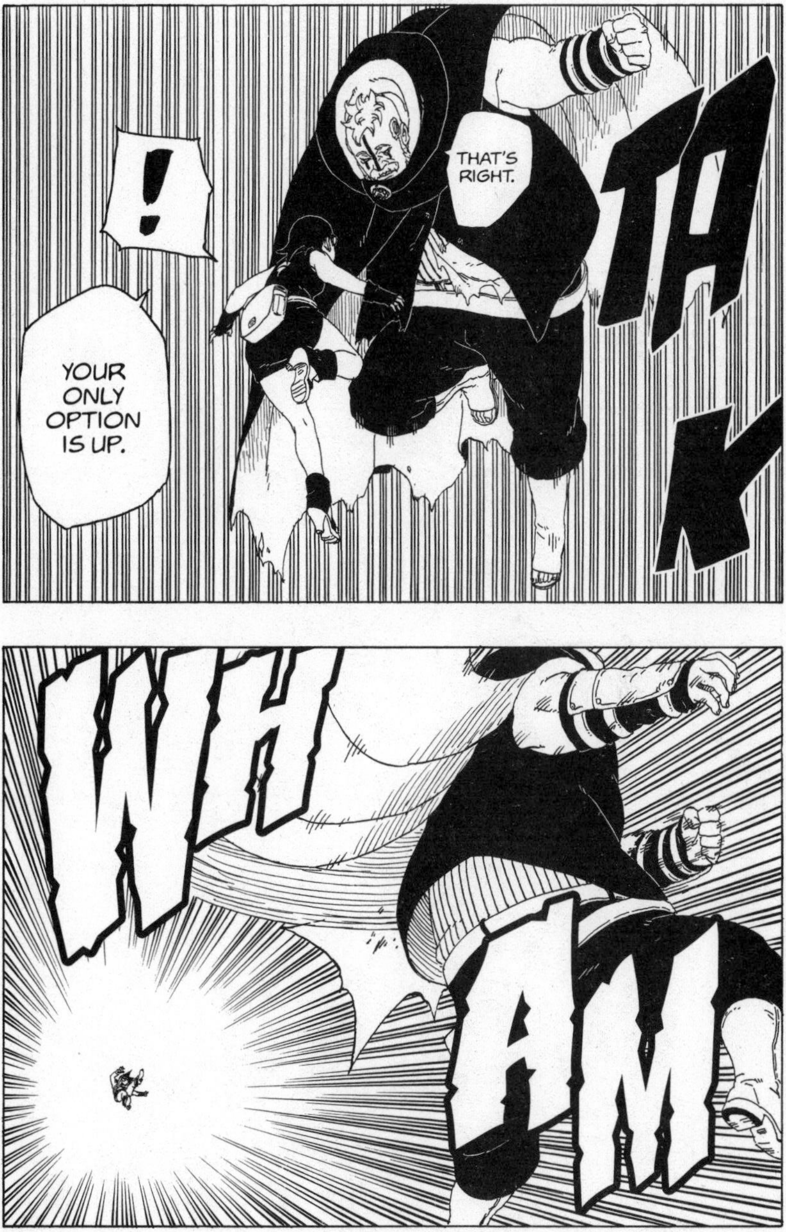
TAK
THAT'S RIGHT.
!
YOUR ONLY OPTION IS UP.
WHAM

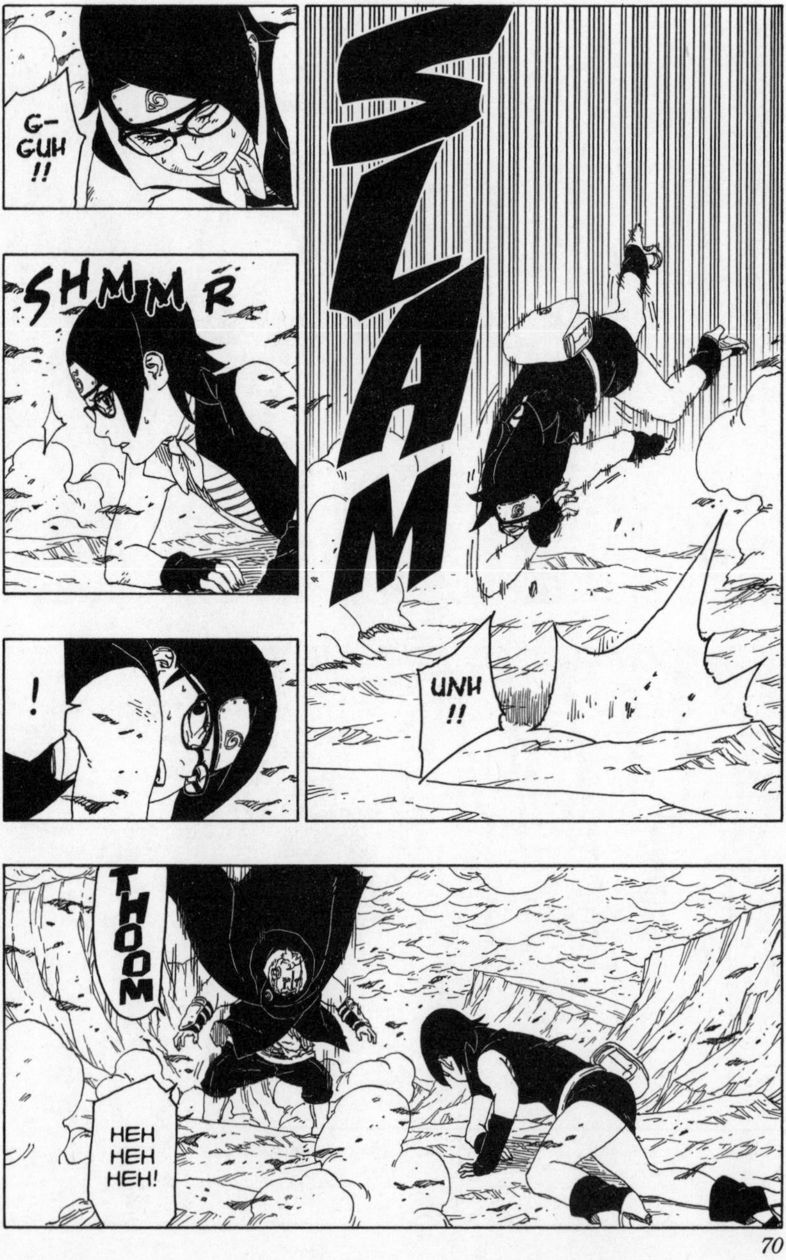
SLAM
UNH!!
G-GUH!!
SHMMR
!
THOOM
HEH HEH HEH!

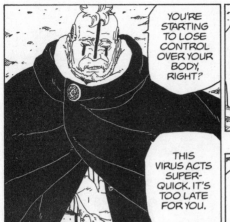

YOU'RE STARTING TO LOSE CONTROL OVER YOUR BODY, RIGHT?

THIS VIRUS ACTS SUPER-QUICK. IT'S TOO LATE FOR YOU.

QUIVV

....!

GUH...

SHUP

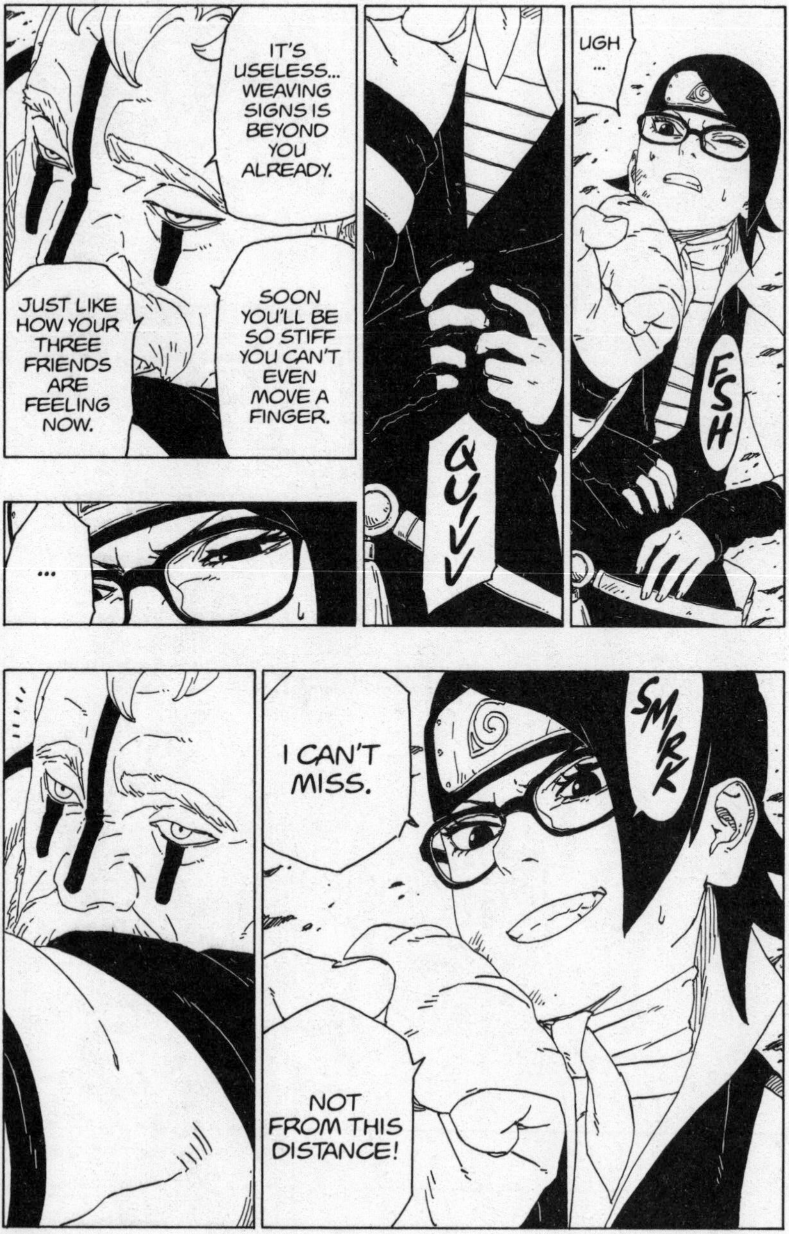

UGH ...
FSH
QUIVVV
IT'S USELESS... WEAVING SIGNS IS BEYOND YOU ALREADY.
SOON YOU'LL BE SO STIFF YOU CAN'T EVEN MOVE A FINGER.
JUST LIKE HOW YOUR THREE FRIENDS ARE FEELING NOW.
...
SMIRK
I CAN'T MISS.
NOT FROM THIS DISTANCE!

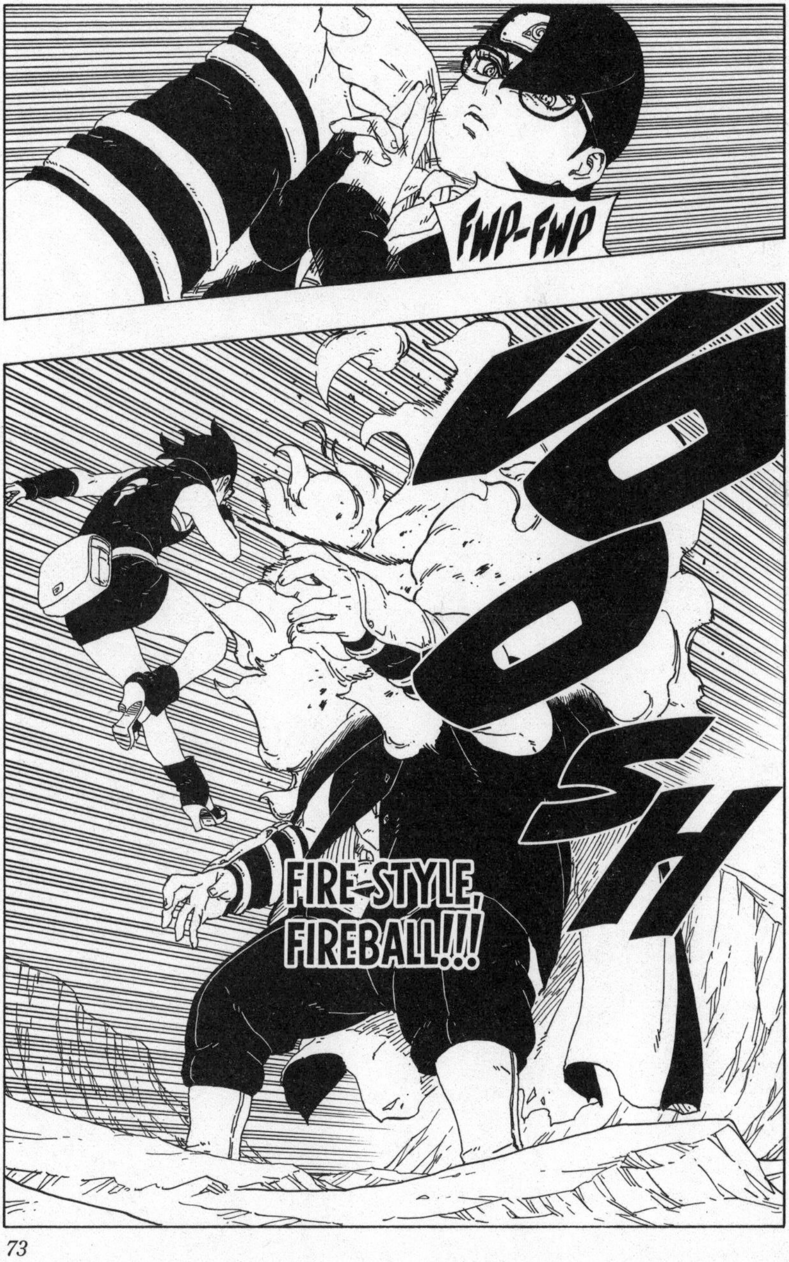
FWP-FWP
WOOSH
FIRE STYLE, FIREBALL!!!

KA
VOOSH
URG!!
WHAT THE--?!
HOW IS SHE ABLE TO MOVE?!!
TAKE ...
THWAK
... THAT!!!!

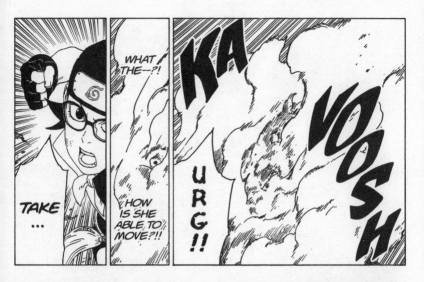

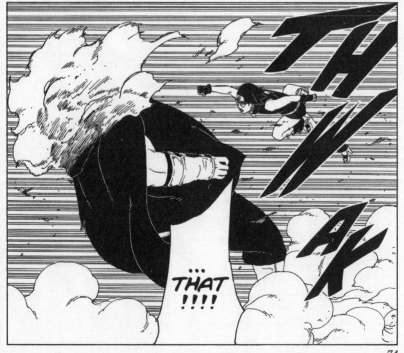

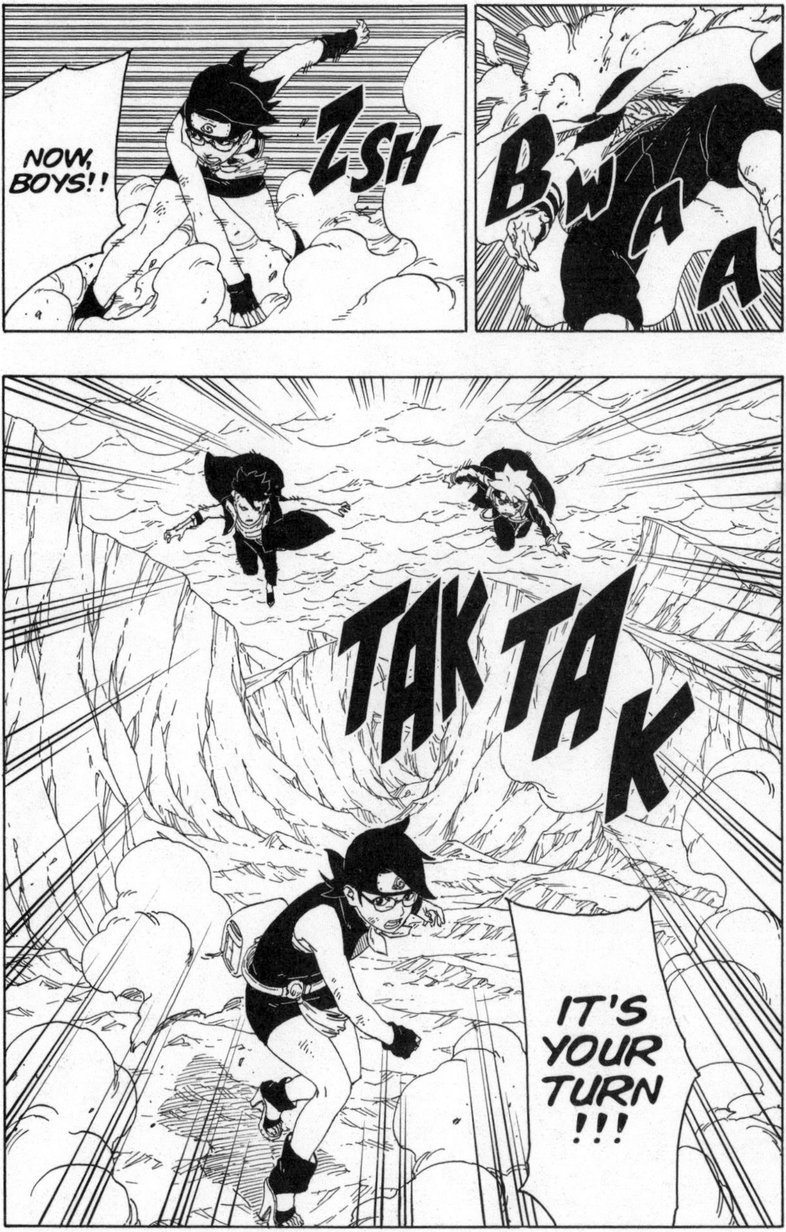
BWAA
ZSH
NOW, BOYS!!
TAKTAK
IT'S YOUR TURN!!!

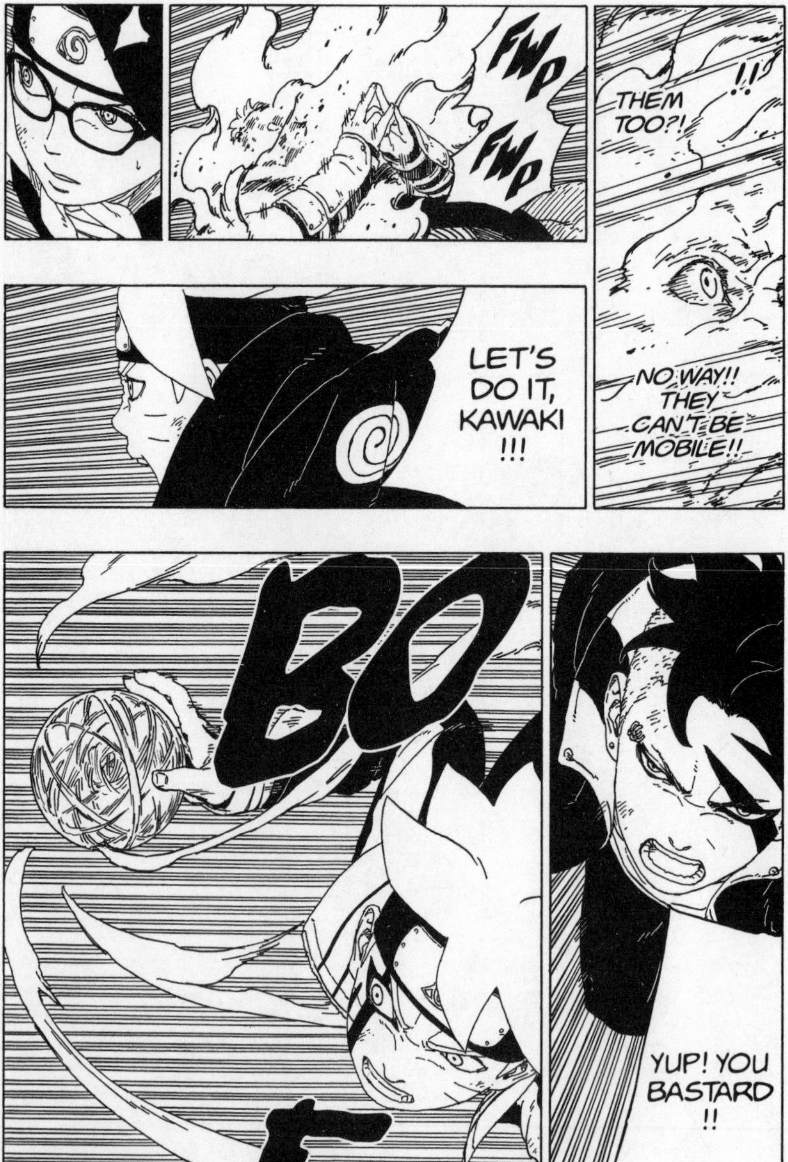
!!
THEM TOO?!
NO WAY!! THEY CAN'T BE MOBILE!!
FWP FWP
LET'S DO IT, KAWAKI !!!
YUP! YOU BASTARD !!
BO
F

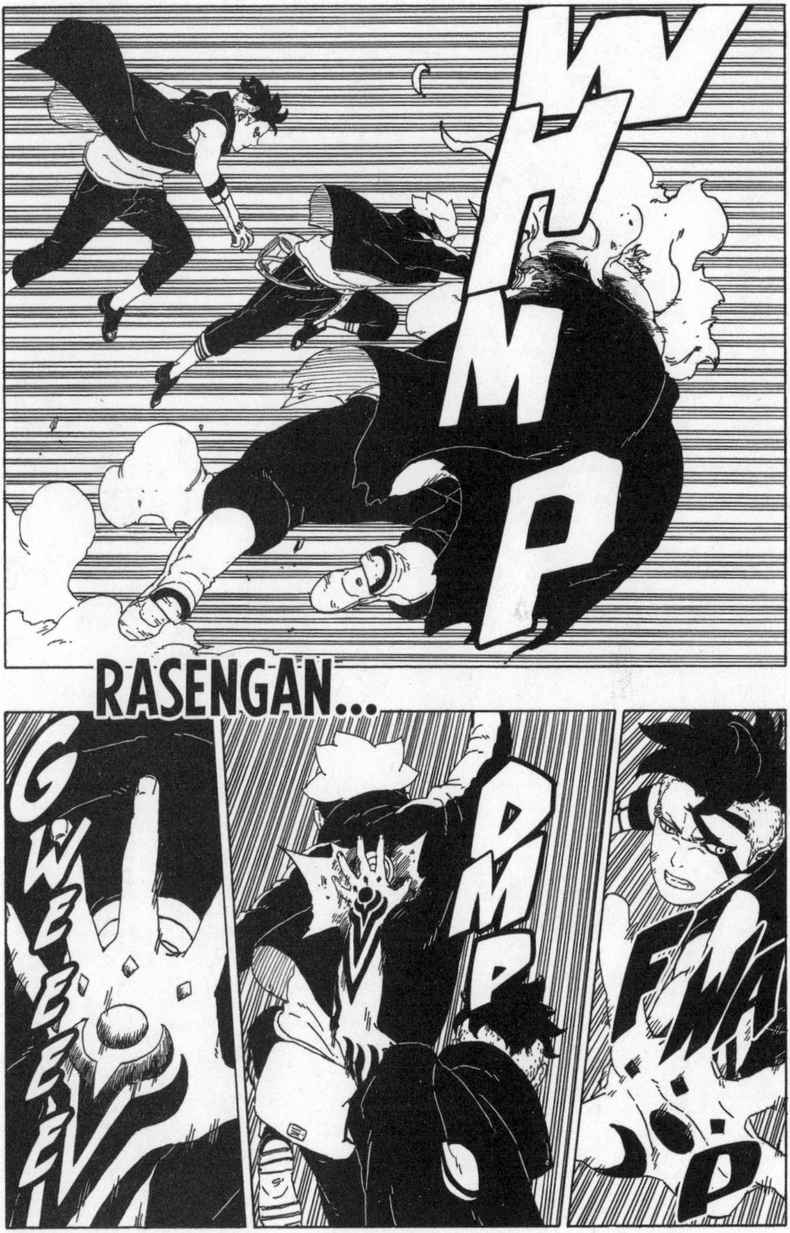
WHMP
RASENGAN...
FWAP
DMP
GWEEEEN

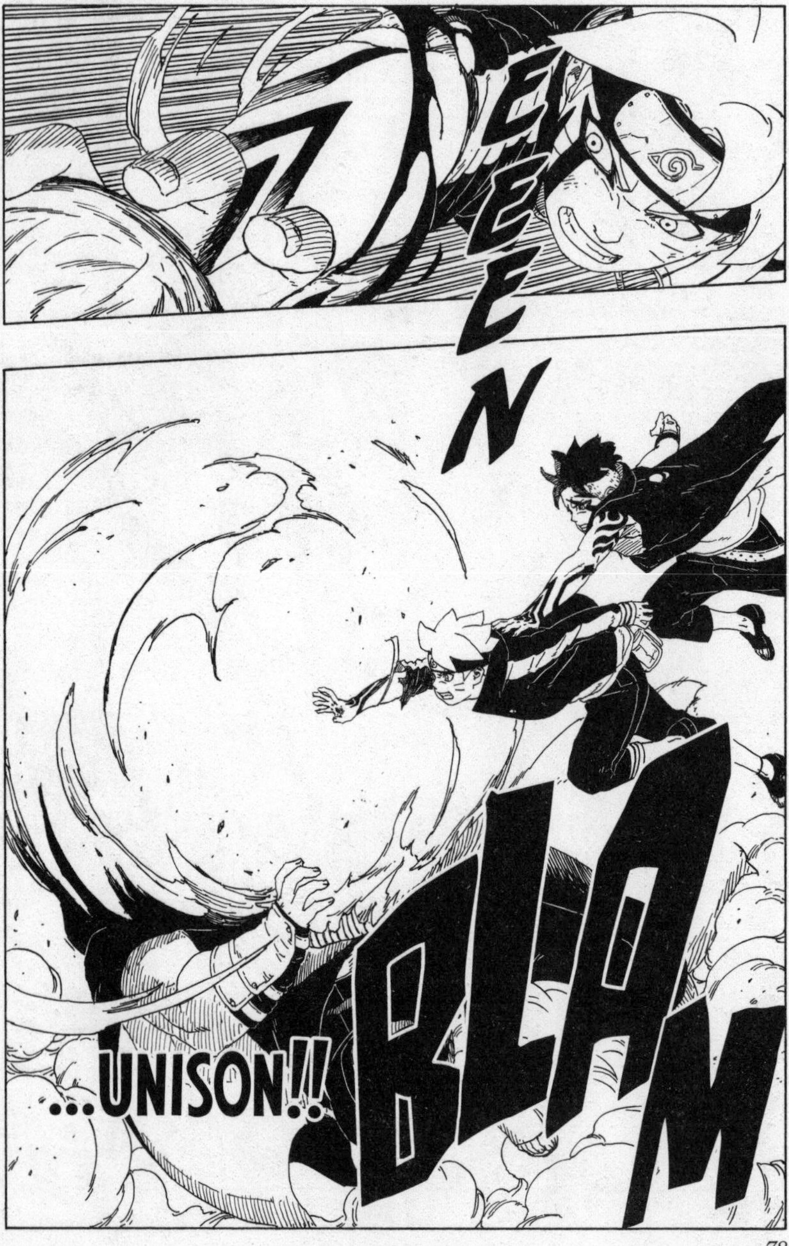
EEEN
...UNISON!!
BLAM

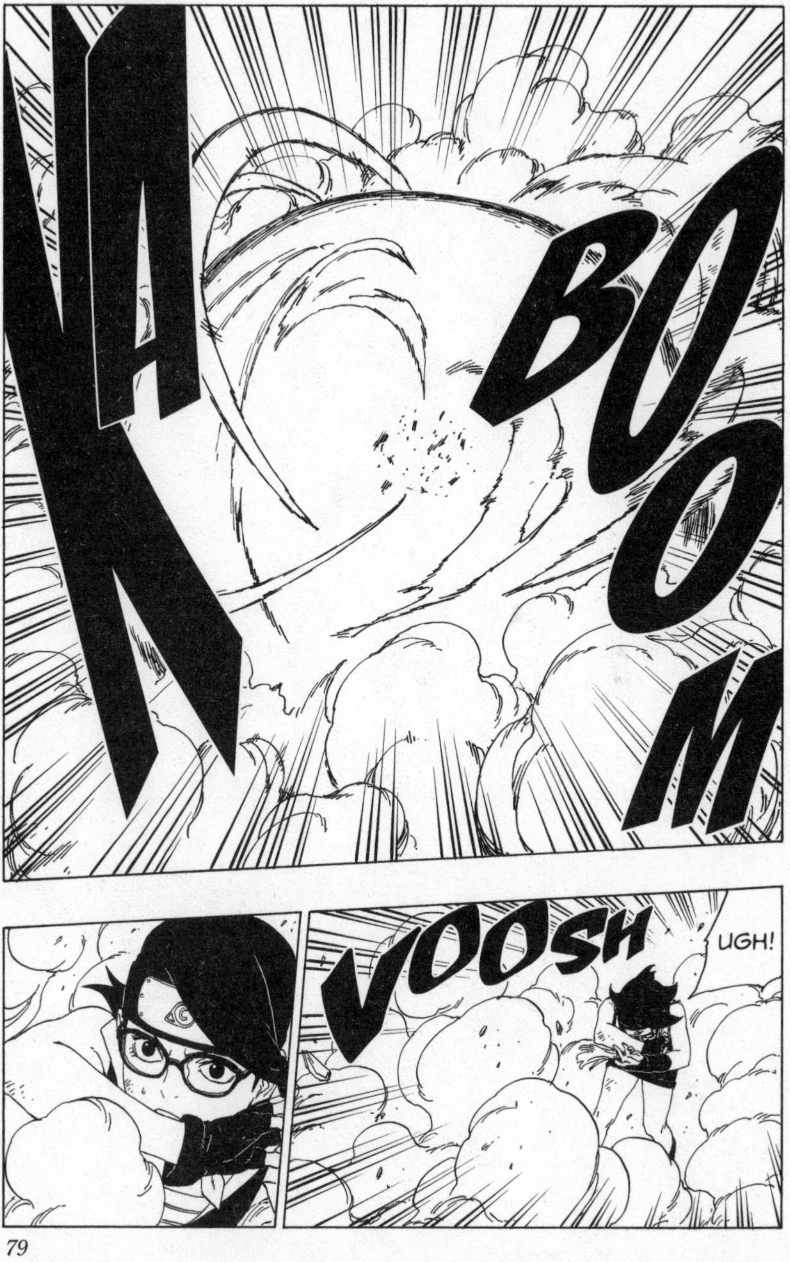
KA
BOOM
VOOSH
UGH!

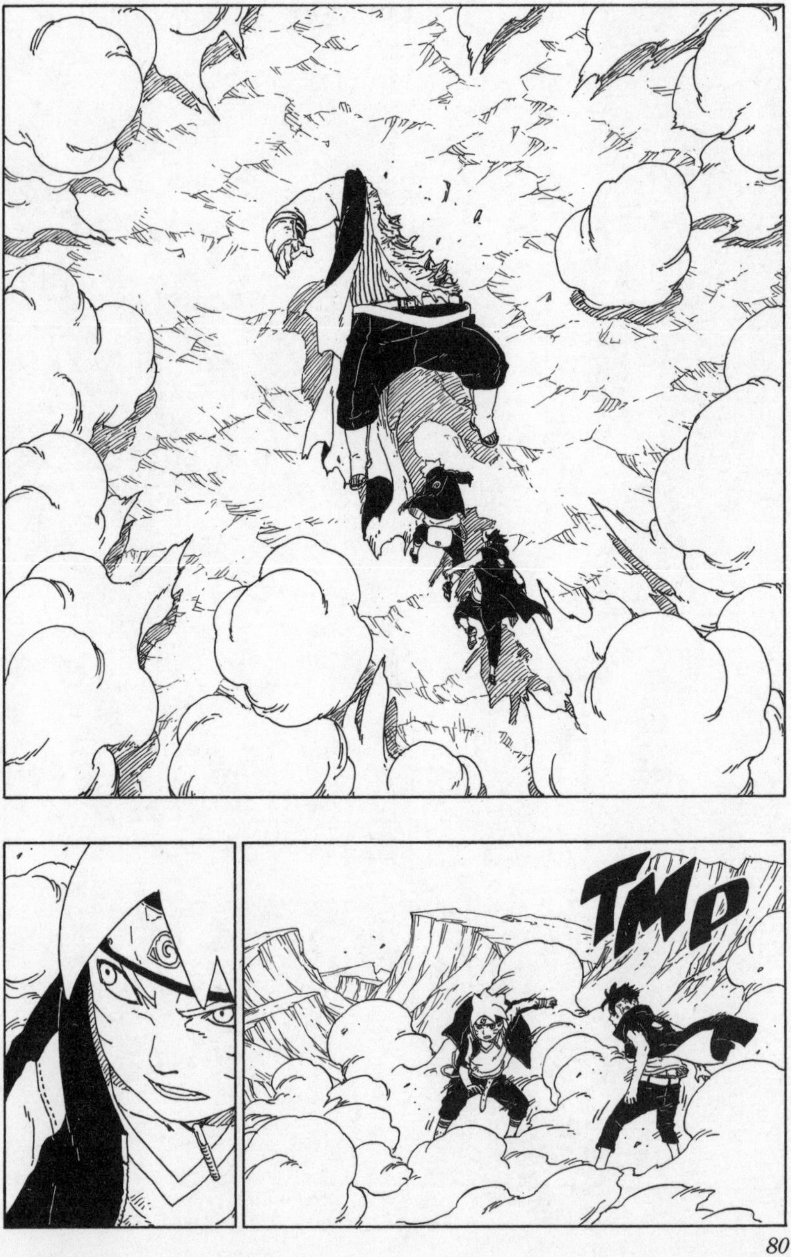
TMP

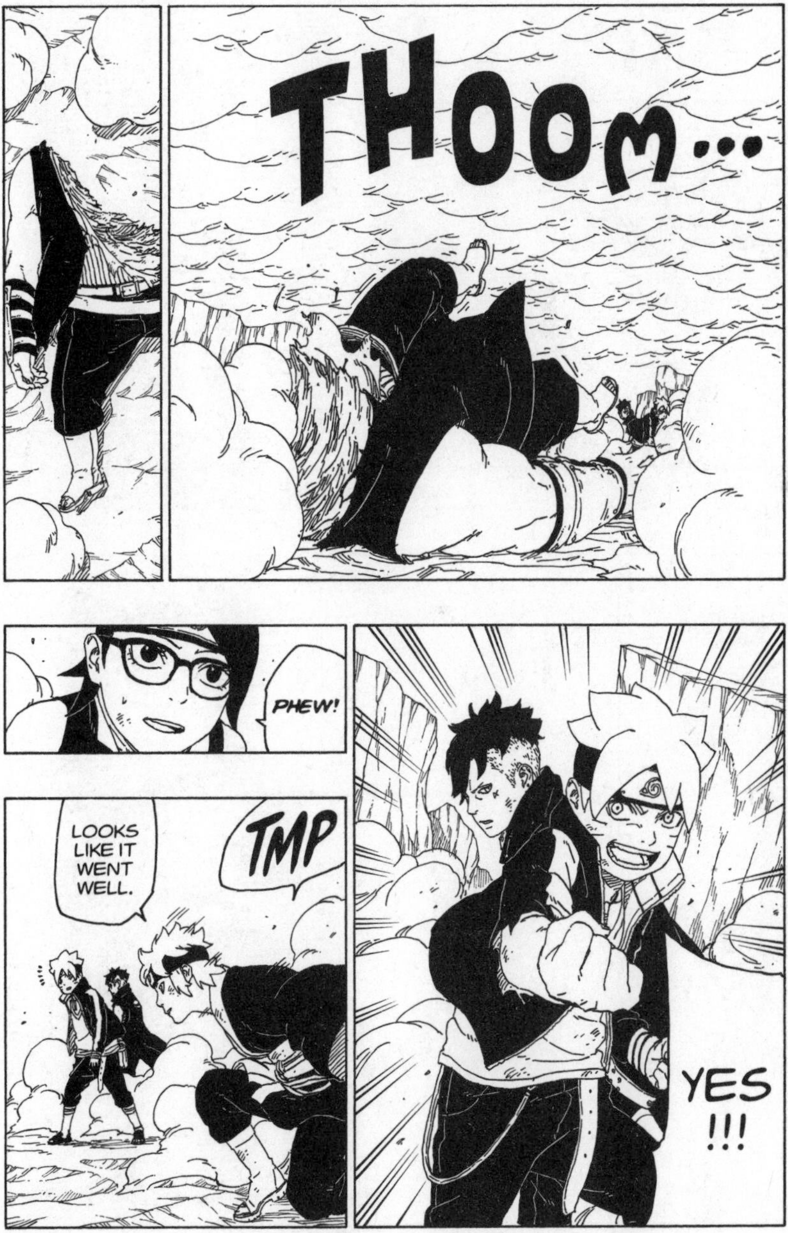
THOOM...
YES !!!
PHEW!
TMP
LOOKS LIKE IT WENT WELL.

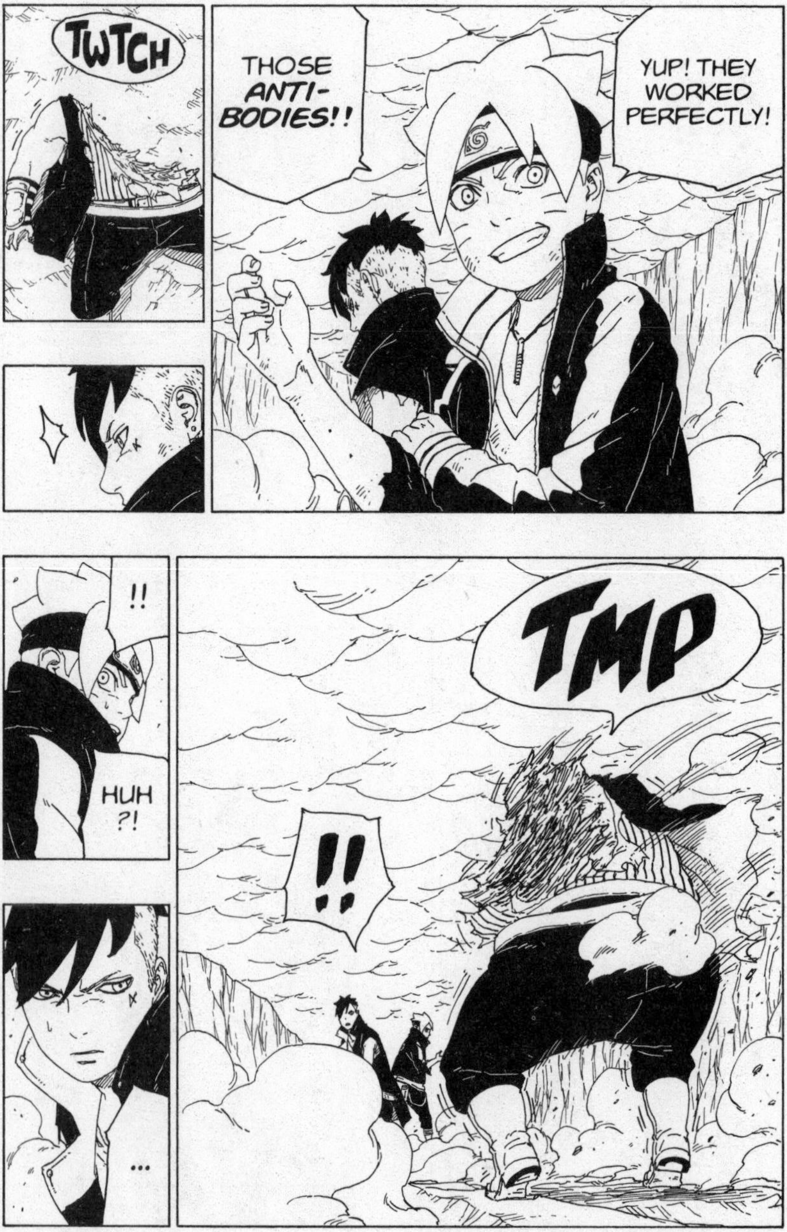
YUP! THEY WORKED PERFECTLY!
THOSE ANTI-BODIES!!
TWTCH
TMP
!!
!!
HUH ?!
...

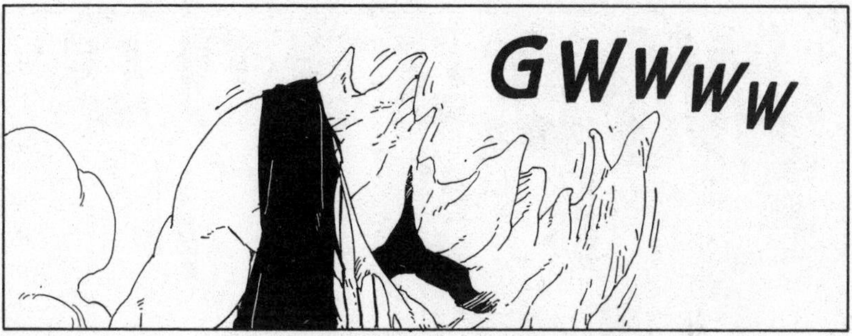
GWWWW

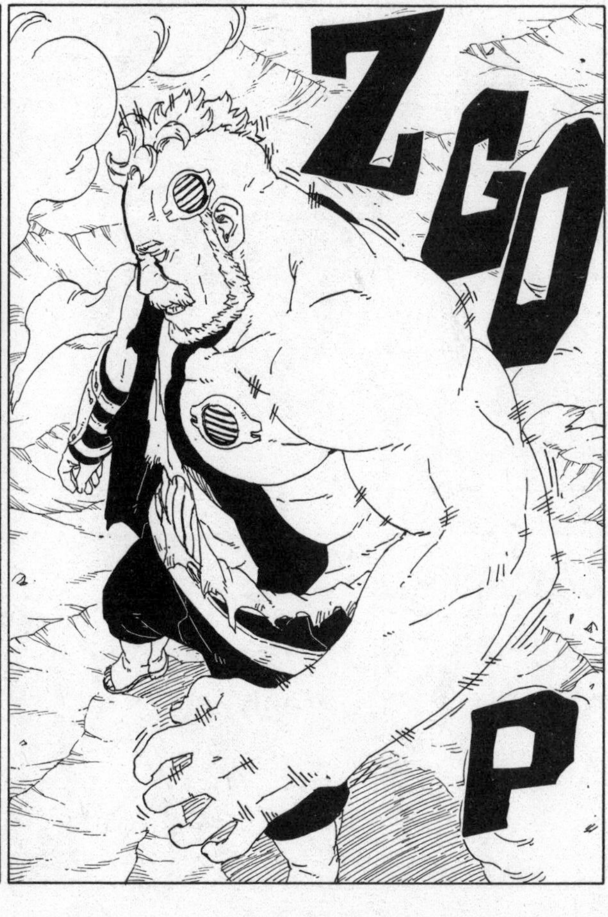
ZGOP

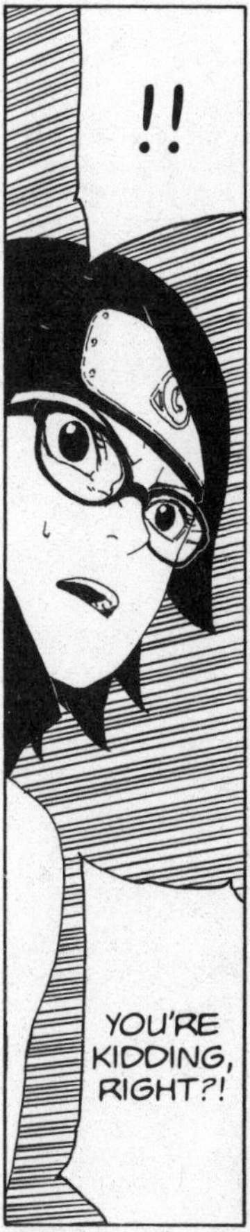
!!
YOU'RE KIDDING, RIGHT?!

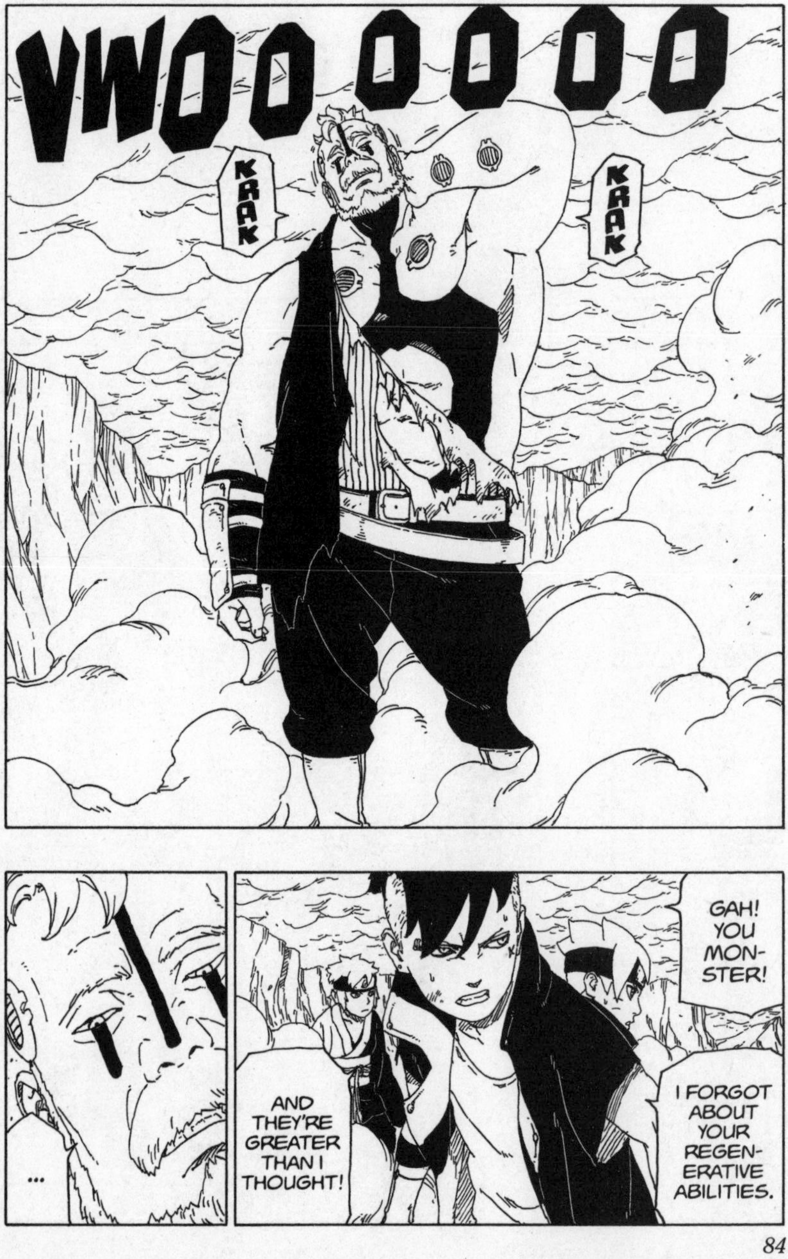
VWOOOOOO
KRAK
KRAK
GAH! YOU MONSTER!
I FORGOT ABOUT YOUR REGENERATIVE ABILITIES.
AND THEY'RE GREATER THAN I THOUGHT!
...

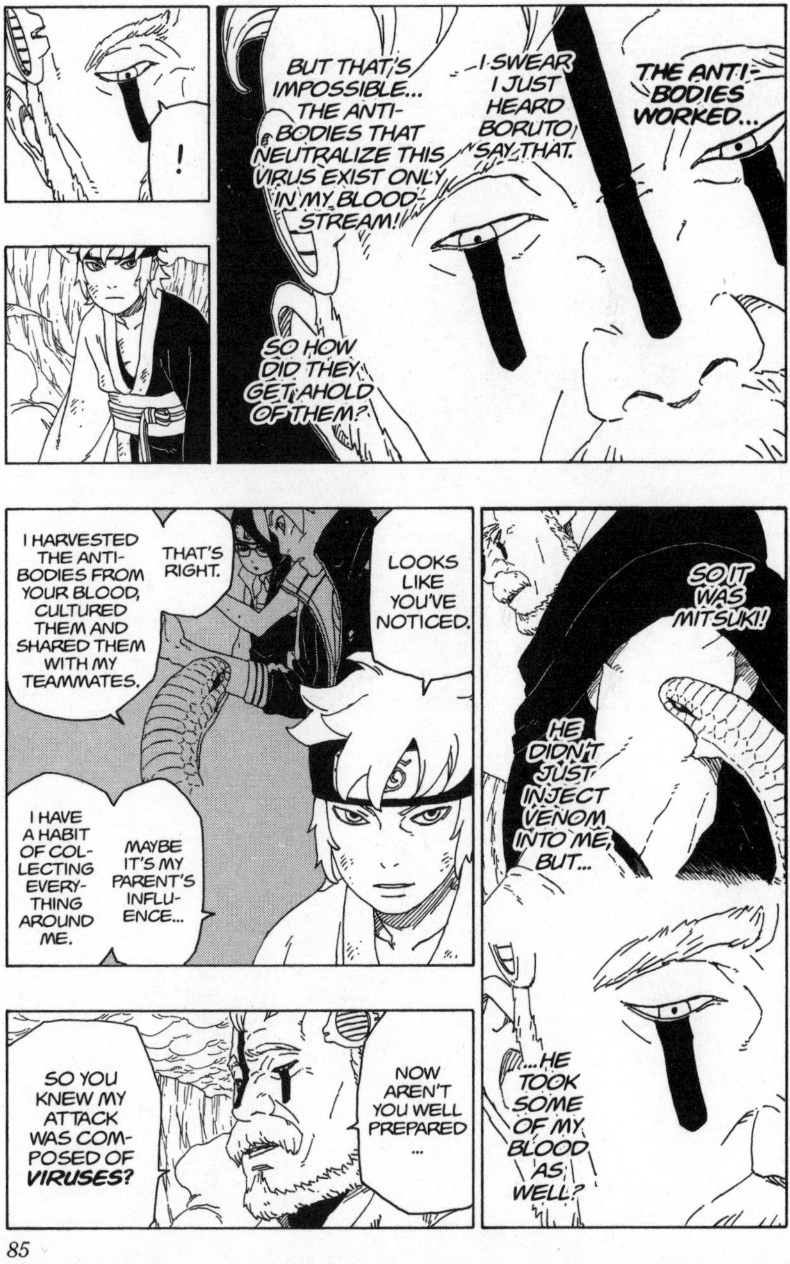
THE ANTIBODIES WORKED...
I SWEAR I JUST HEARD BORUTO SAY THAT.
BUT THAT'S IMPOSSIBLE... THE ANTIBODIES THAT NEUTRALIZE THIS VIRUS EXIST ONLY IN MY BLOODSTREAM!
SO HOW DID THEY GET AHOLD OF THEM?
!
SO IT WAS MITSUKI!
HE DIDN'T JUST INJECT VENOM INTO ME, BUT...
...HE TOOK SOME OF MY BLOOD AS WELL?
LOOKS LIKE YOU'VE NOTICED.
THAT'S RIGHT.
I HARVESTED THE ANTIBODIES FROM YOUR BLOOD, CULTURED THEM AND SHARED THEM WITH MY TEAMMATES.
MAYBE IT'S MY PARENT'S INFLUENCE...
I HAVE A HABIT OF COLLECTING EVERYTHING AROUND ME.
NOW AREN'T YOU WELL PREPARED...
SO YOU KNEW MY ATTACK WAS COMPOSED OF ***VIRUSES?***

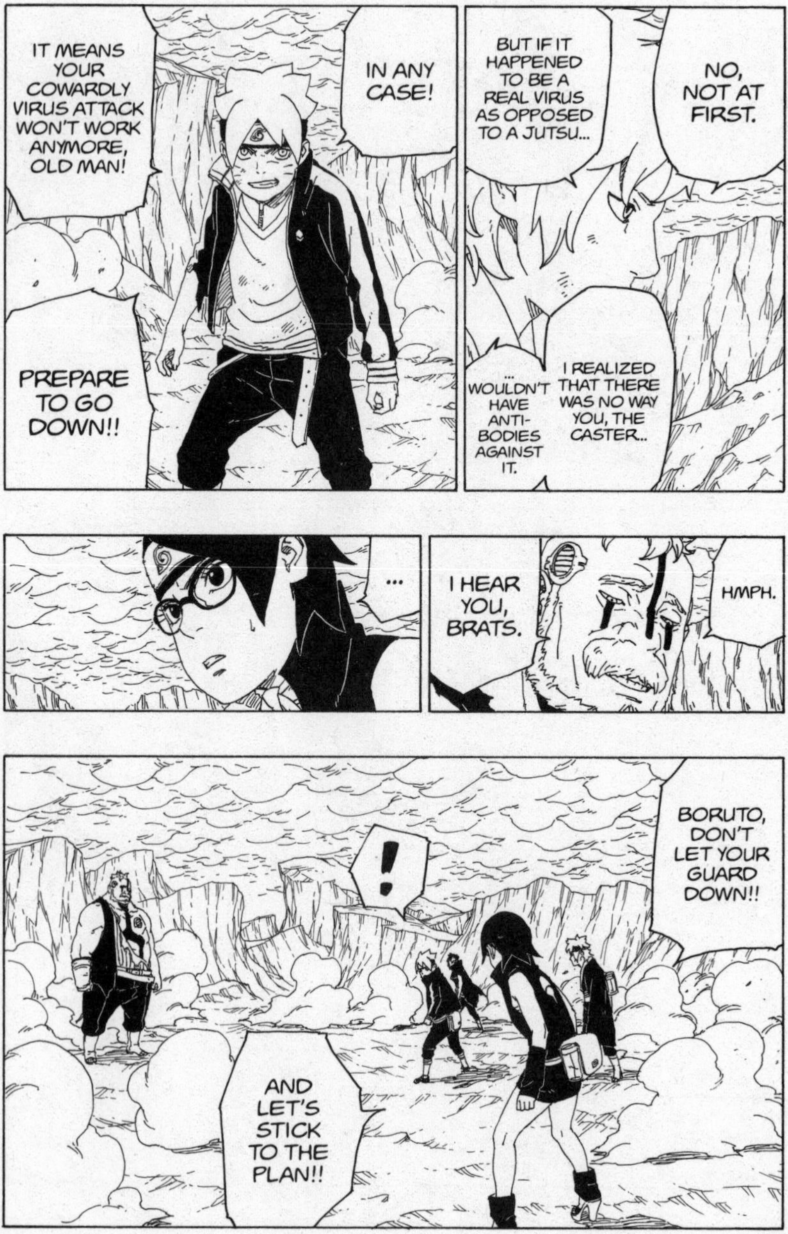
NO, NOT AT FIRST.
BUT IF IT HAPPENED TO BE A REAL VIRUS AS OPPOSED TO A JUTSU...
I REALIZED THAT THERE WAS NO WAY YOU, THE CASTER...
...WOULDN'T HAVE ANTI-BODIES AGAINST IT.
IN ANY CASE!
IT MEANS YOUR COWARDLY VIRUS ATTACK WON'T WORK ANYMORE, OLD MAN!
PREPARE TO GO DOWN!!
HMPH.
I HEAR YOU, BRATS.
...
BORUTO, DON'T LET YOUR GUARD DOWN!!
!
AND LET'S STICK TO THE PLAN!!

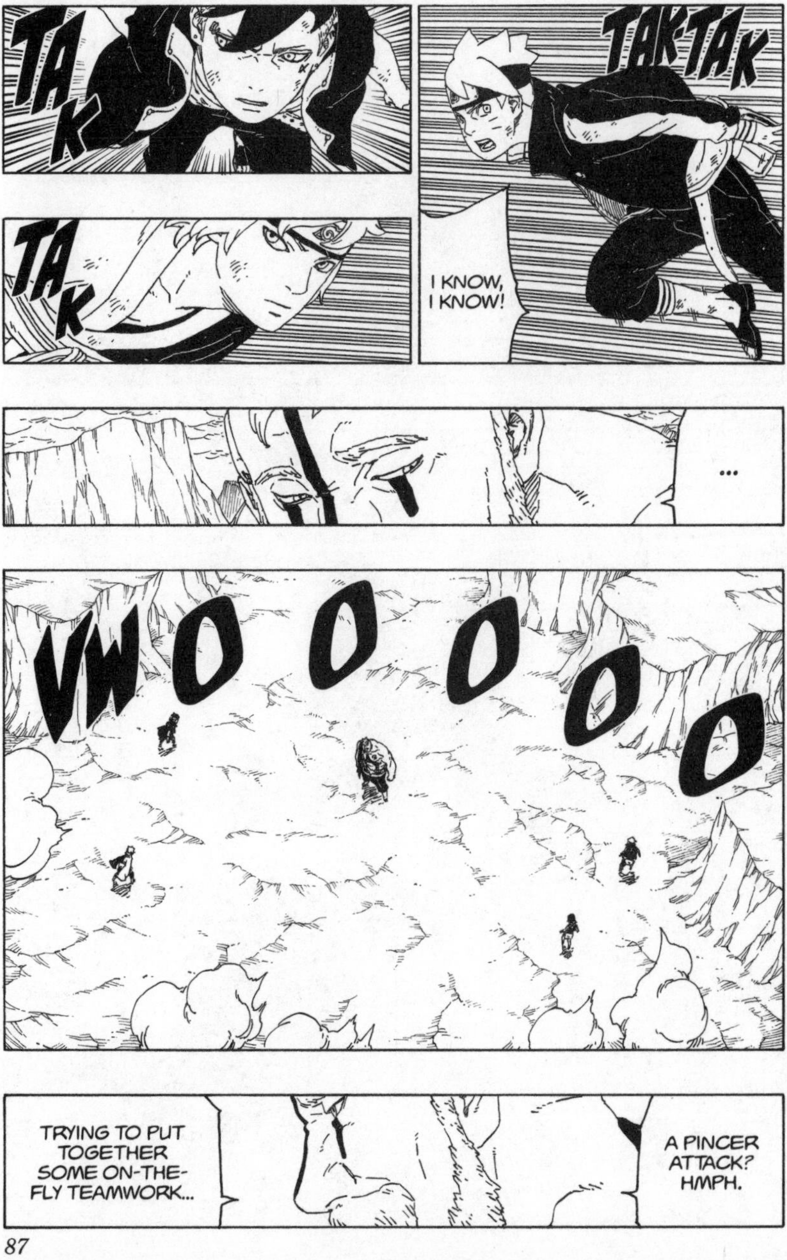
TAKTAK
I KNOW, I KNOW!
TAK
TAK
...
VWOOOOO
A PINCER ATTACK? HMPH.
TRYING TO PUT TOGETHER SOME ON-THE-FLY TEAMWORK...

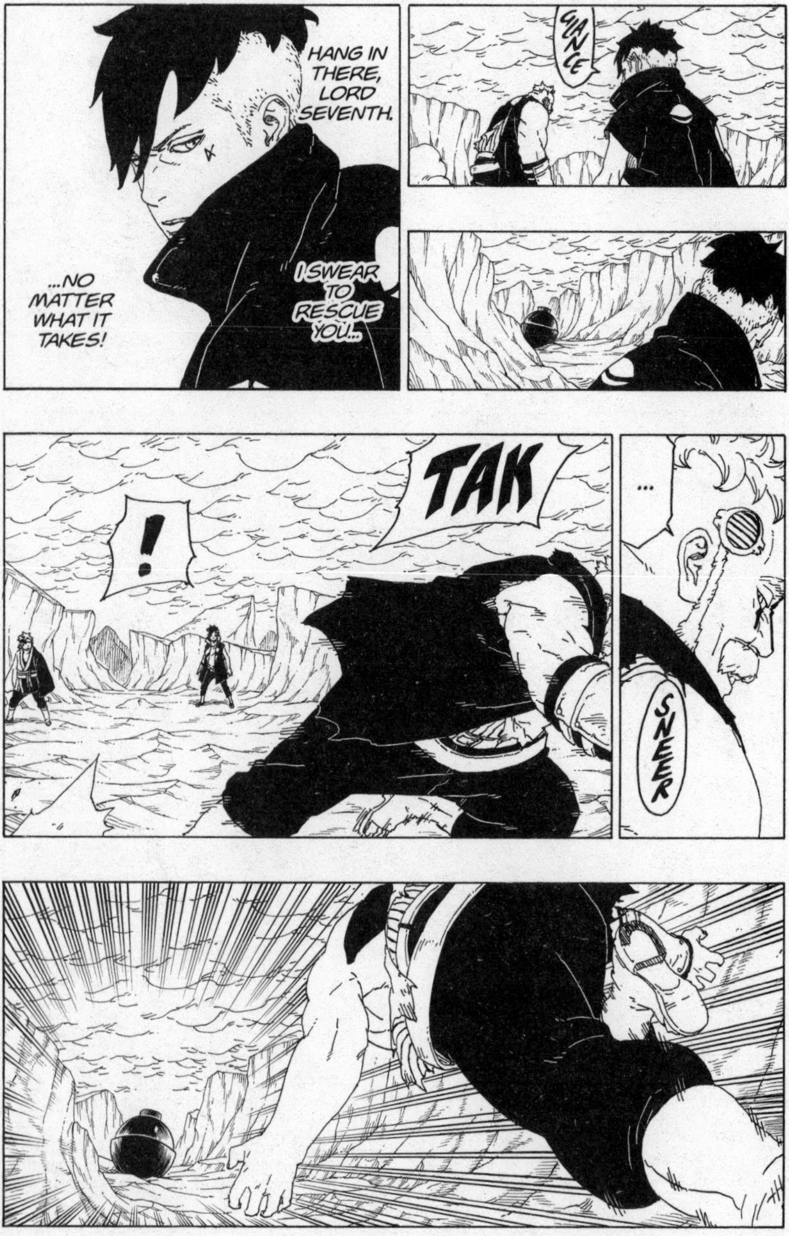
GLANCE
HANG IN THERE, LORD SEVENTH.
I SWEAR TO RESCUE YOU...
...NO MATTER WHAT IT TAKES!
...
SNEER
TAK
!

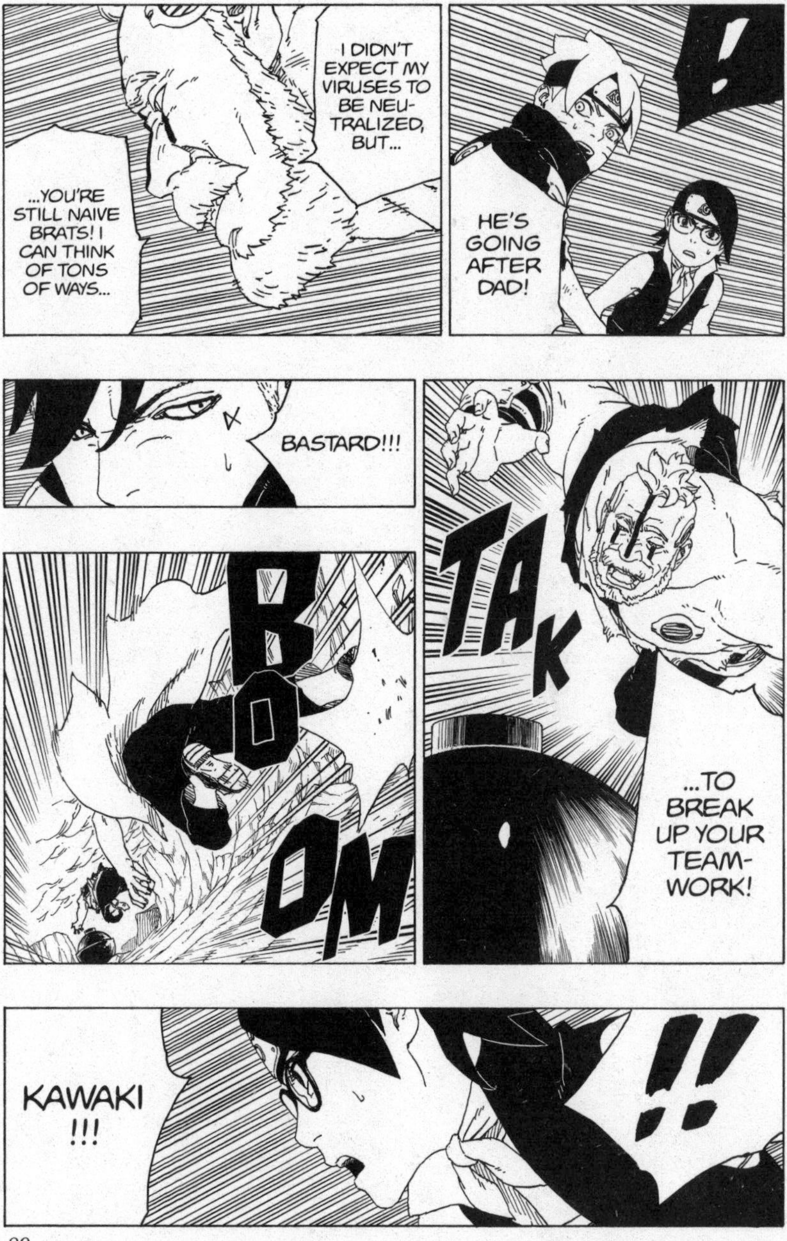
!
HE'S GOING AFTER DAD!
I DIDN'T EXPECT MY VIRUSES TO BE NEU-TRALIZED, BUT...
...YOU'RE STILL NAIVE BRATS! I CAN THINK OF TONS OF WAYS...
TAK
...TO BREAK UP YOUR TEAM-WORK!
BASTARD!!!
BOOM
!!
KAWAKI !!!

# Number 42: Regeneration

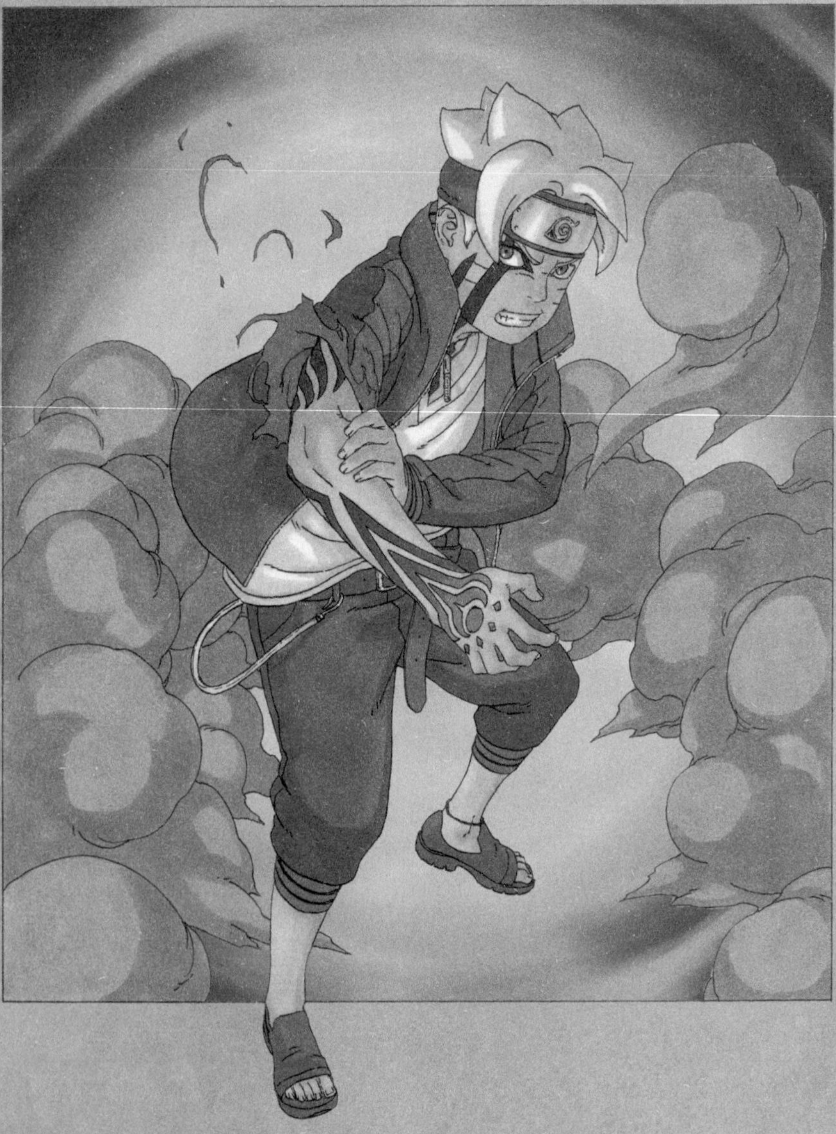

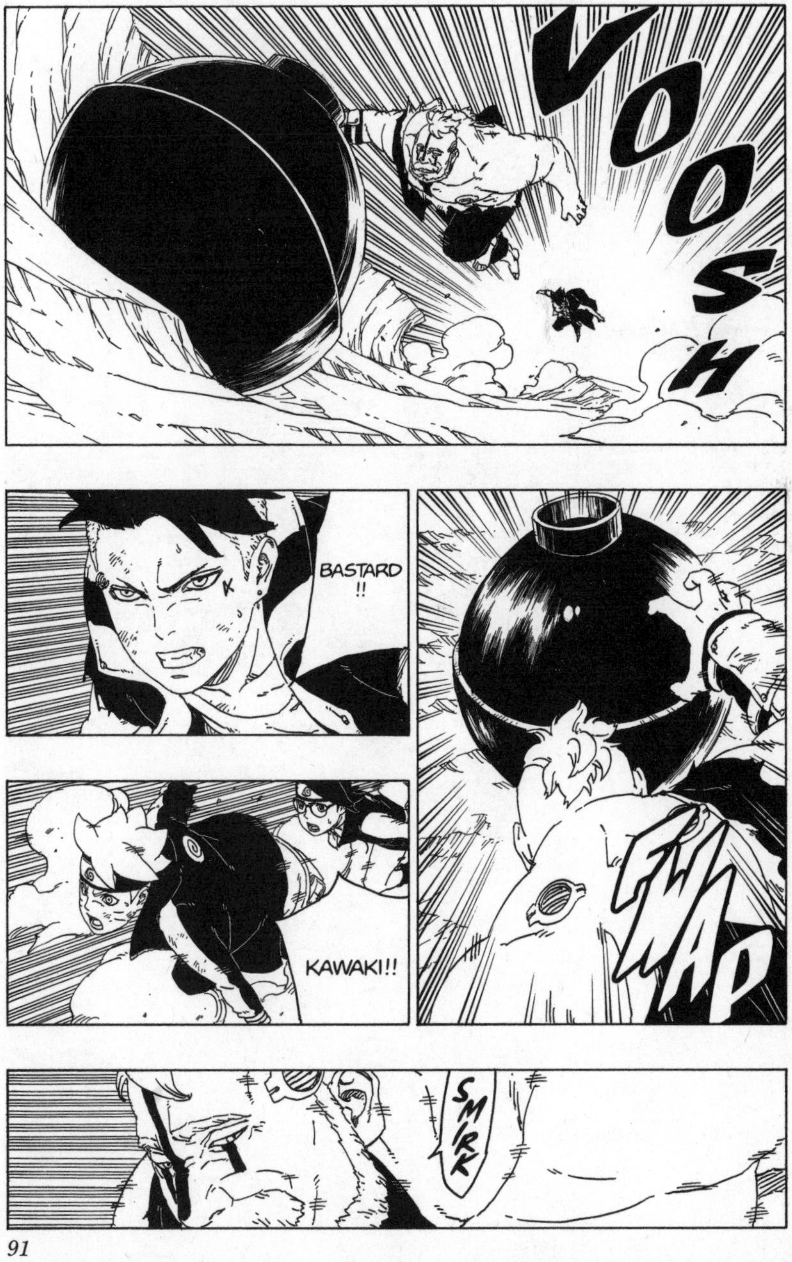

VOOSH
THWAP
BASTARD !!
KAWAKI!!
SMIRK

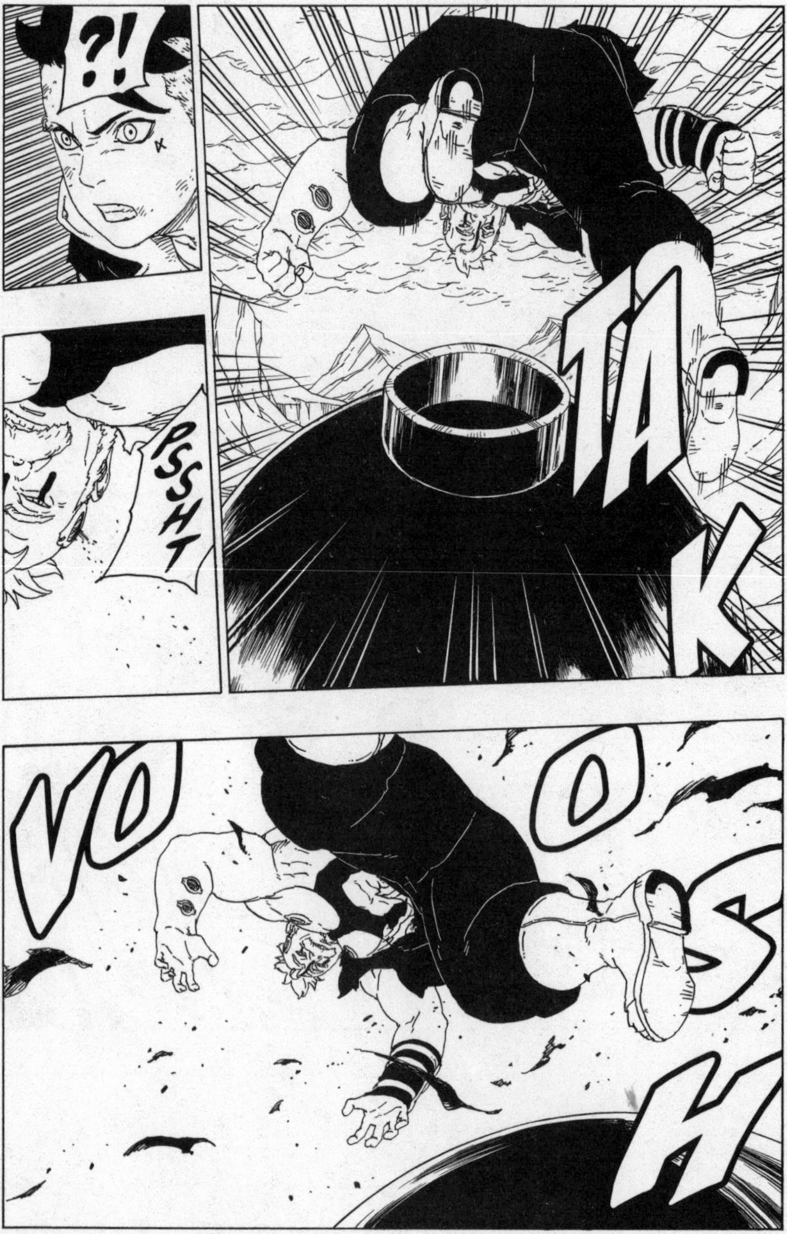
TAK
?!
PSSHT
VOOSH

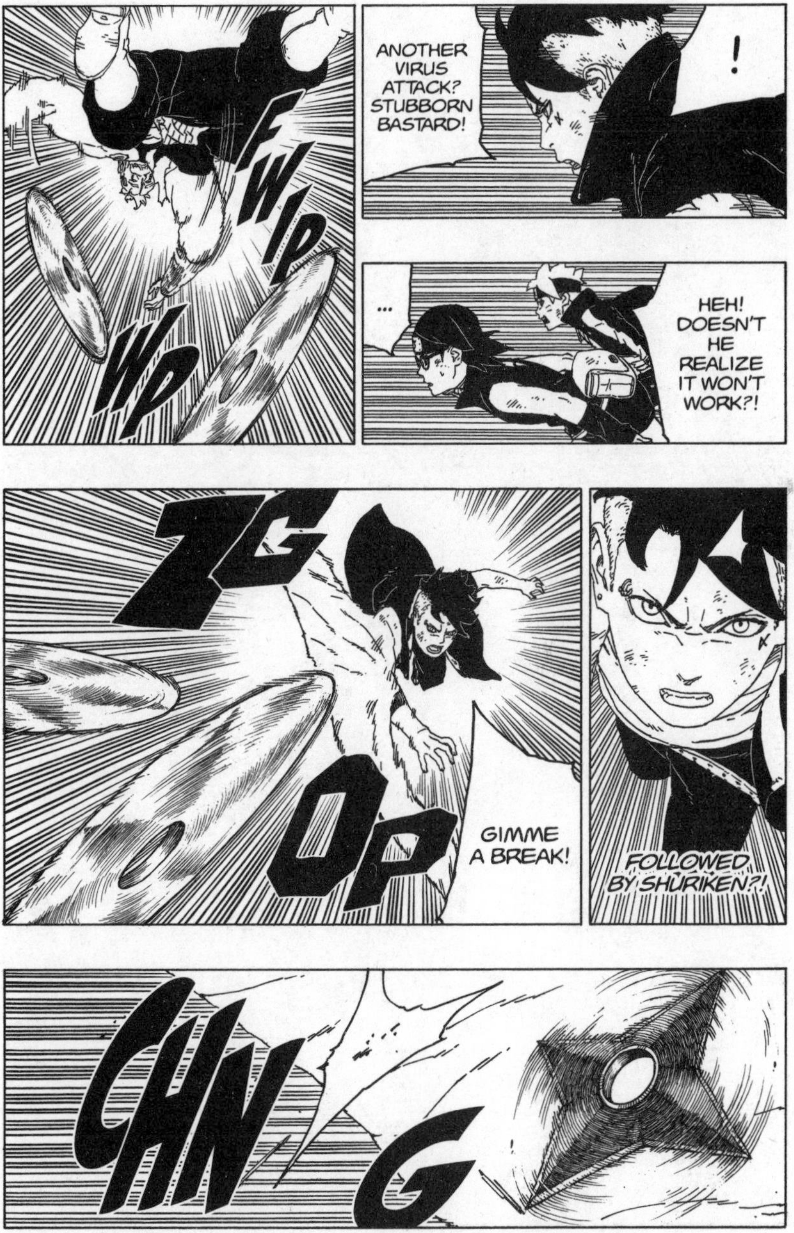

!
ANOTHER VIRUS ATTACK? STUBBORN BASTARD!
HEH! DOESN'T HE REALIZE IT WON'T WORK?!
...
FWIP
WP
FOLLOWED BY SHURIKEN?!
ZG
GIMME A BREAK!
OP
CHIN
G

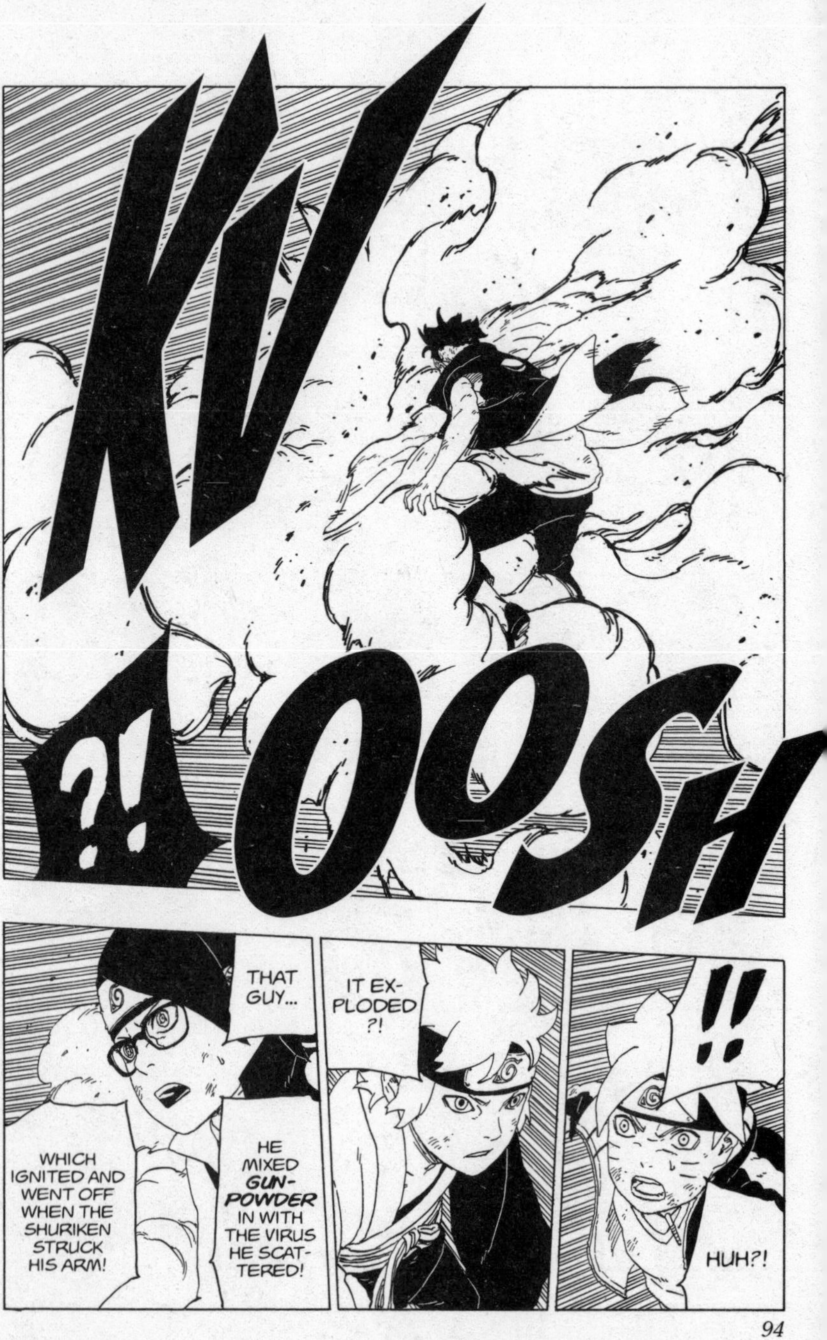
KWOOSH
?!
!!
HUH?!
IT EX-
PLODED
?!
THAT
GUY...
HE MIXED GUN-POWDER IN WITH THE VIRUS HE SCATTERED!
WHICH IGNITED AND WENT OFF WHEN THE SHURIKEN STRUCK HIS ARM!

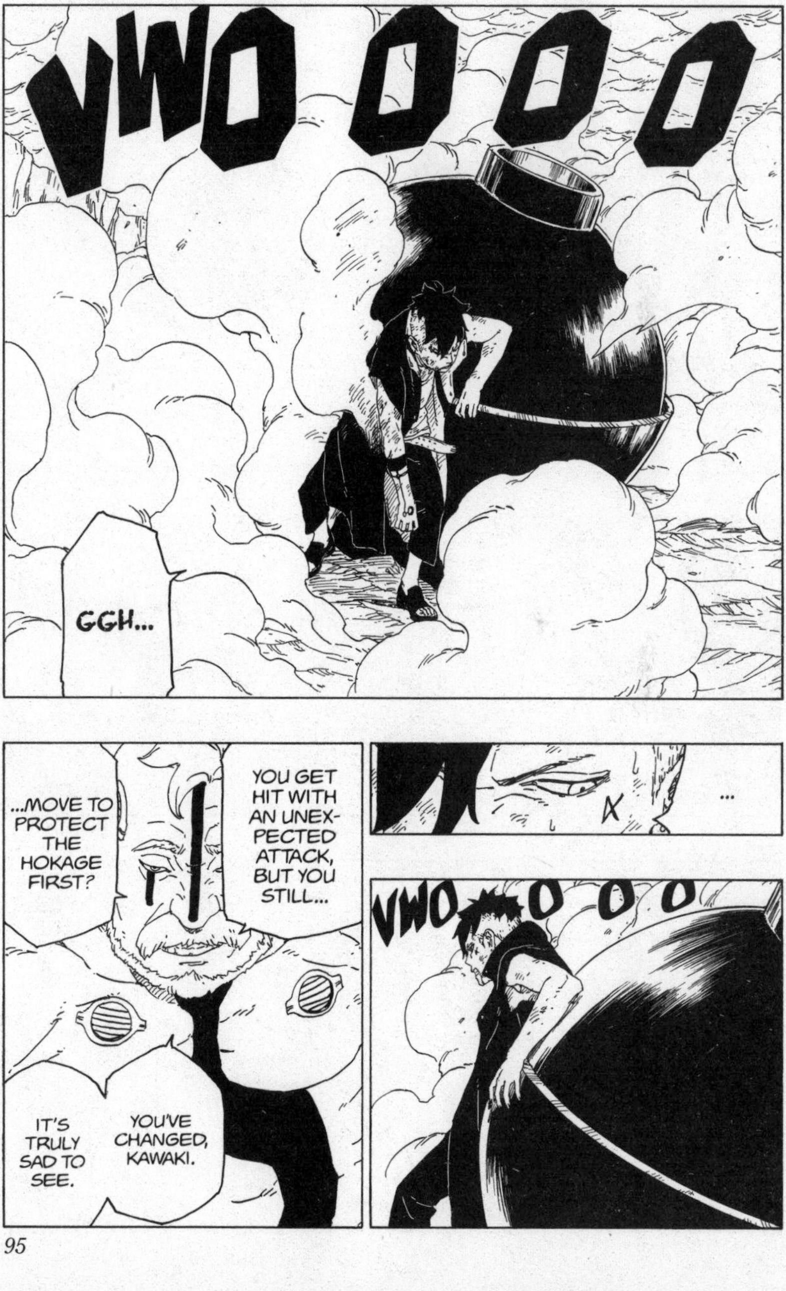
VWO O O O
GGH...
...
VWO O O O
YOU GET HIT WITH AN UNEX-PECTED ATTACK, BUT YOU STILL...
...MOVE TO PROTECT THE HOKAGE FIRST?
YOU'VE CHANGED, KAWAKI.
IT'S TRULY SAD TO SEE.

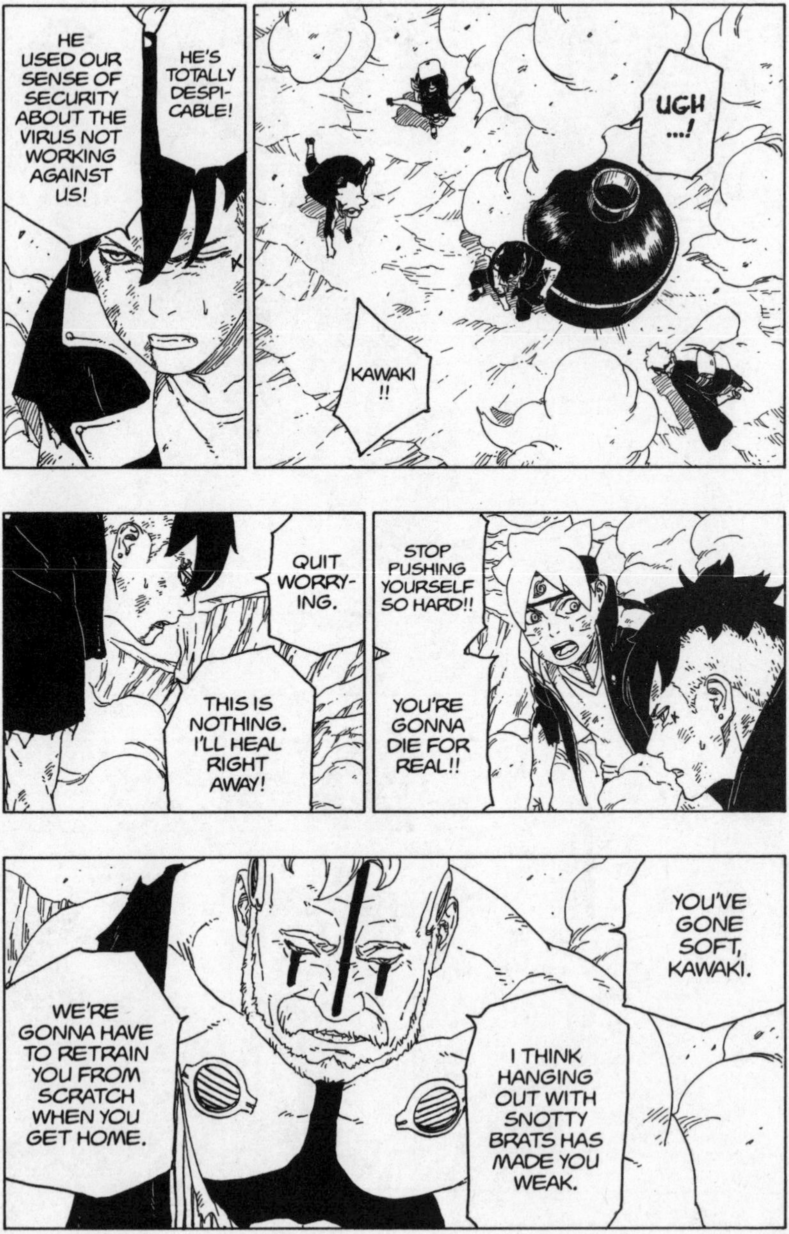
UGH ...!
KAWAKI !!
HE'S TOTALLY DESPI-CABLE!
HE USED OUR SENSE OF SECURITY ABOUT THE VIRUS NOT WORKING AGAINST US!
STOP PUSHING YOURSELF SO HARD!!
YOU'RE GONNA DIE FOR REAL!!
QUIT WORRY-ING.
THIS IS NOTHING. I'LL HEAL RIGHT AWAY!
YOU'VE GONE SOFT, KAWAKI.
I THINK HANGING OUT WITH SNOTTY BRATS HAS MADE YOU WEAK.
WE'RE GONNA HAVE TO RETRAIN YOU FROM SCRATCH WHEN YOU GET HOME.

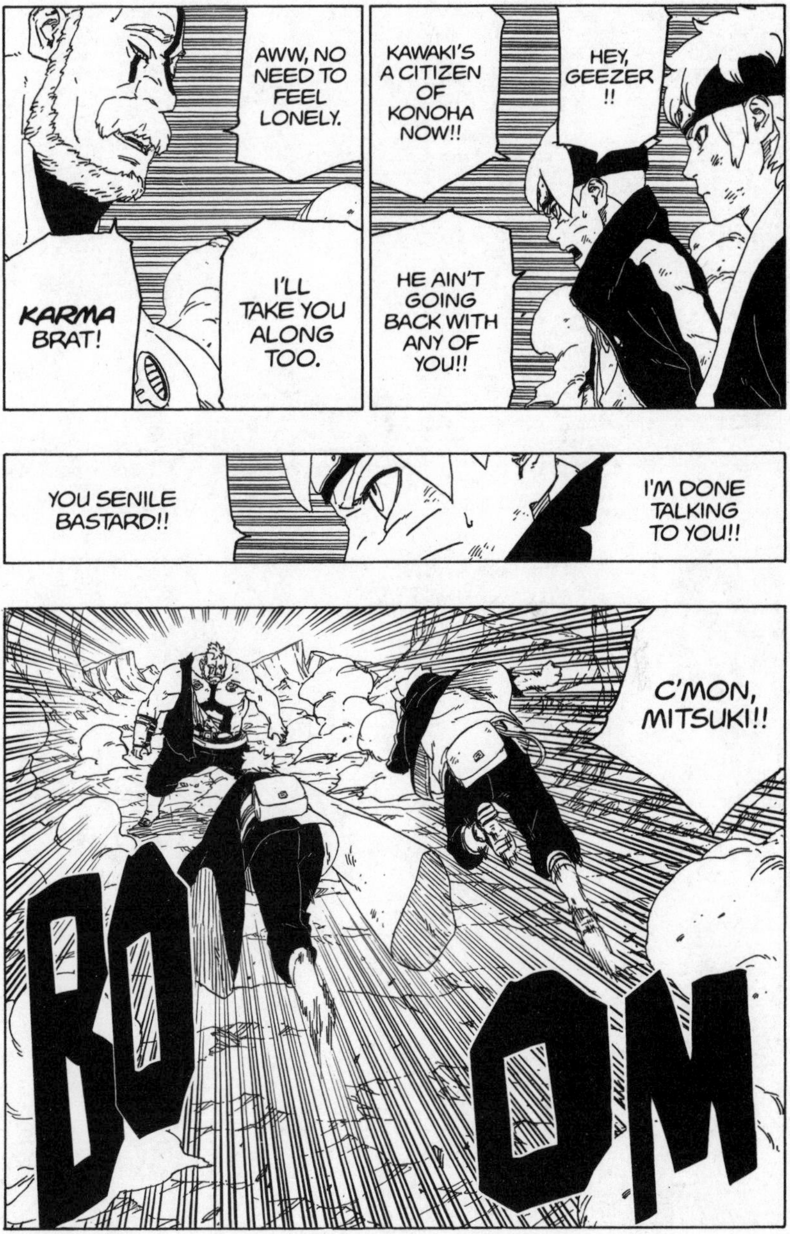
HEY, GEEZER !!
KAWAKI'S A CITIZEN OF KONOHA NOW!!
HE AIN'T GOING BACK WITH ANY OF YOU!!
AWW, NO NEED TO FEEL LONELY.
I'LL TAKE YOU ALONG TOO.
*KARMA* BRAT!
I'M DONE TALKING TO YOU!!
YOU SENILE BASTARD!!
C'MON, MITSUKI!!
BOOM

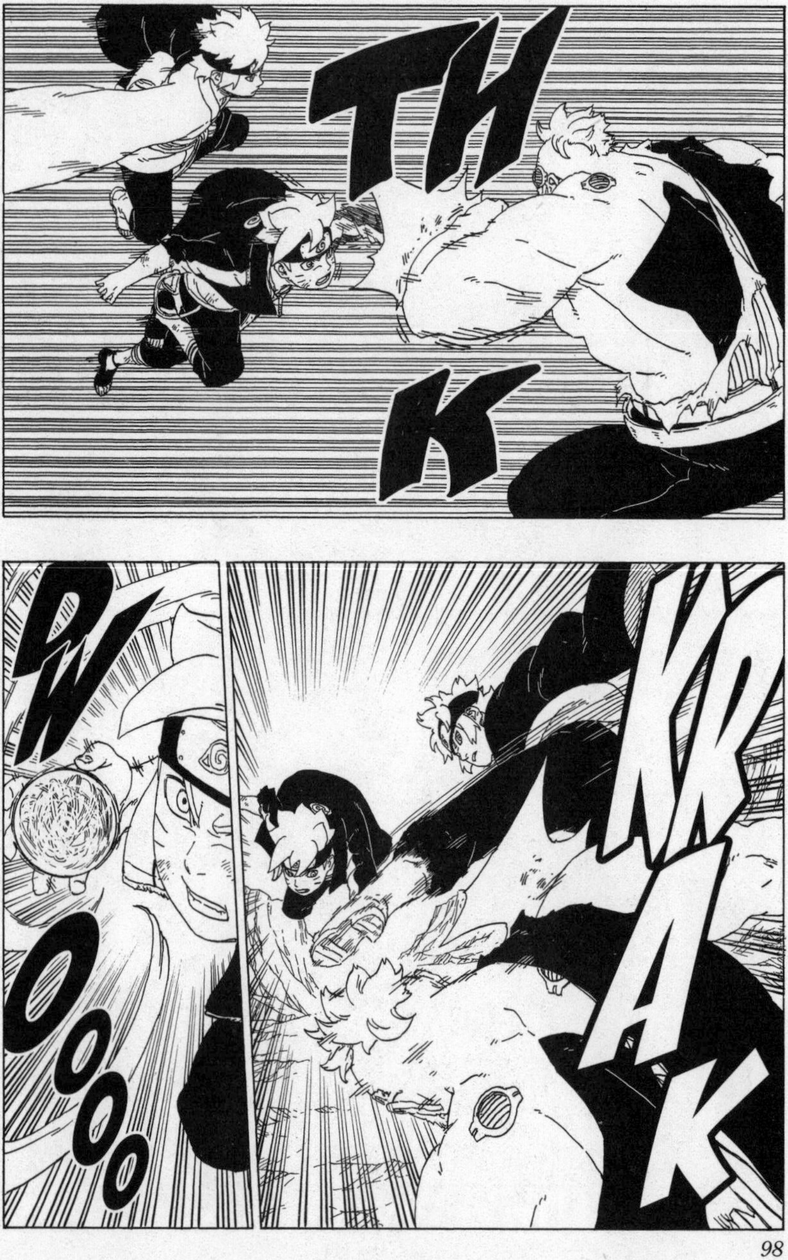
THK
KRAAK
DWOOOO

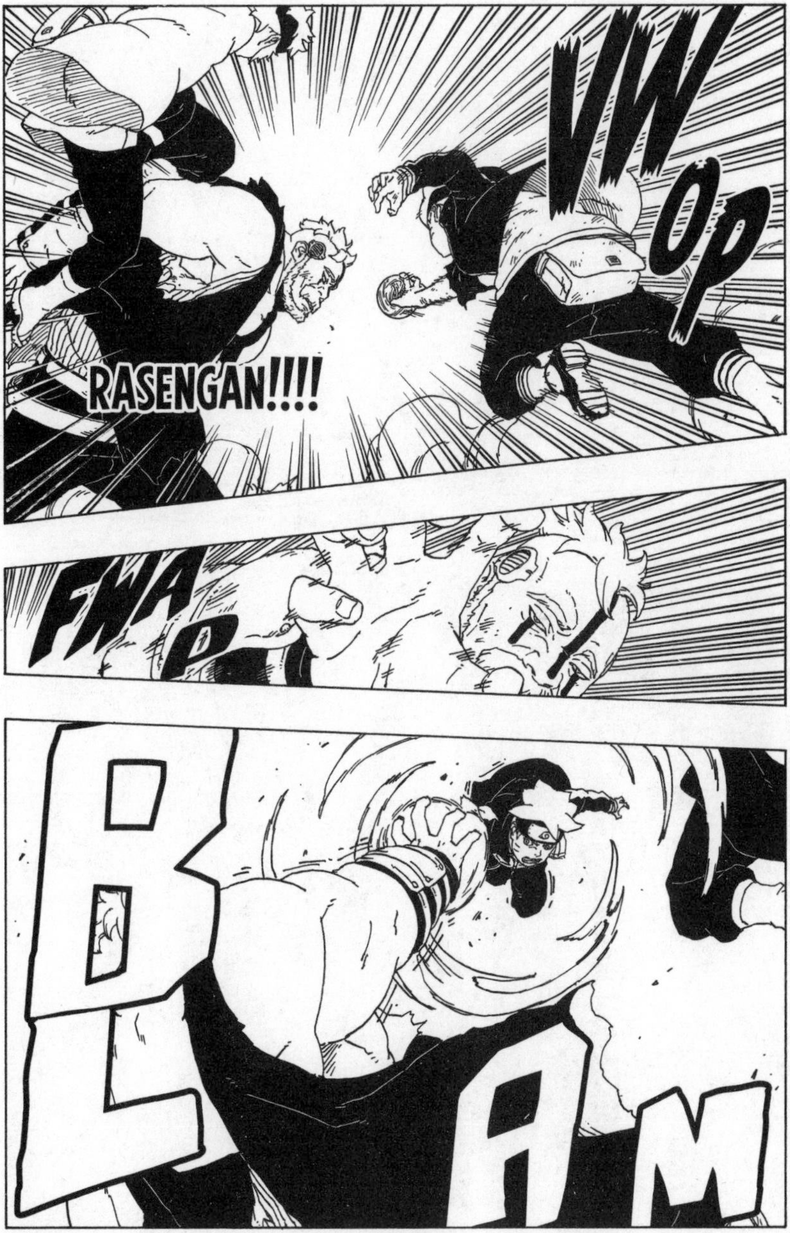
VWOP
RASENGAN!!!!
FWAP
BLAM

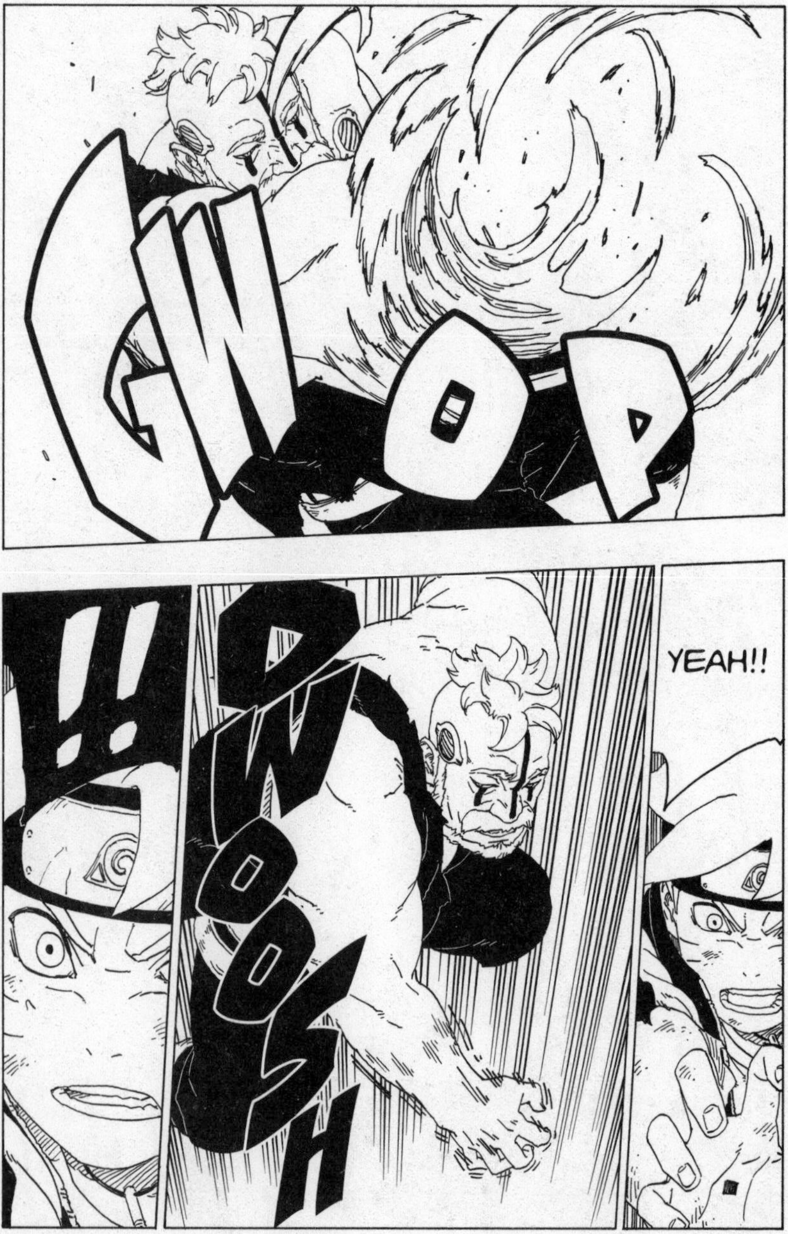
GWOOP
YEAH!!
DWOOOSH
!!

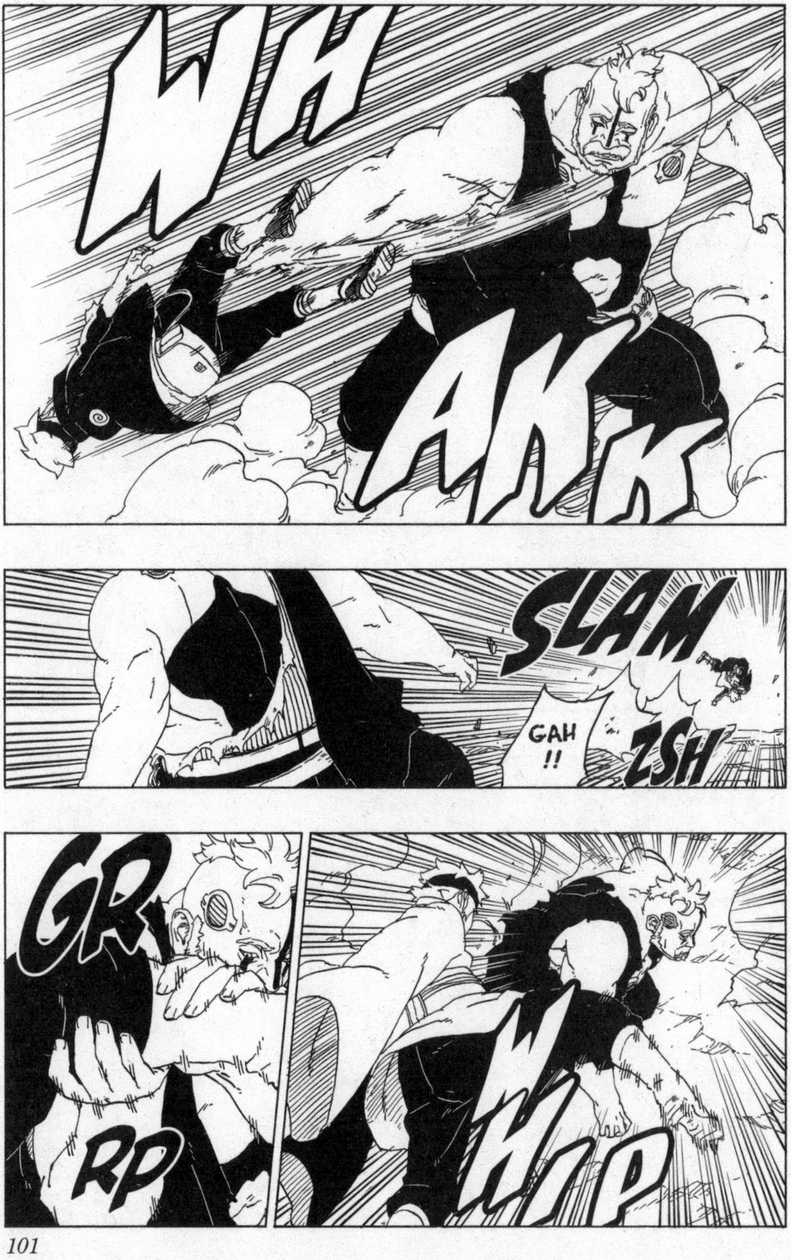
WH
ACK
SLAM
GAH!!
ZSH
WHIP
GR
RP

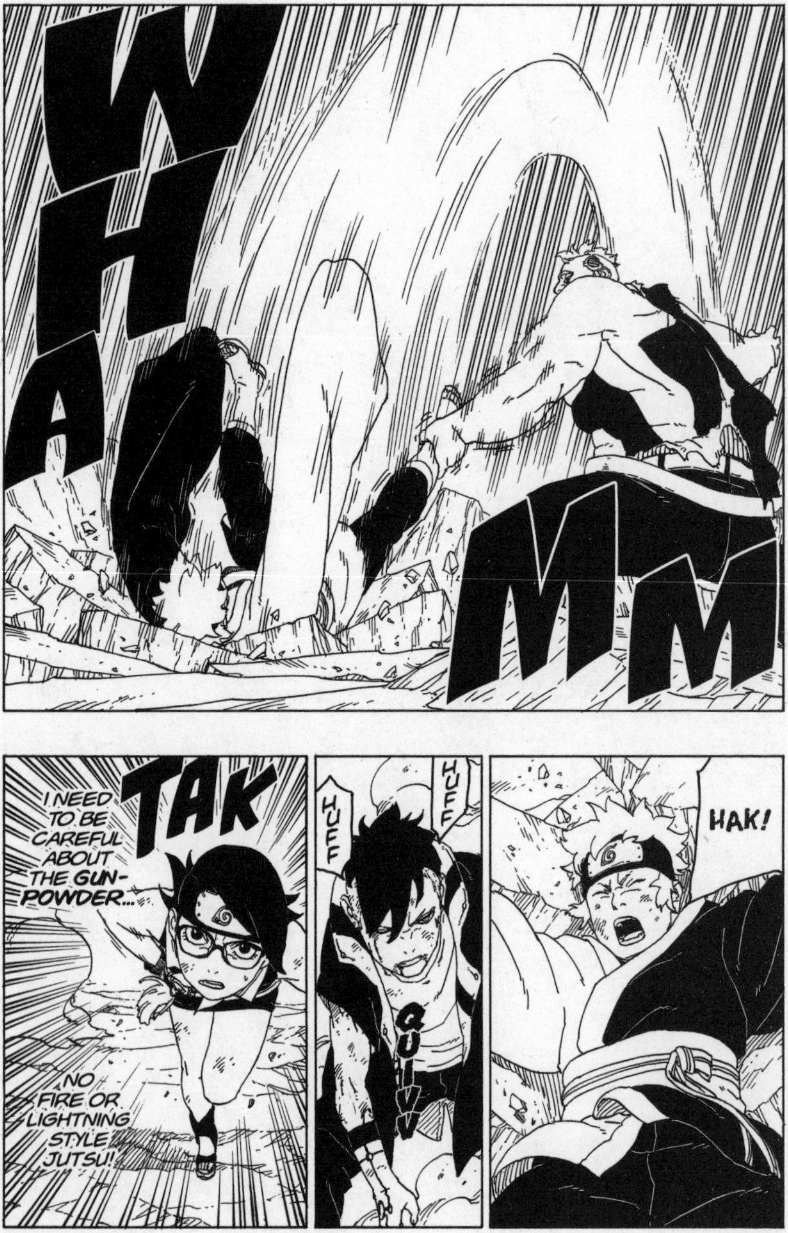
WHAMM
HAK!
HUFF
HUFF
QUIVV
TAK
I NEED TO BE CAREFUL ABOUT THE GUN-POWDER...
NO FIRE OR LIGHTNING STYLE JUTSU!

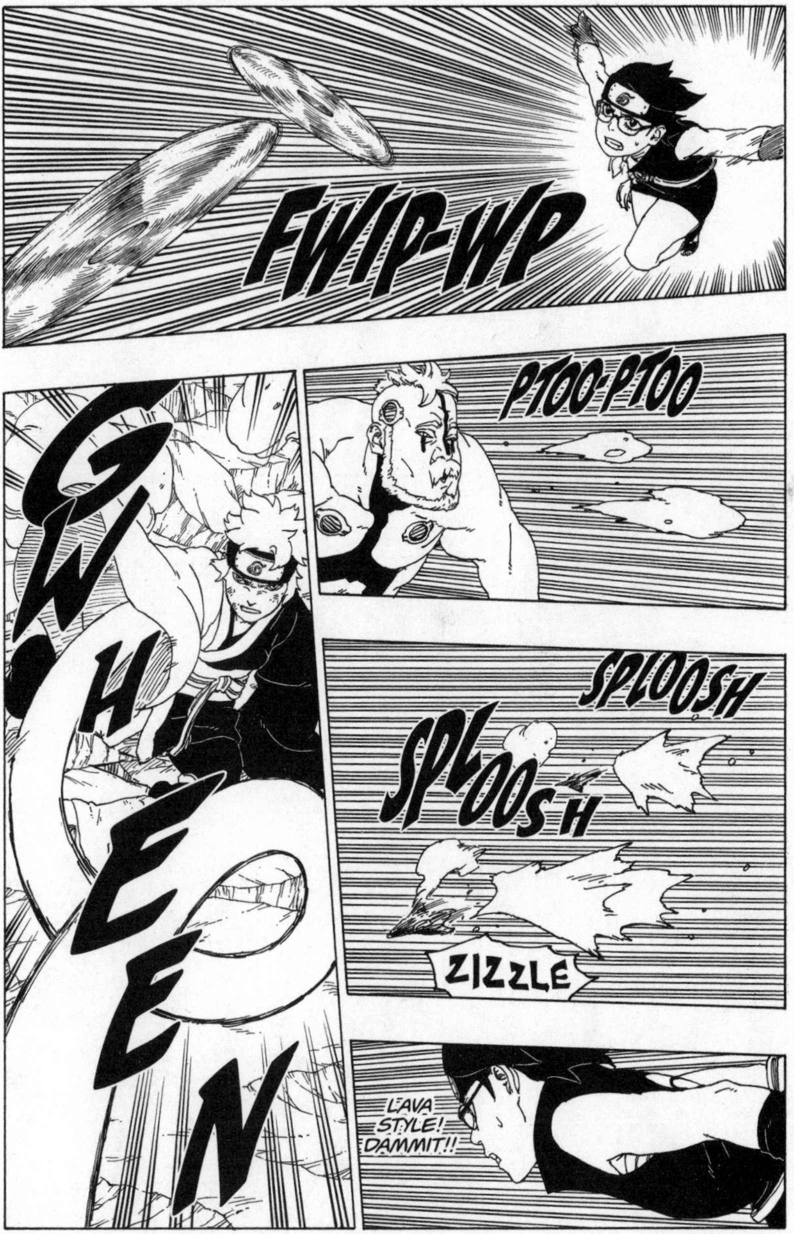
FWIP-WP
PTOO-PTOO
SPLOOSH
SPLOOSH
ZIZZLE
LAVA STYLE! DAMMIT!!
GWHEEEN

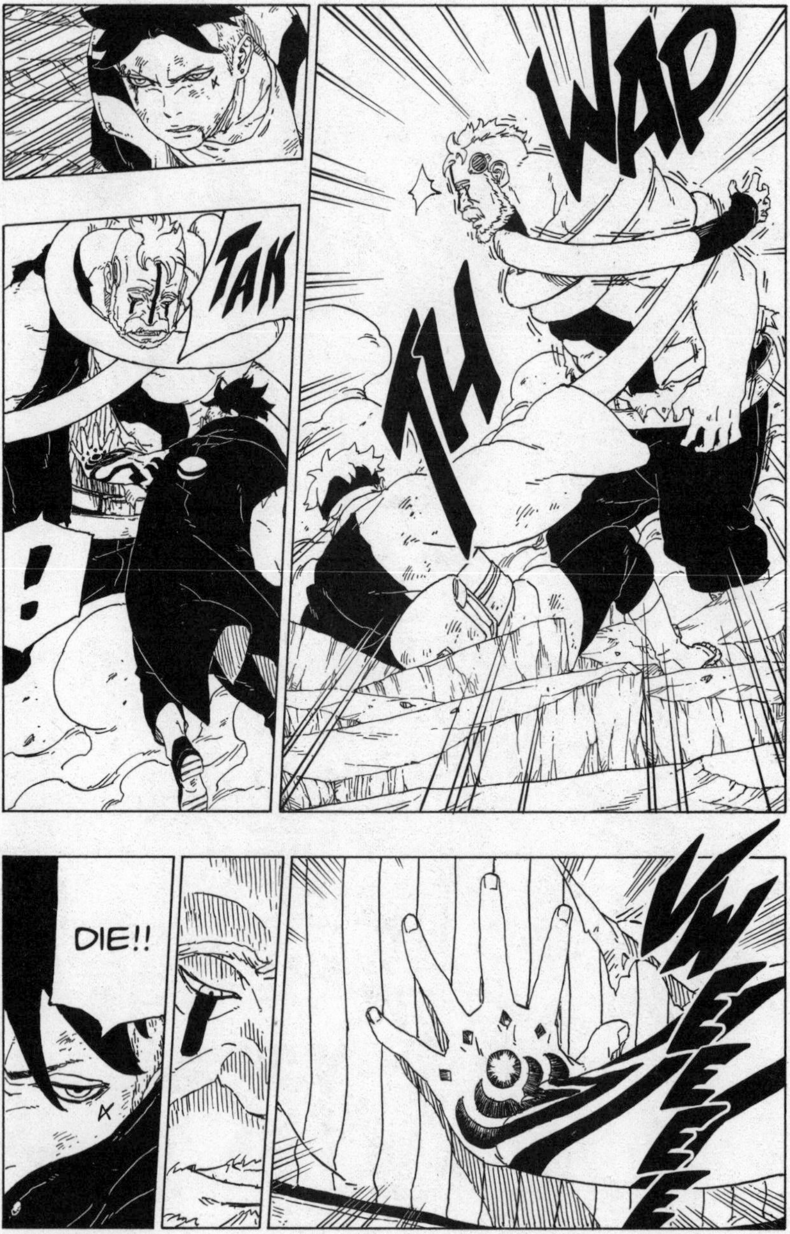
WAP
TH
TAK
!
VWEEEE
DIE!!

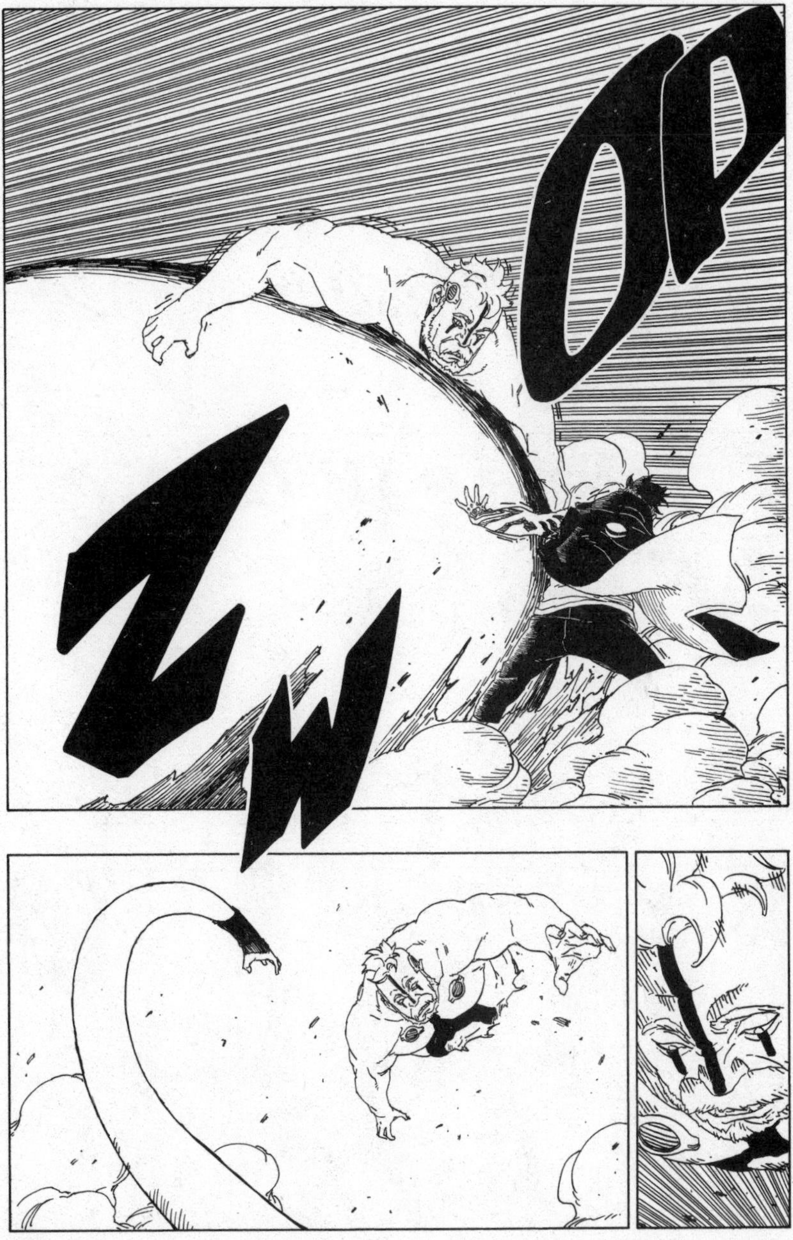
ZWOP

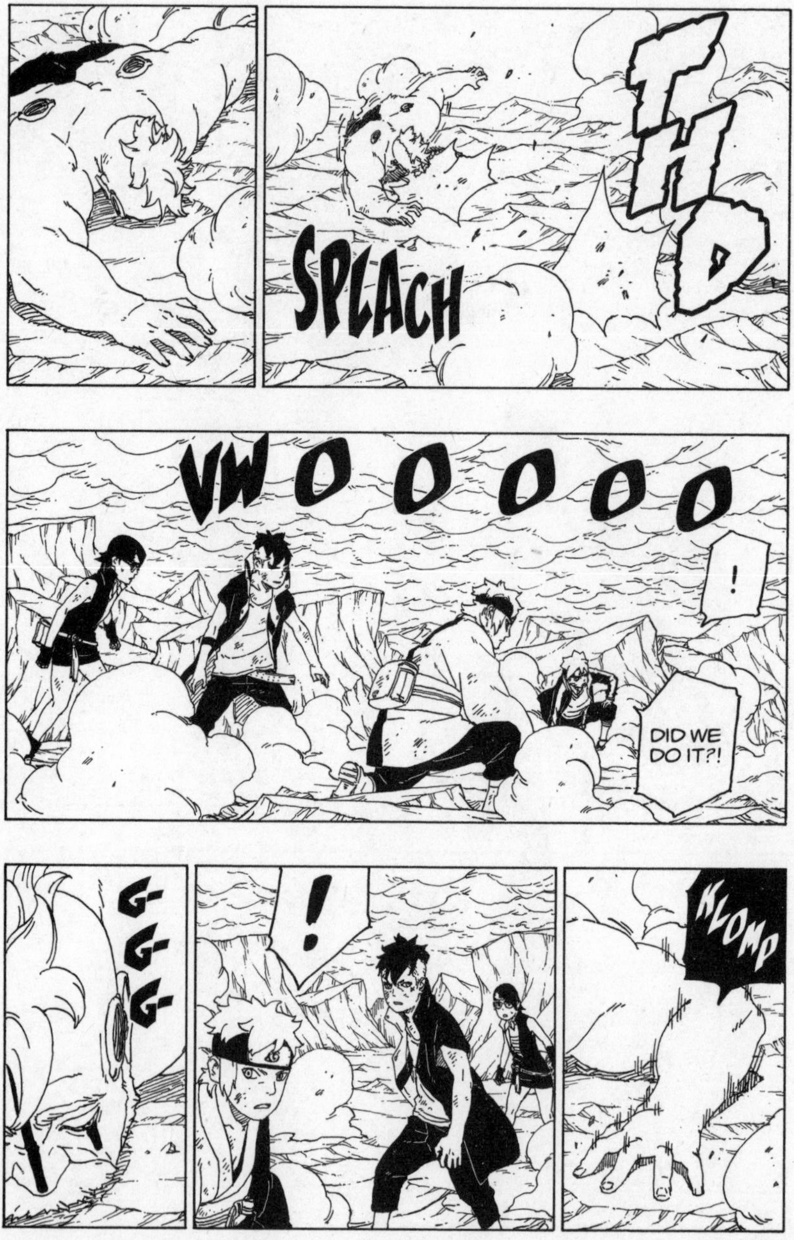
THD
SPLACH
VWOOOOOO
!
DID WE DO IT?!
KLOMP
!
G-G-G-

ZRPP
!
HE REALLY IS A FREAKING MONSTER!!
VWOOOOO
YOU JUST NOTICED?
NOT THE BRIGHTEST, ARE YOU?

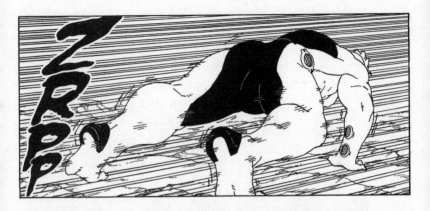

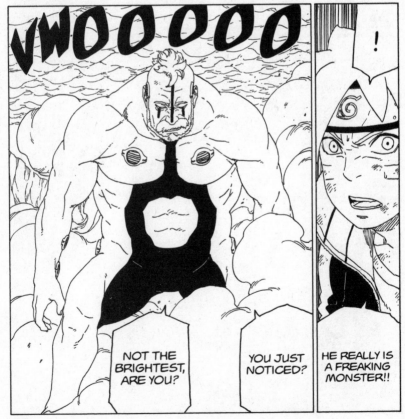

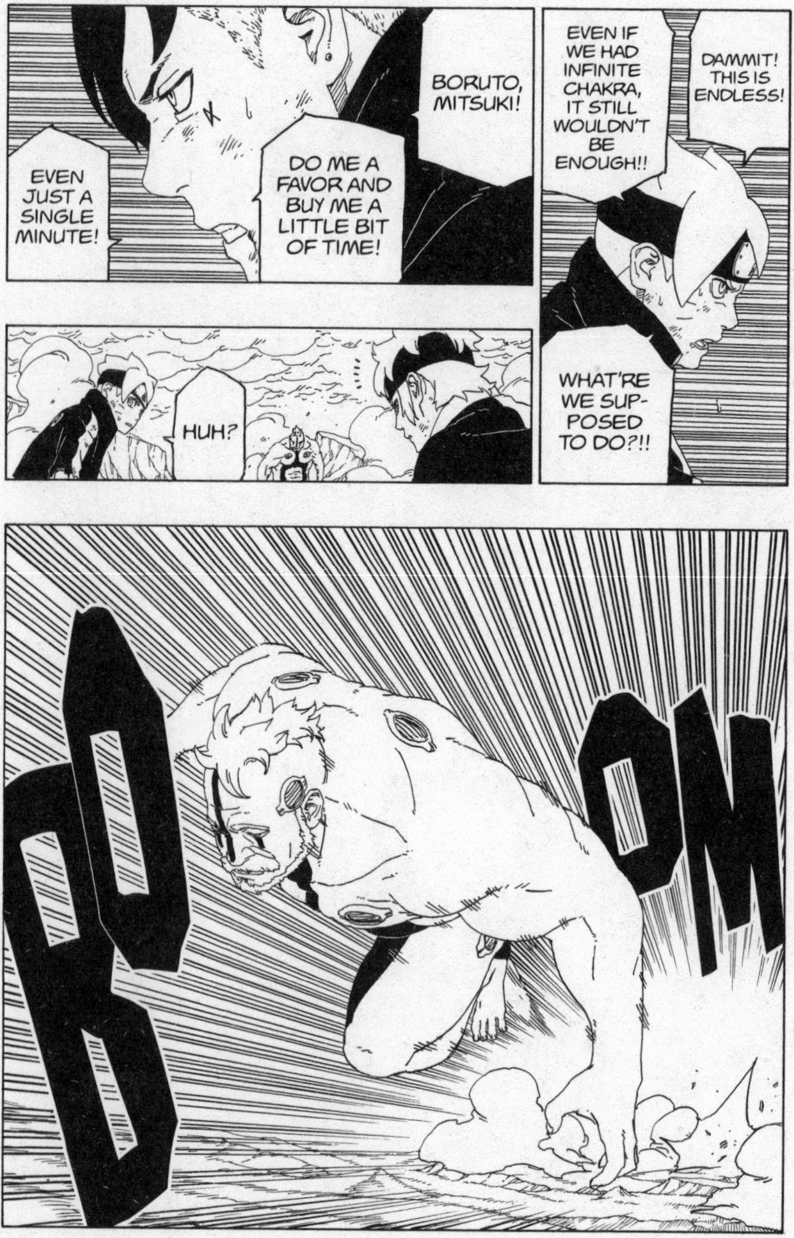
DAMMIT! THIS IS ENDLESS!
EVEN IF WE HAD INFINITE CHAKRA, IT STILL WOULDN'T BE ENOUGH!!
WHAT'RE WE SUP-POSED TO DO?!!
BORUTO, MITSUKI!
DO ME A FAVOR AND BUY ME A LITTLE BIT OF TIME!
EVEN JUST A SINGLE MINUTE!
HUH?
BOOM

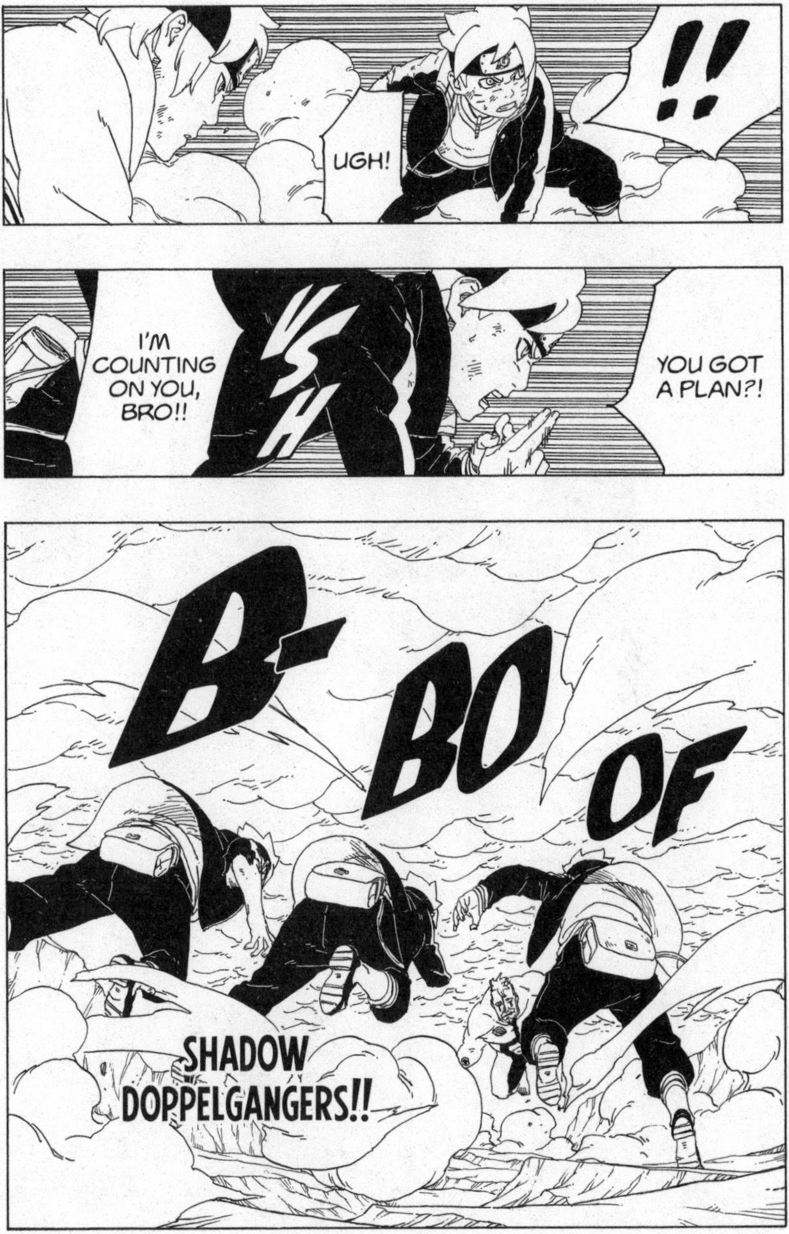
!!
UGH!
YOU GOT A PLAN?!
VSH
I'M COUNTING ON YOU, BRO!!
B-BOOF
SHADOW DOPPELGANGERS!!

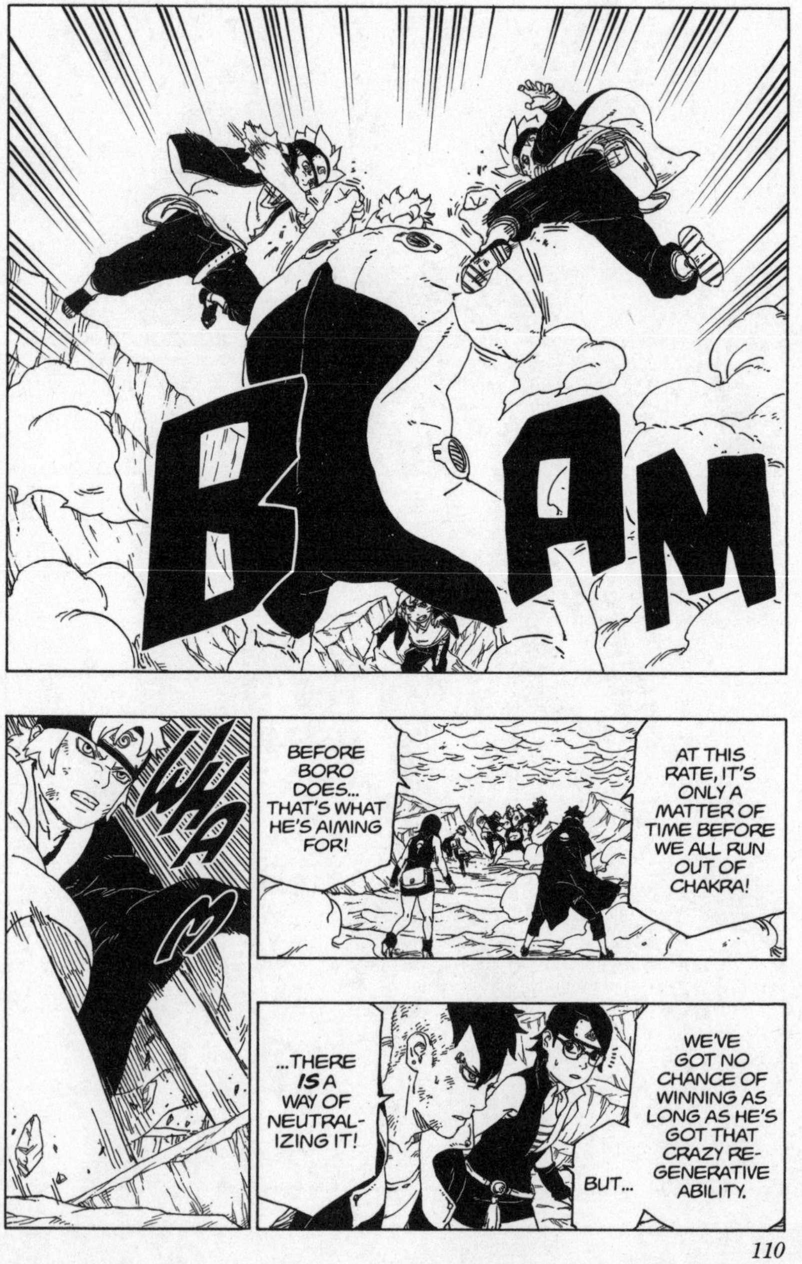
BAM
AT THIS RATE, IT'S ONLY A MATTER OF TIME BEFORE WE ALL RUN OUT OF CHAKRA!
BEFORE BORO DOES... THAT'S WHAT HE'S AIMING FOR!
WE'VE GOT NO CHANCE OF WINNING AS LONG AS HE'S GOT THAT CRAZY RE-GENERATIVE ABILITY.
BUT...
...THERE *IS* A WAY OF NEUTRAL-IZING IT!
WHAM

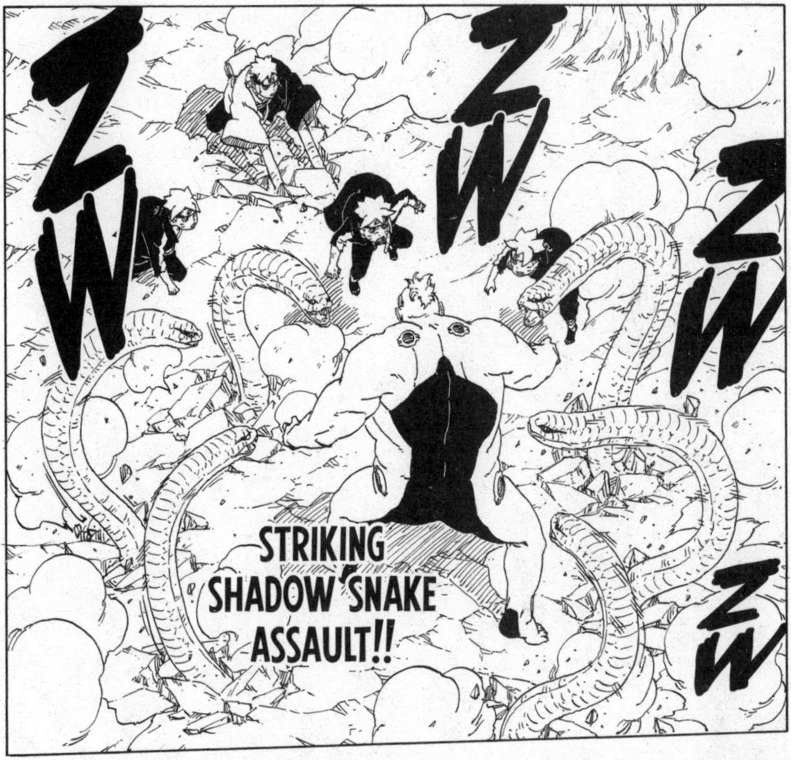
ZW
ZW
ZW
ZW
STRIKING SHADOW SNAKE ASSAULT!!

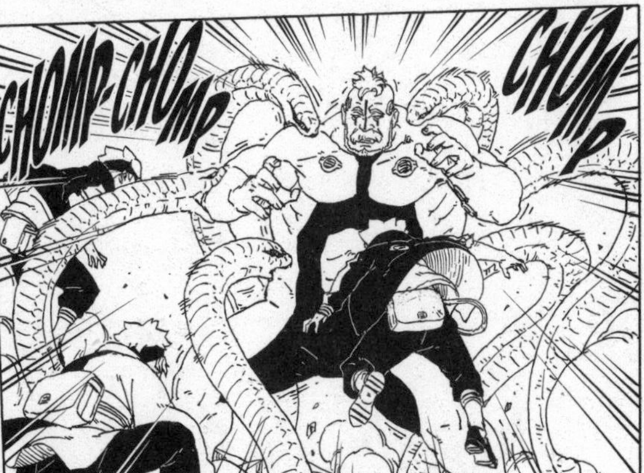
CHOMP-CHOMP
CHOMP

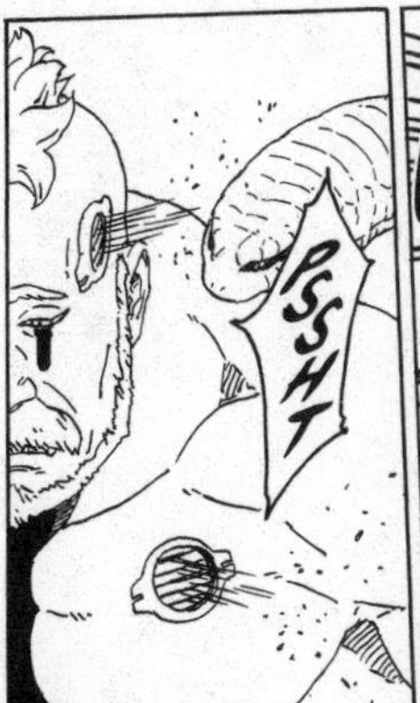
PSSH

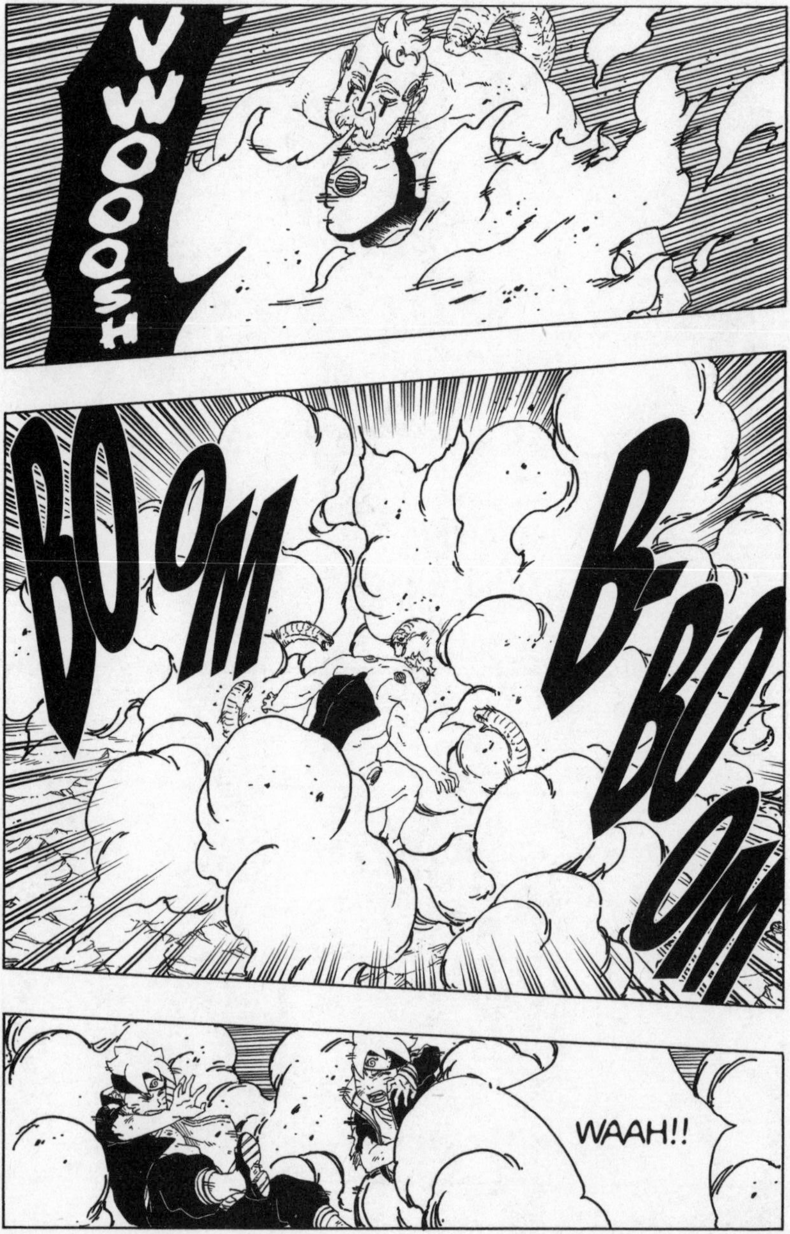
VWOOOSH
BOOM
B-BOOM
WAAH!!

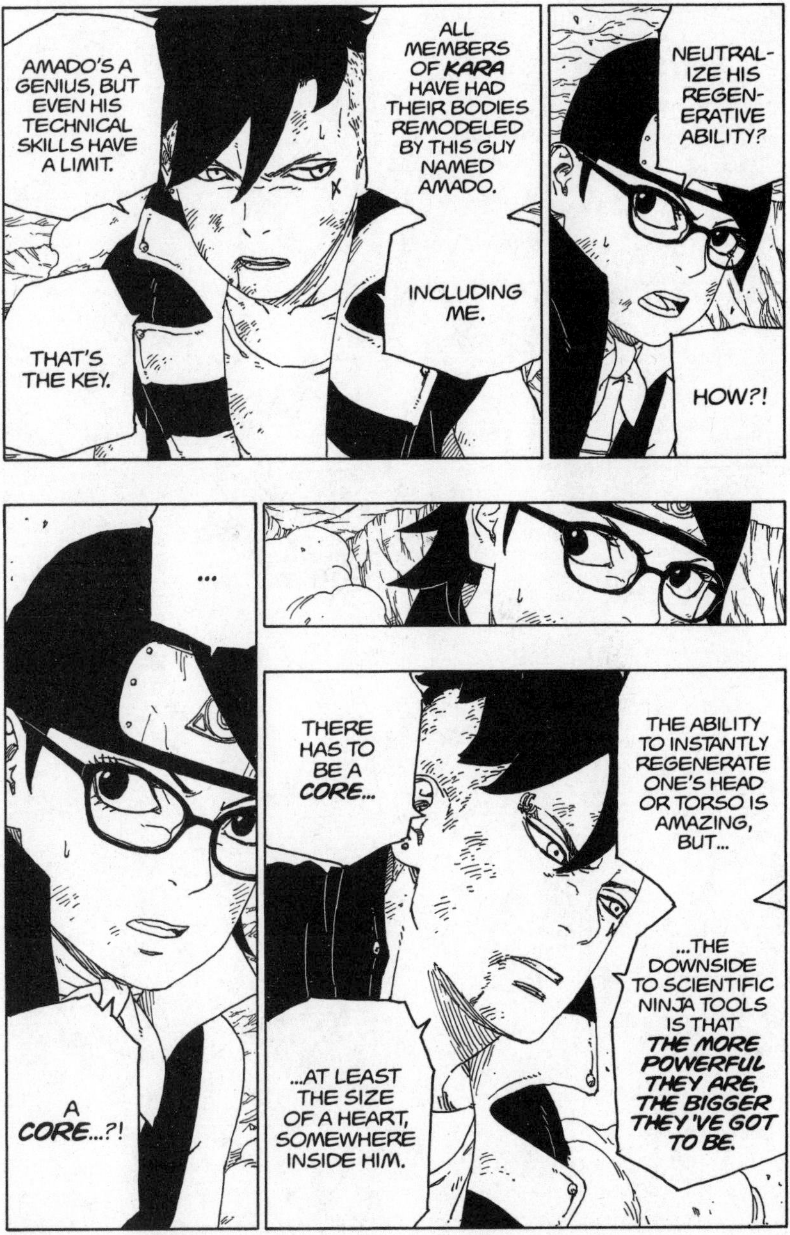
NEUTRALIZE HIS REGENERATIVE ABILITY?
HOW?!
ALL MEMBERS OF ***KARA*** HAVE HAD THEIR BODIES REMODELED BY THIS GUY NAMED AMADO.
INCLUDING ME.
AMADO'S A GENIUS, BUT EVEN HIS TECHNICAL SKILLS HAVE A LIMIT.
THAT'S THE KEY.
THE ABILITY TO INSTANTLY REGENERATE ONE'S HEAD OR TORSO IS AMAZING, BUT...
...THE DOWNSIDE TO SCIENTIFIC NINJA TOOLS IS THAT ***THE MORE POWERFUL THEY ARE, THE BIGGER THEY'VE GOT TO BE.***
THERE HAS TO BE A ***CORE...***
...AT LEAST THE SIZE OF A HEART, SOMEWHERE INSIDE HIM.
...
A ***CORE...?!***

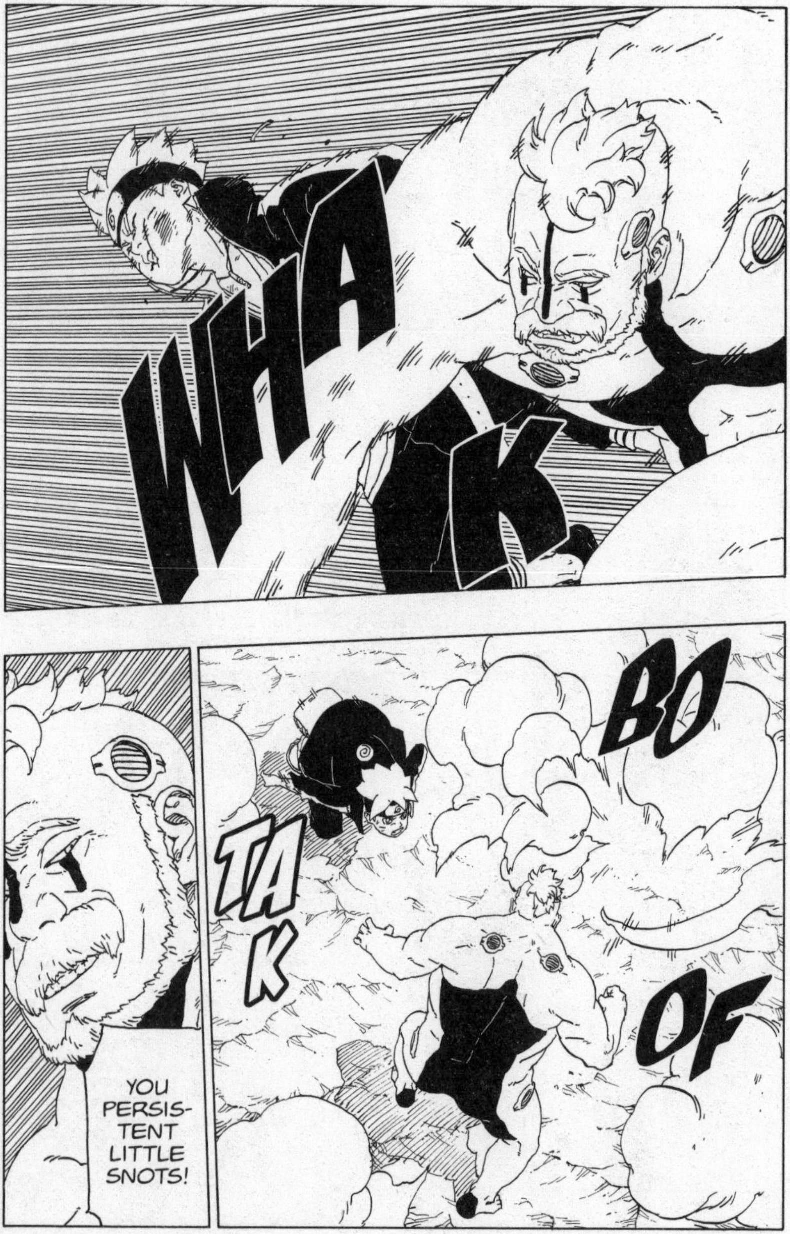
WHAK
BOOF
TAK
YOU PERSIS-TENT LITTLE SNOTS!

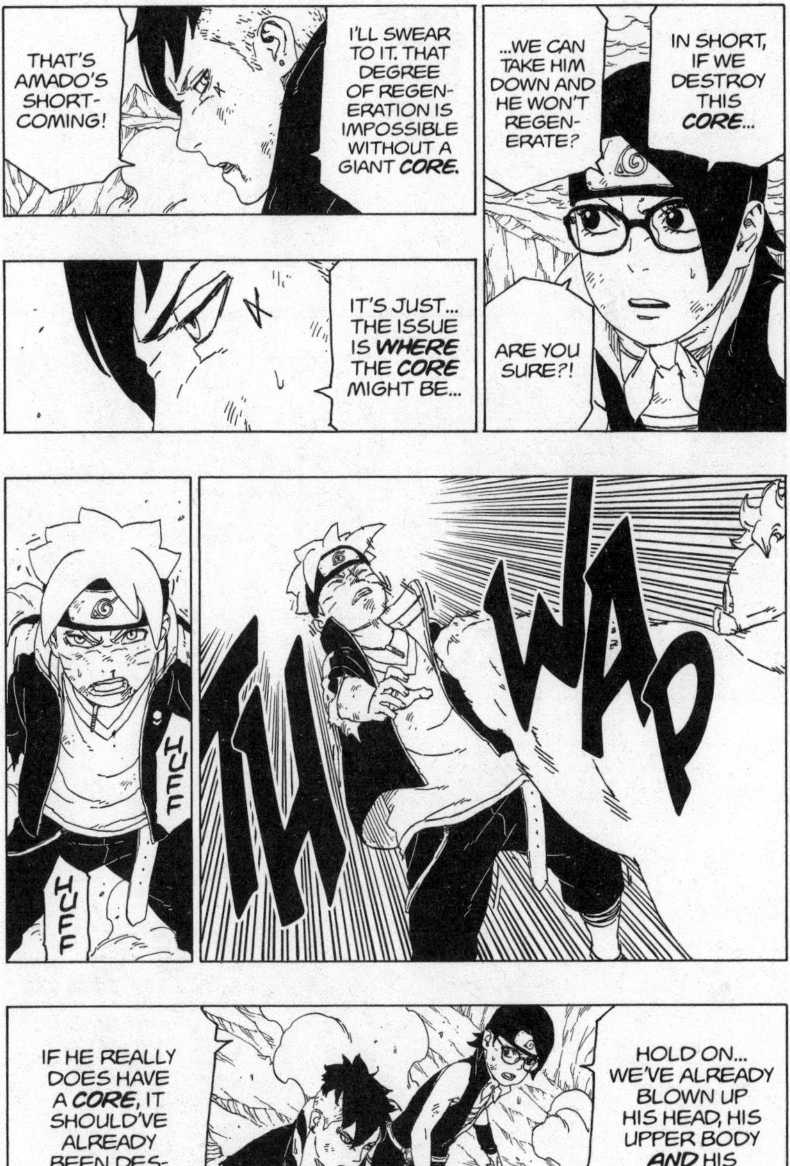
IN SHORT, IF WE DESTROY THIS CORE...
...WE CAN TAKE HIM DOWN AND HE WON'T REGENERATE?
ARE YOU SURE?!
I'LL SWEAR TO IT. THAT DEGREE OF REGENERATION IS IMPOSSIBLE WITHOUT A GIANT CORE.
THAT'S AMADO'S SHORTCOMING!
IT'S JUST... THE ISSUE IS WHERE THE CORE MIGHT BE...
WAP
HUFF
HUFF
HOLD ON... WE'VE ALREADY BLOWN UP HIS HEAD, HIS UPPER BODY AND HIS LOWER BODY!
IF HE REALLY DOES HAVE A CORE, IT SHOULD'VE ALREADY BEEN DESTROYED, NO?!

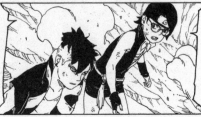

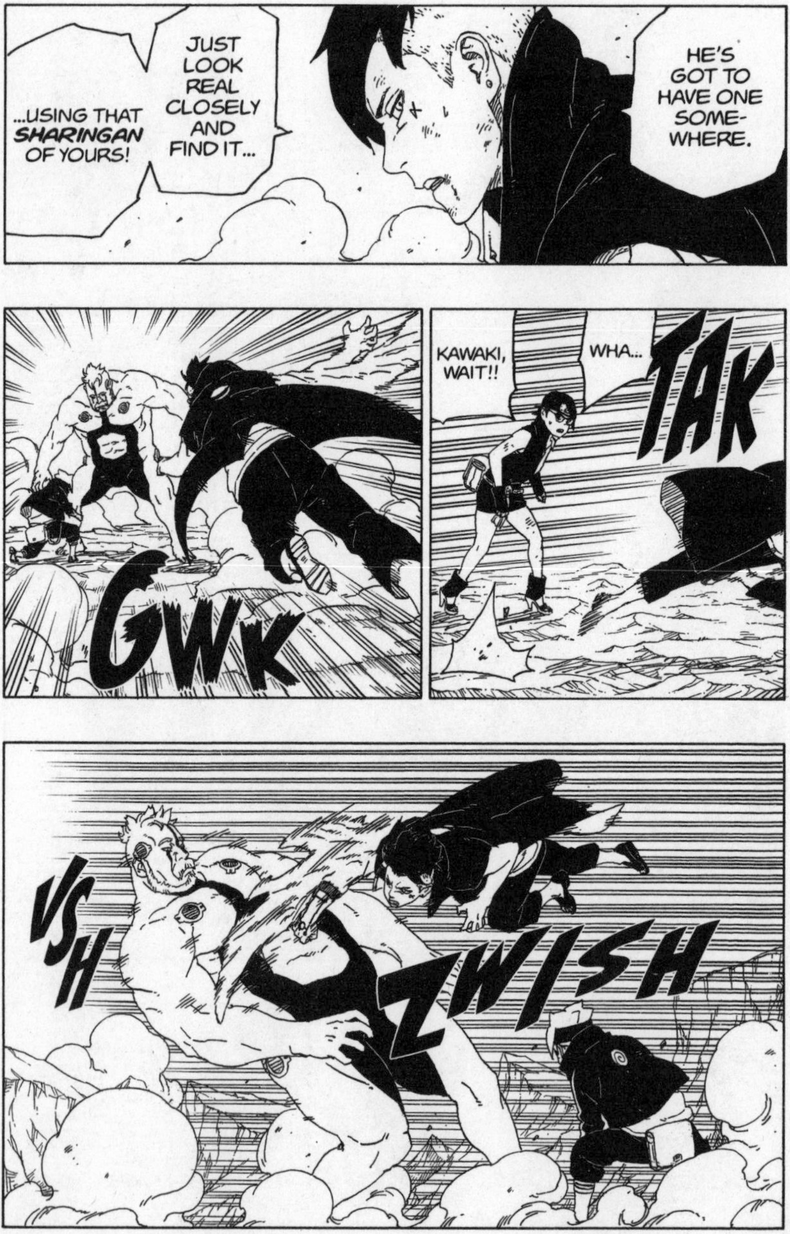

HE'S GOT TO HAVE ONE SOME-WHERE.
JUST LOOK REAL CLOSELY AND FIND IT...
...USING THAT **SHARINGAN** OF YOURS!
TAK
WHA...
KAWAKI, WAIT!!
GWK
ZWISH
VSH

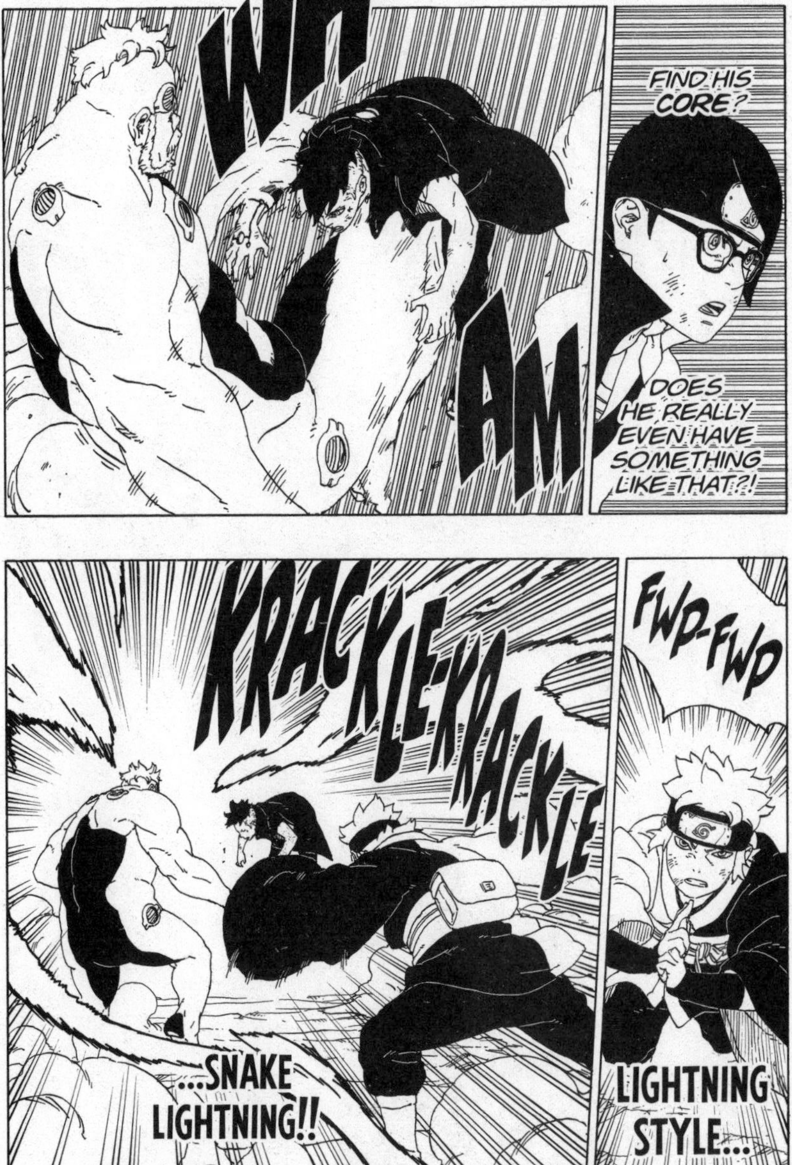
FIND HIS CORE?
DOES HE REALLY EVEN HAVE SOMETHING LIKE THAT?!
WH
AM
FWP-FWP
LIGHTNING STYLE...
KRACKLE-KRACKLE
...SNAKE LIGHTNING!!

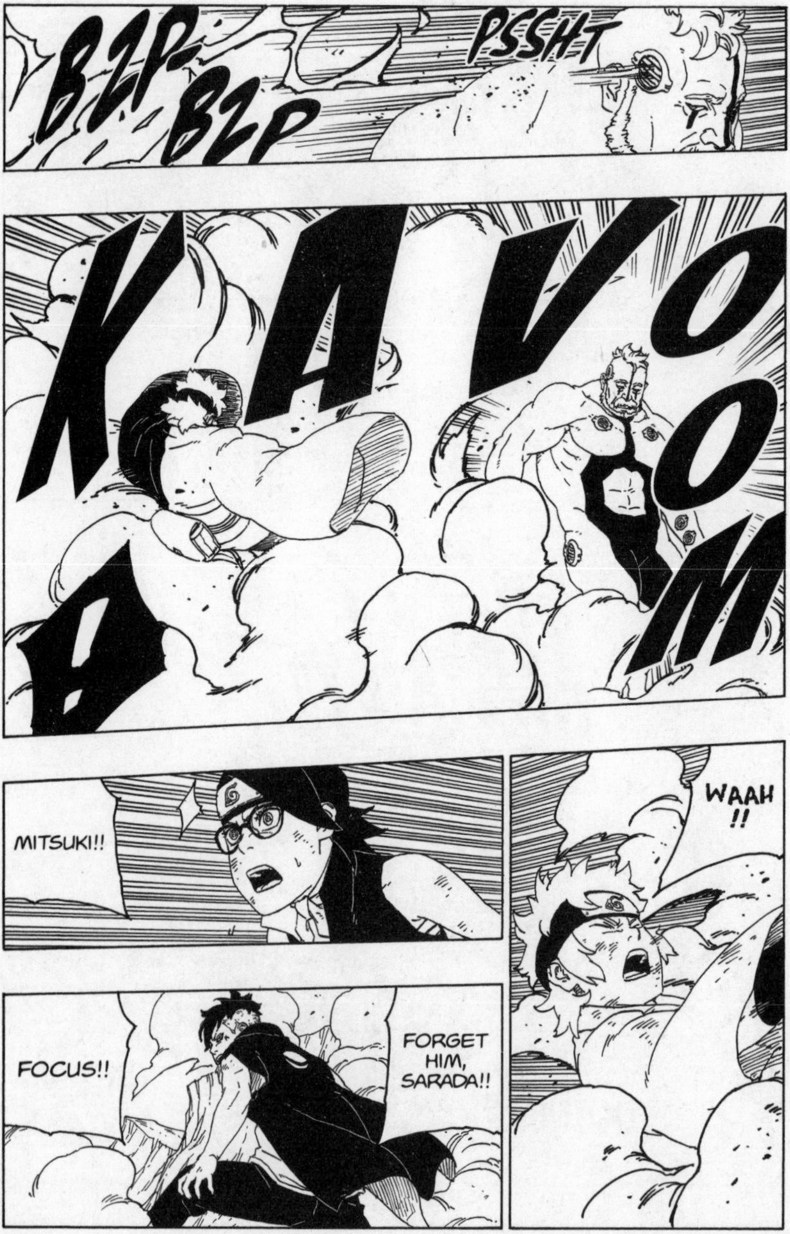

PSSHT
BZZP-BZZP
KAVOOM
WAAH!!
MITSUKI!!
FORGET HIM, SARADA!!
FOCUS!!

HAH!!
WHAKK
UNH!!
DNK
GRIP!
FWP-FWP

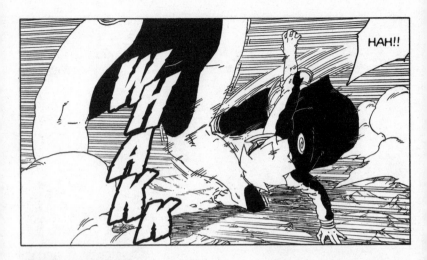

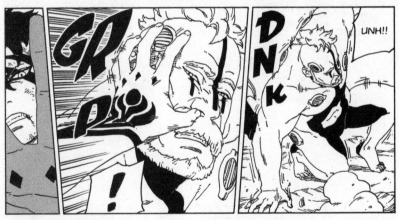

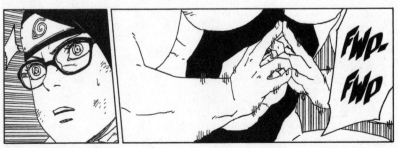

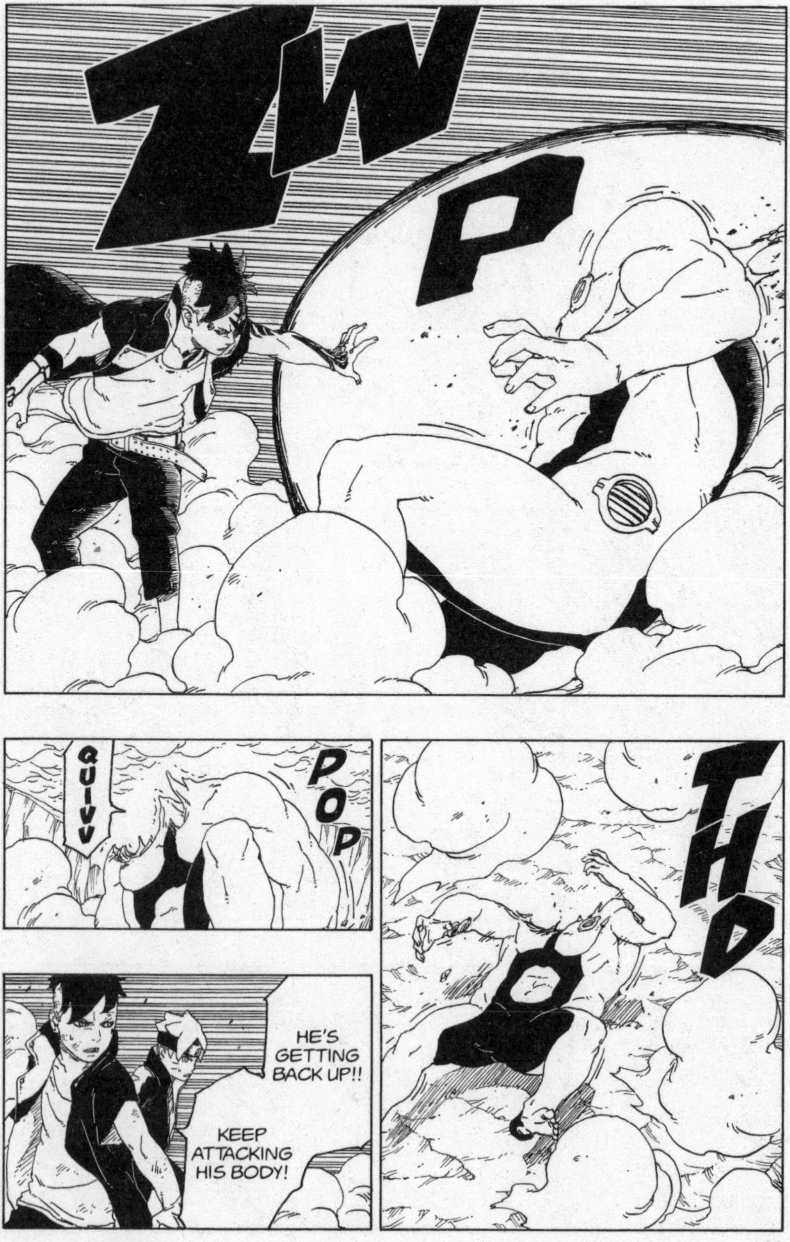
ZWP
THD
POP
QUIVV
HE'S GETTING BACK UP!!
KEEP ATTACKING HIS BODY!

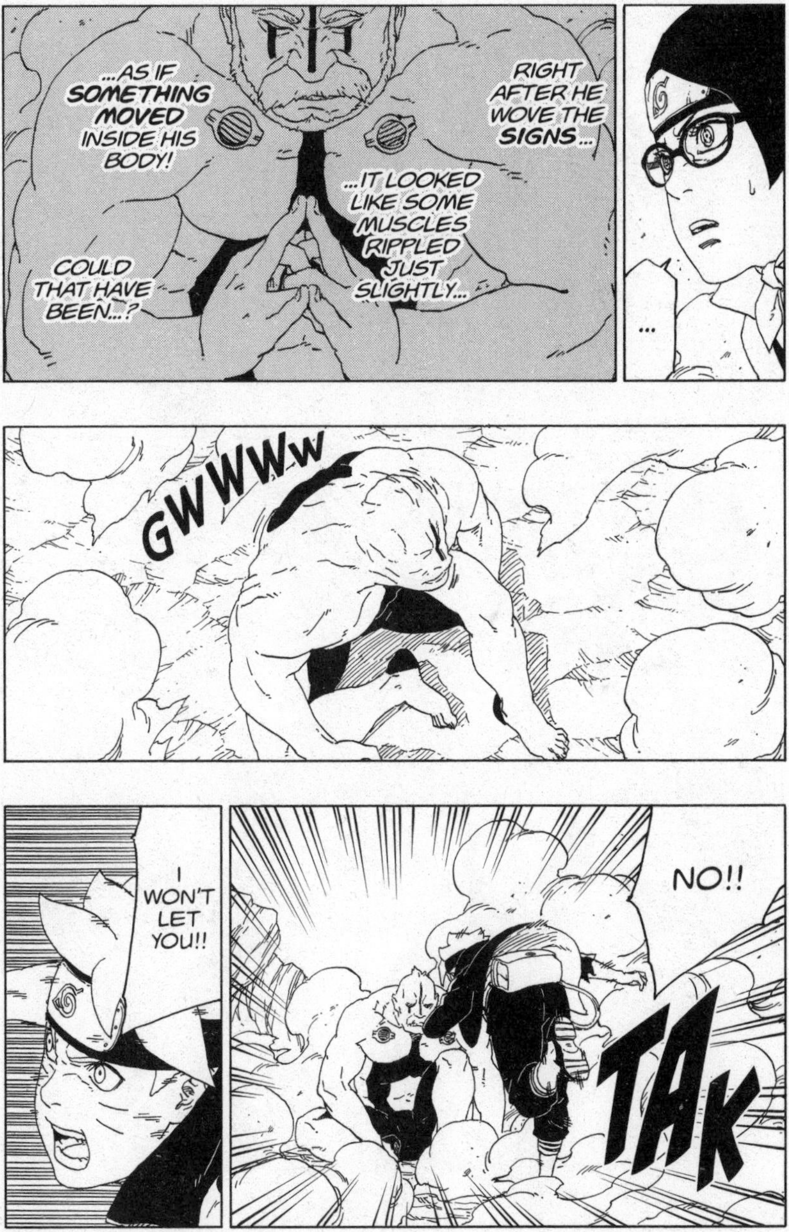
...
RIGHT AFTER HE WOVE THE SIGNS...
...IT LOOKED LIKE SOME MUSCLES RIPPLED JUST SLIGHTLY...
...AS IF SOMETHING MOVED INSIDE HIS BODY!
COULD THAT HAVE BEEN...?
GWWWW
NO!!
TAK
I WON'T LET YOU!!

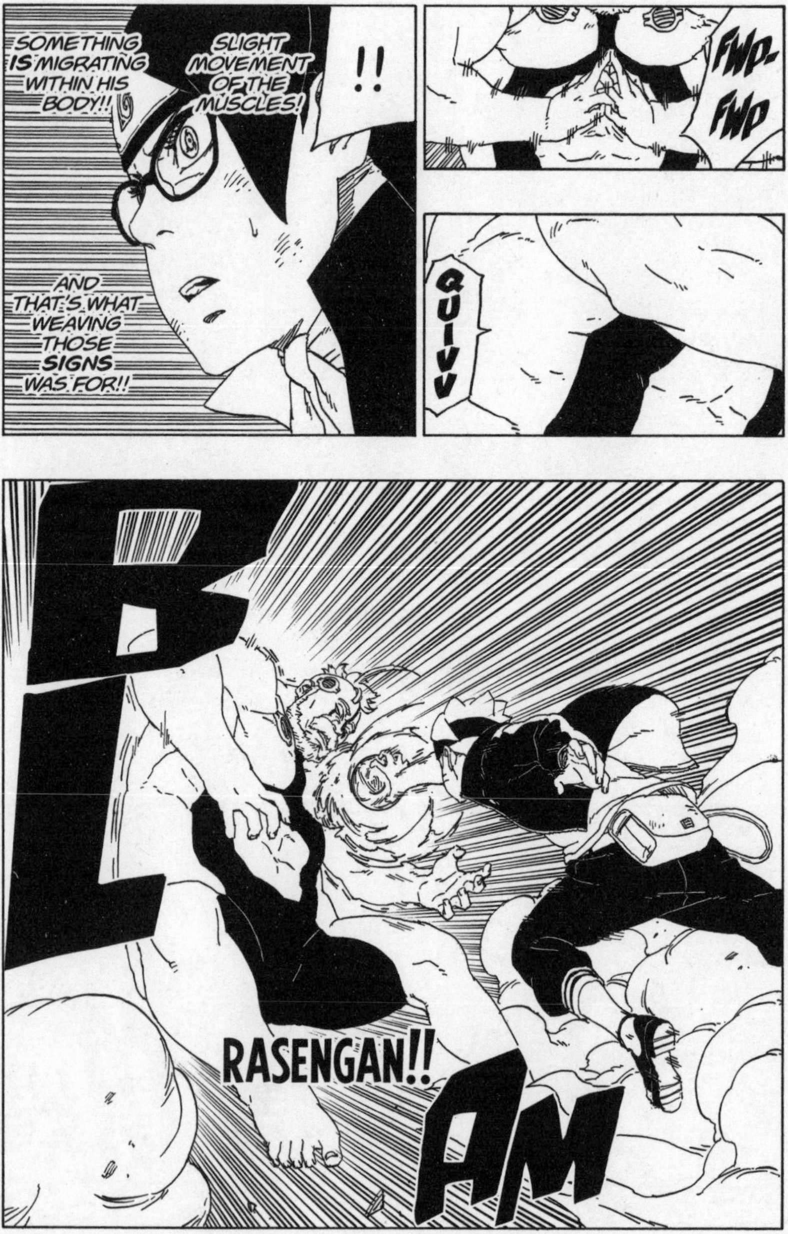
FWP FWP
QUIVV
!!
SLIGHT MOVEMENT OF THE MUSCLES!
SOMETHING IS MIGRATING WITHIN HIS BODY!!
AND THAT'S WHAT WEAVING THOSE SIGNS WAS FOR!!
BAM
RASENGAN!!

GWWW

ZSHH

HUFF

HUFF

THAT WAS MY LAST RASENGAN.

I DON'T HAVE ENOUGH CHAKRA LEFT FOR MORE!

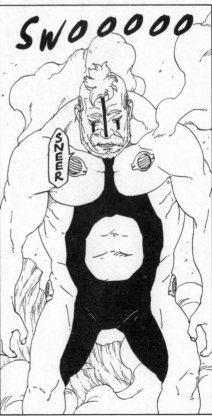

SWOOOOOO

SNEER

...

DAMMIT!

HUFF

HUFF

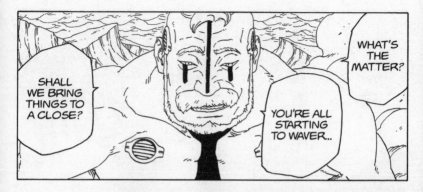

WHAT'S THE MATTER?
YOU'RE ALL STARTING TO WAVER...
SHALL WE BRING THINGS TO A CLOSE?
VWOOOOOO
...
HIS RIGHT FLANK.
NO MISTAKE, THAT'S WHERE...
...HIS CORE IS RIGHT NOW!!
BUT NOW WHAT?
EVEN IF I TELL KAWAKI AND THE OTHERS...
...ONCE BORO CATCHES ON THAT THEY KNOW, HE'LL JUST MOVE IT AGAIN!

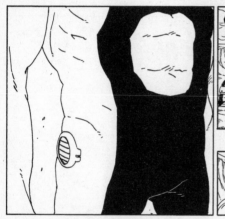

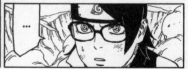

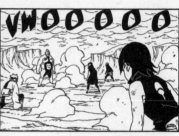

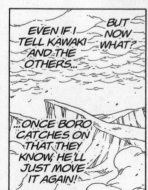

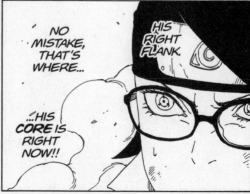

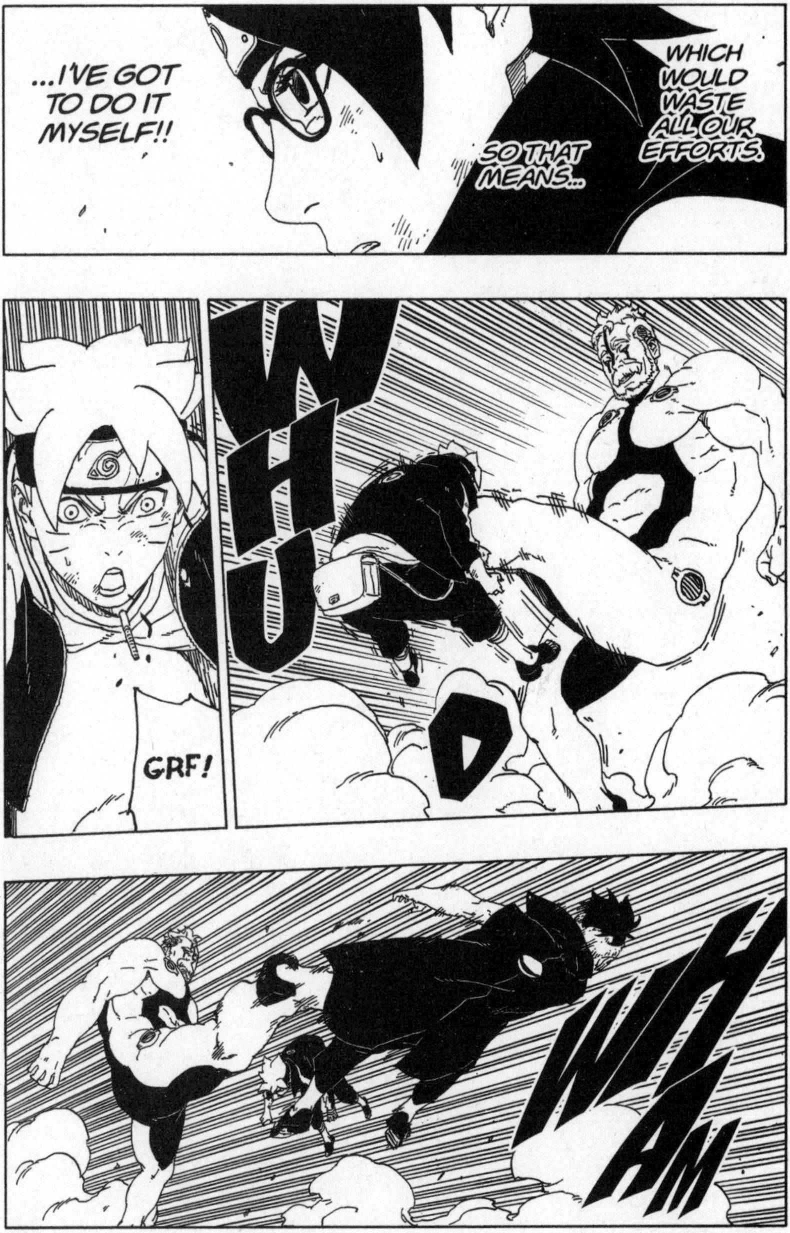
WHICH WOULD WASTE ALL OUR EFFORTS.
SO THAT MEANS...
...I'VE GOT TO DO IT MYSELF!!
WHUD
GRF!
WHAM

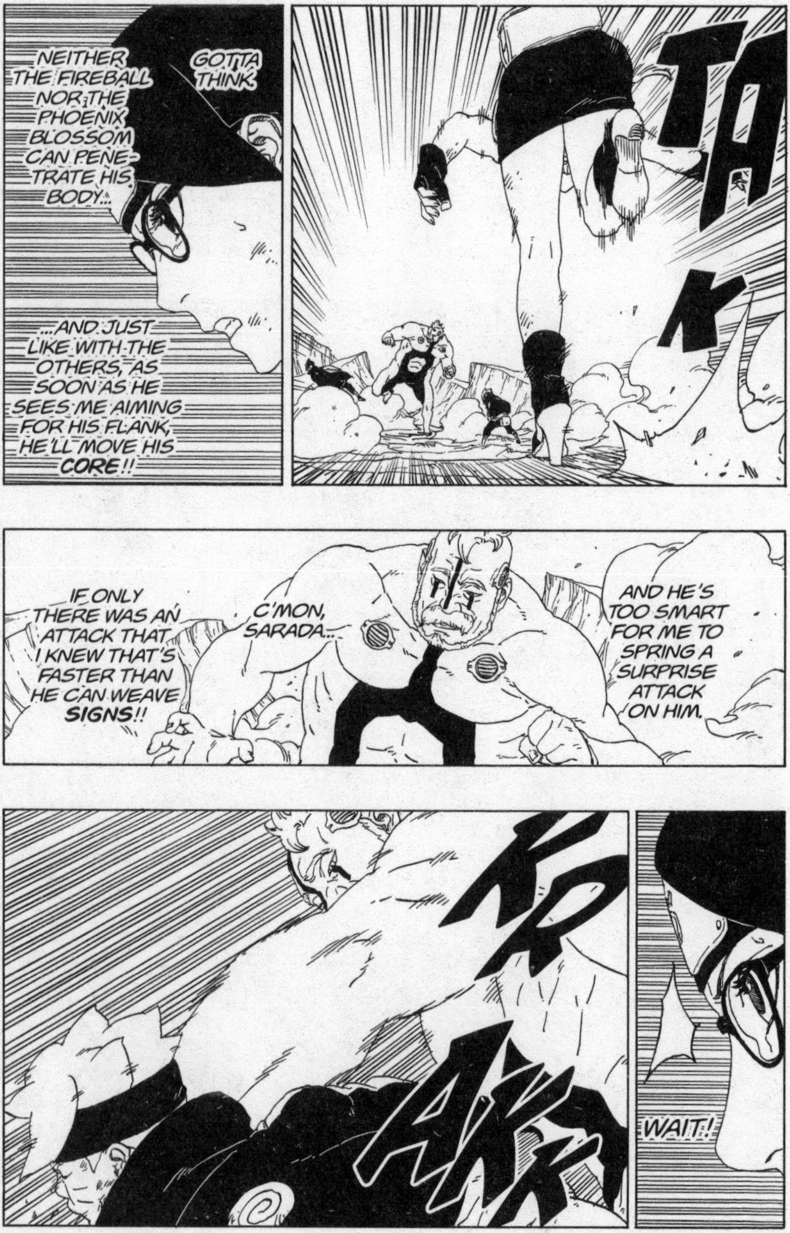
TAK
GOTTA THINK
NEITHER THE FIREBALL NOR THE PHOENIX BLOSSOM CAN PENETRATE HIS BODY...
...AND JUST LIKE WITH THE OTHERS, AS SOON AS HE SEES ME AIMING FOR HIS FLANK, HE'LL MOVE HIS **CORE**!!
AND HE'S TOO SMART FOR ME TO SPRING A SURPRISE ATTACK ON HIM.
C'MON, SARADA...
IF ONLY THERE WAS AN ATTACK THAT I KNEW THAT'S FASTER THAN HE CAN WEAVE **SIGNS**!!
WAIT!
KRAK

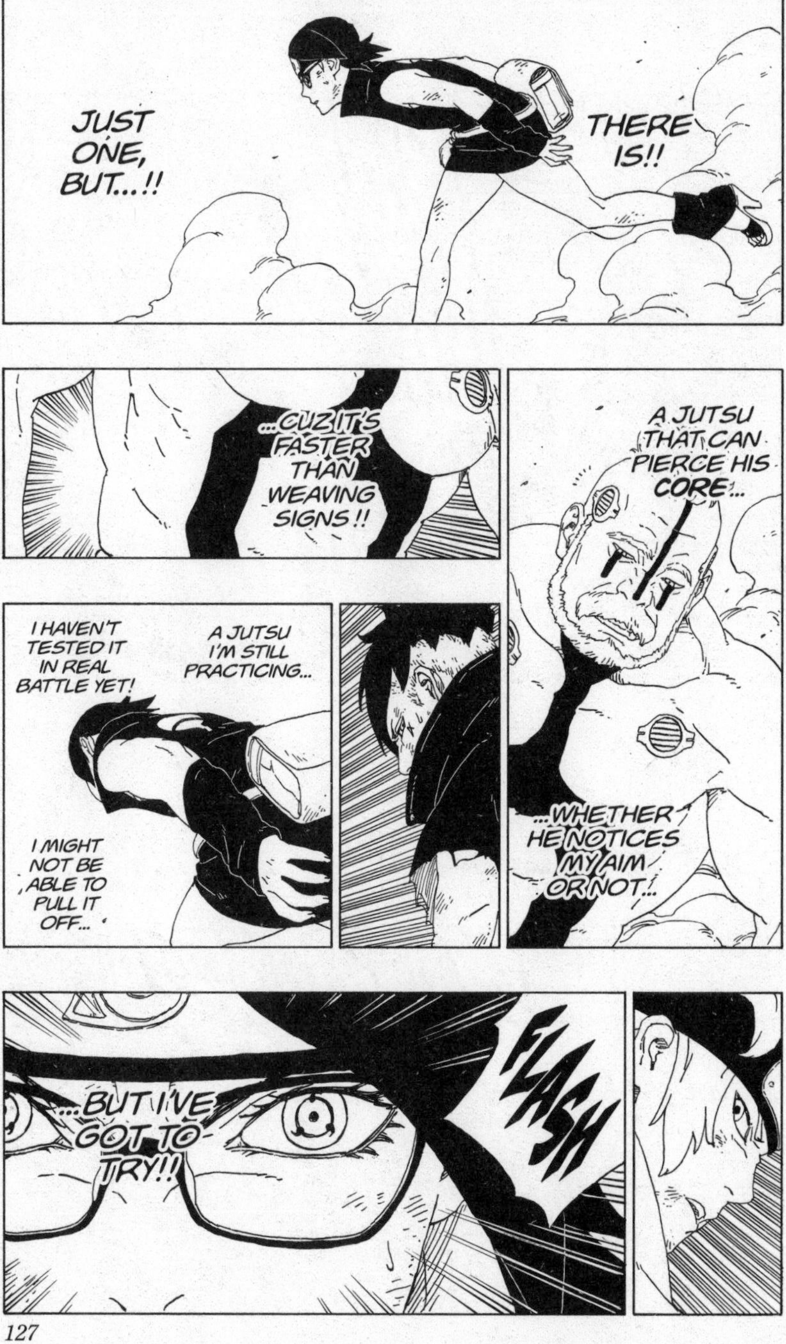
THERE IS!!
JUST ONE, BUT...!!
A JUTSU THAT CAN PIERCE HIS CORE...
...WHETHER HE NOTICES MY AIM OR NOT...
...CUZ IT'S FASTER THAN WEAVING SIGNS!!
A JUTSU I'M STILL PRACTICING...
I HAVEN'T TESTED IT IN REAL BATTLE YET!
I MIGHT NOT BE ABLE TO PULL IT OFF...
FLASH
...BUT I'VE GOT TO TRY!!

ISN'T THAT...?!!

OLD MAN SASUKE'S...

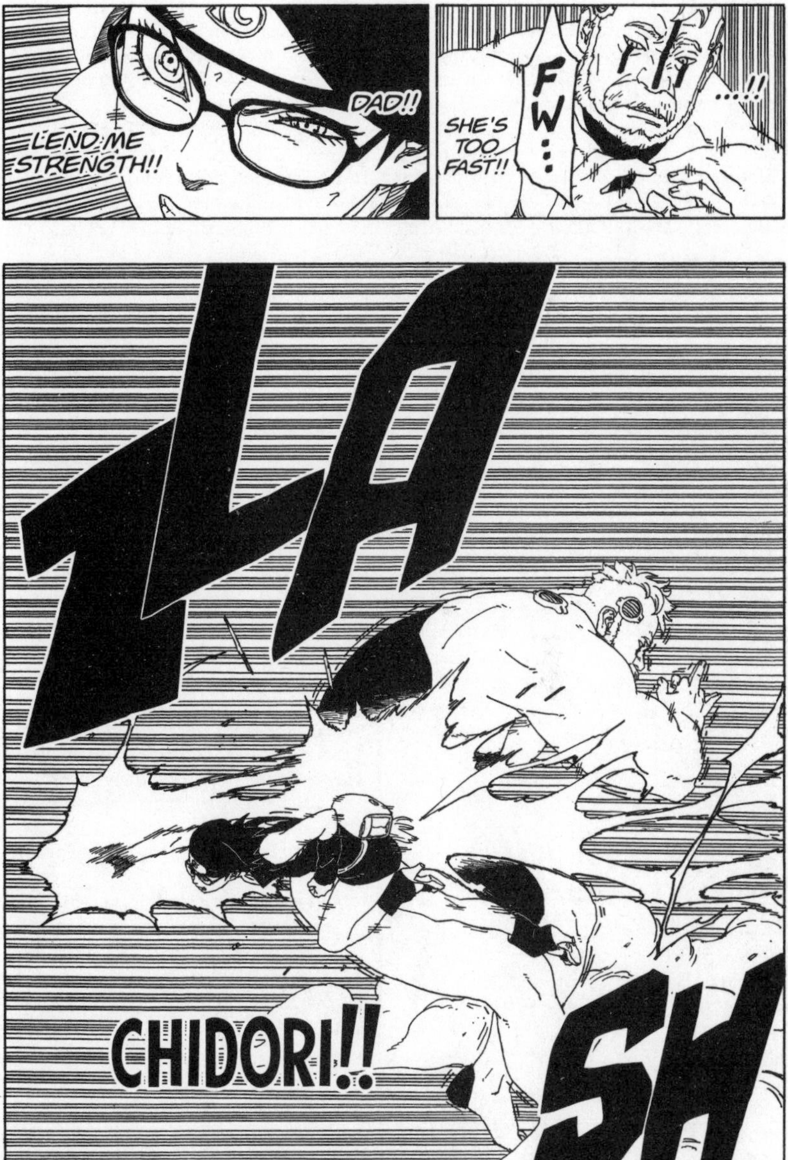
...!!
FW...
SHE'S TOO FAST!!
DAD!!
LEND ME STRENGTH!!
ZZA
CHIDORI!!
SH

④ Advanced Technology Types
Traditional Ninja Tools updated using the latest science and technology.

For example, kunai knives made of superhard ceramic, highly heat-retaining and stab-resistant combat wear, only nanometer-thick high-strength wire, miniaturized communicators and remote-controlled drone weapons. More broadly, mine vehicles and computers would probably also fall under this category.

The importance of shinobi who are experts in such hi-tech Ninja Tools has grown greater and greater in recent years. There even exist shinobi who are weak at ninjutsu, taijutsu and genjutsu but top-notch in science and technology (such as Boruto's contemporary Kaminarimon Denki), and just like medic ninja and sensory ninja, they are becoming an indispensable part of any ninja squad.

## Kara's Secret Maneuverings

Kara's **Outers** are greatly influencing the spread of Scientific Tools behind the scenes. They have infiltrated various scientists and Village technicians, majorly advanced their tech and then taken those technologies back to Kara. It is this conglomeration of the latest technology, compiled by central **Inner** figure Jigen and his right-hand man, the scientist Amado, that was utilized to produce Kawaki, the fruit of their labors.

TRY TO ABSORB THIS.
GWEEEEEN
ALL RIGHT?
DON'T DODGE IT!
KRI-KRI-KRIK...

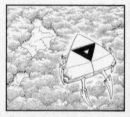

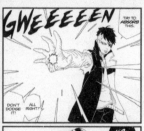

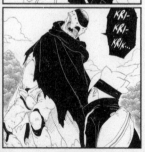

Most Outers believe that Kara's purpose is to expand the power of the secret society, or for human evolution through technological advancement. However, only the Inners and Jigen know the organization's true objectives–and they have no intention of sharing their spoils of victory with anyone but themselves.

As both Katasuke and Ao state, Scientific Ninja Tools are neither good nor evil on their own. They are just a type of tech, no more. But what of the ambitions squirming in the shadow of their rapid development...?

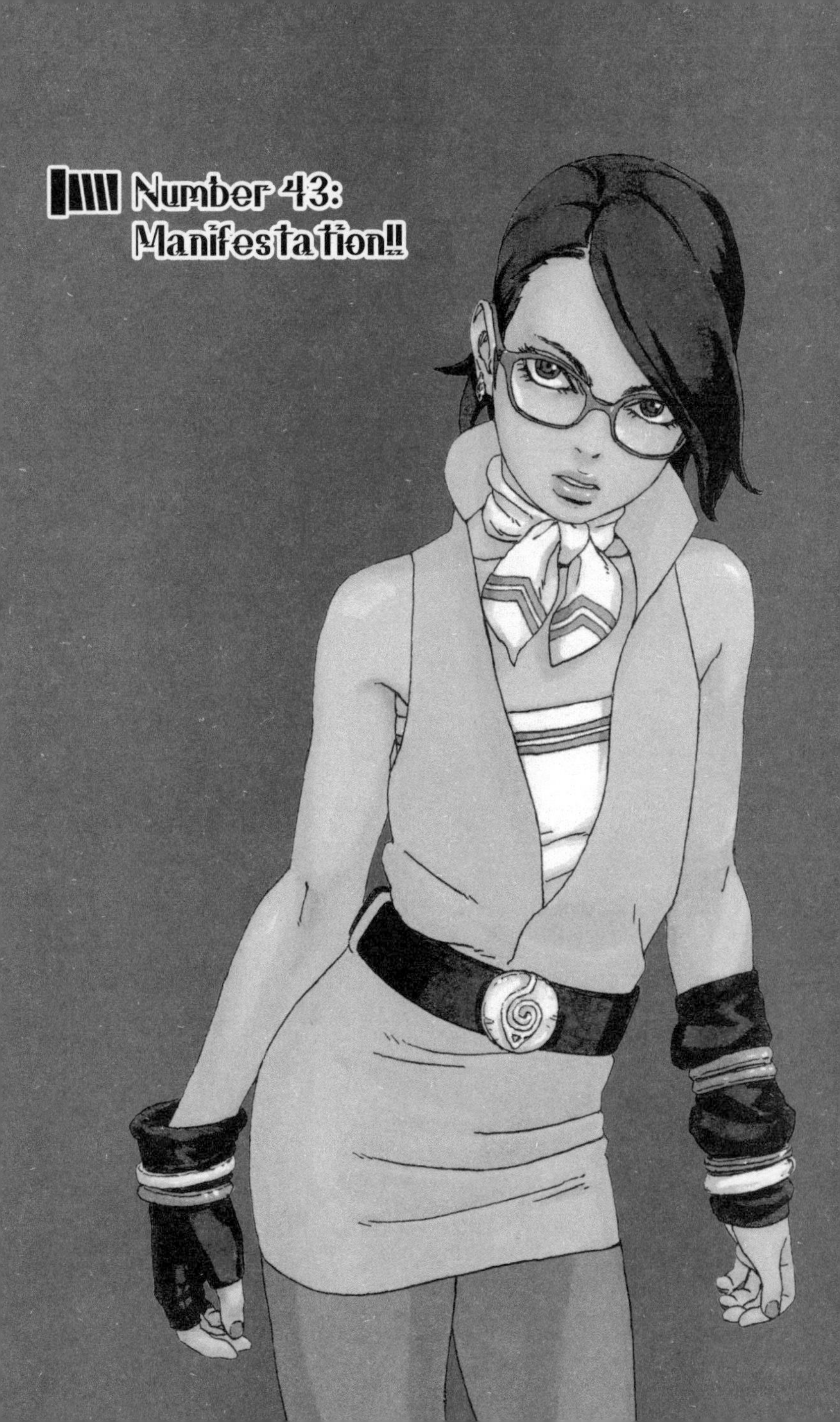
Number 43:
Manifestation!!

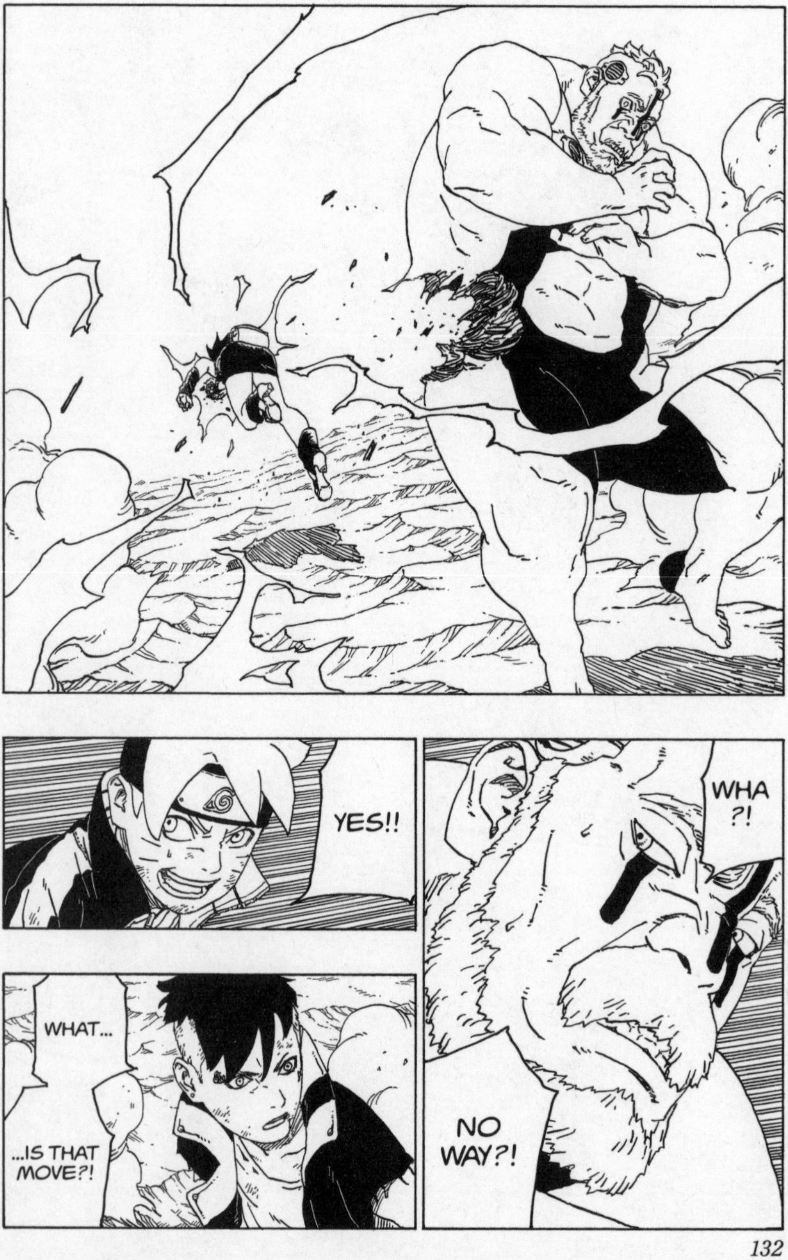
WHA ?!
NO WAY?!
YES!!
WHAT...
...IS THAT MOVE?!

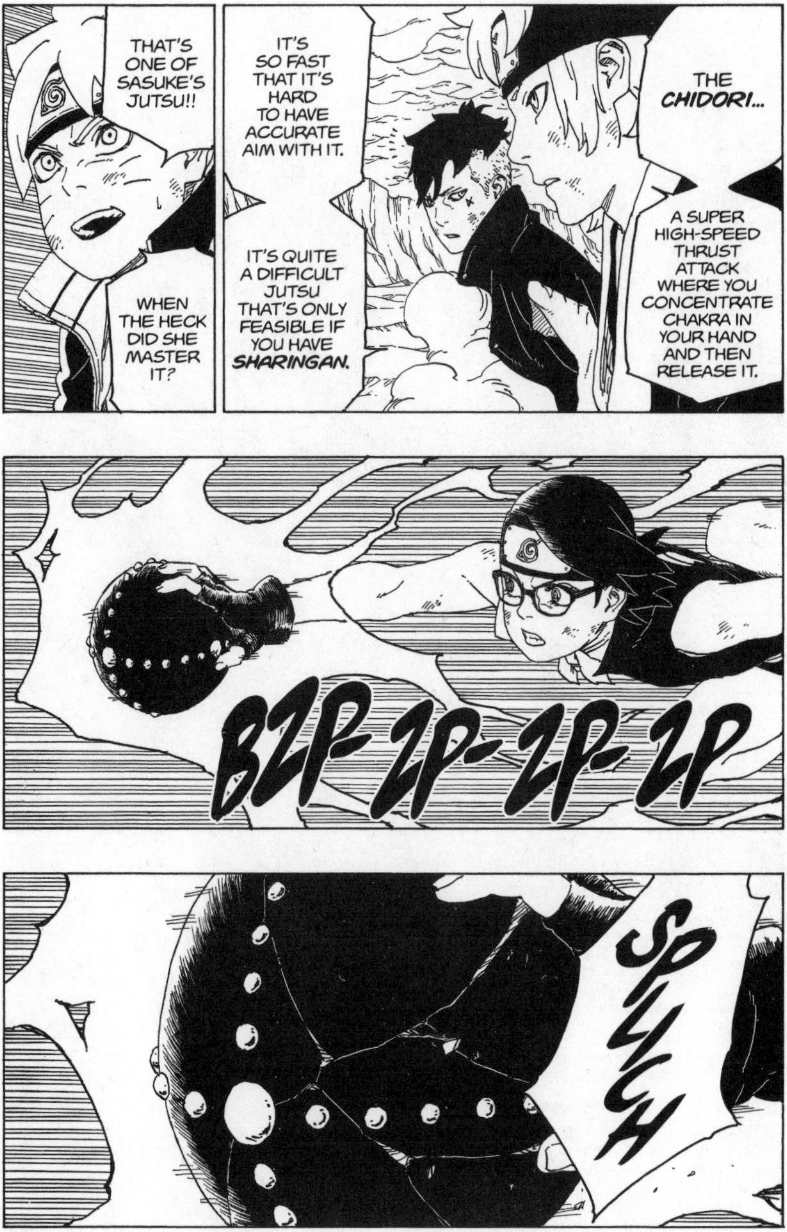

THE *CHIDORI*...
A SUPER HIGH-SPEED THRUST ATTACK WHERE YOU CONCENTRATE CHAKRA IN YOUR HAND AND THEN RELEASE IT.
IT'S SO FAST THAT IT'S HARD TO HAVE ACCURATE AIM WITH IT.
IT'S QUITE A DIFFICULT JUTSU THAT'S ONLY FEASIBLE IF YOU HAVE *SHARINGAN*.
THAT'S ONE OF SASUKE'S JUTSU!!
WHEN THE HECK DID SHE MASTER IT?
BZP-ZP-ZP-ZP
SPLUCH

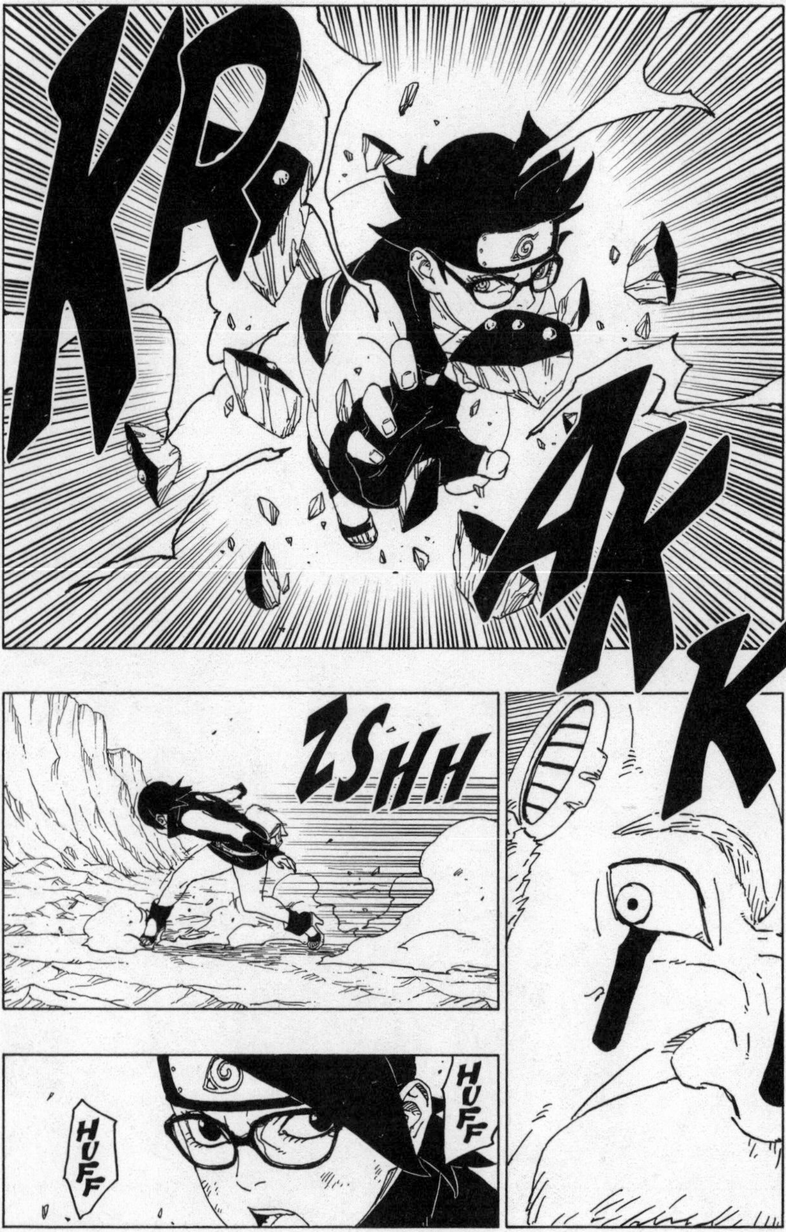
KRAKK
ZSHH
HUFF
HUFF

YOU STUPID...

...LITTLE GIRL!!

PSHHHHHHH

...YOÜU-UUU...

HOW...

...DARE...

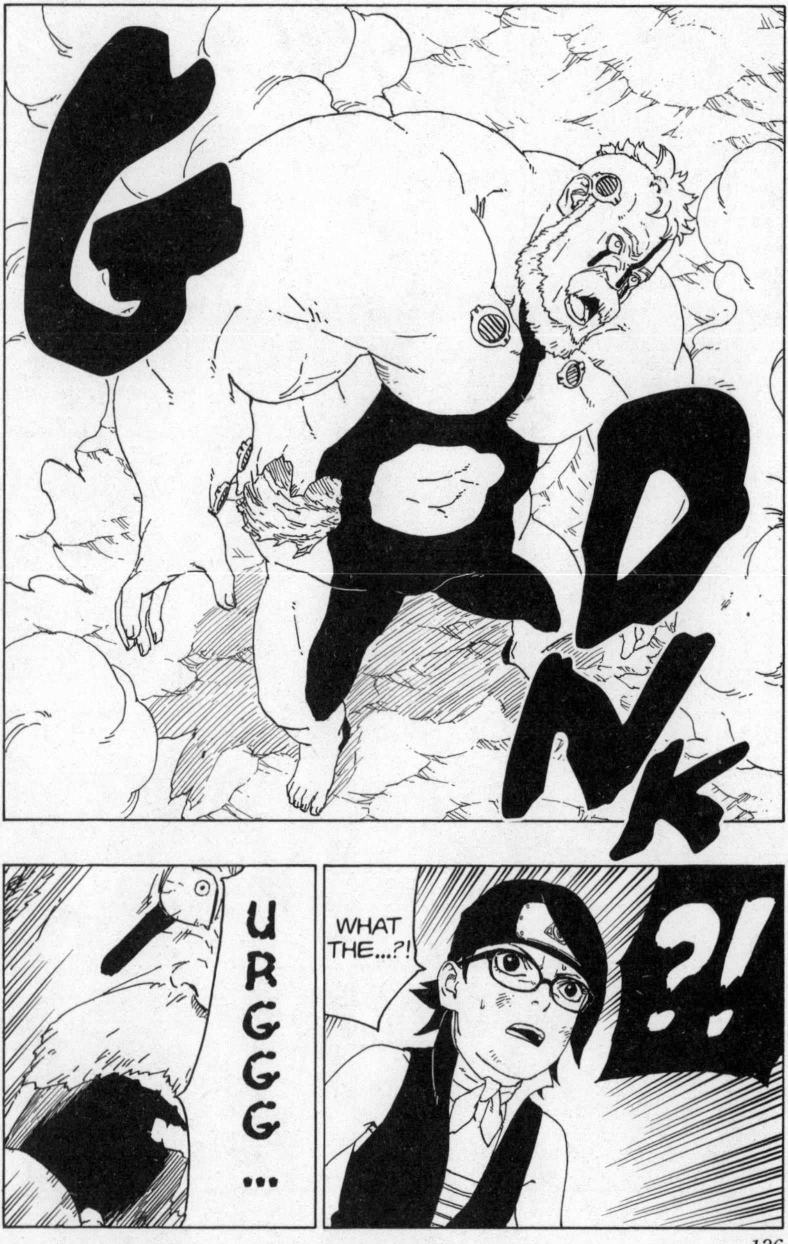
WHAT THE...?!
?!
URGGG...

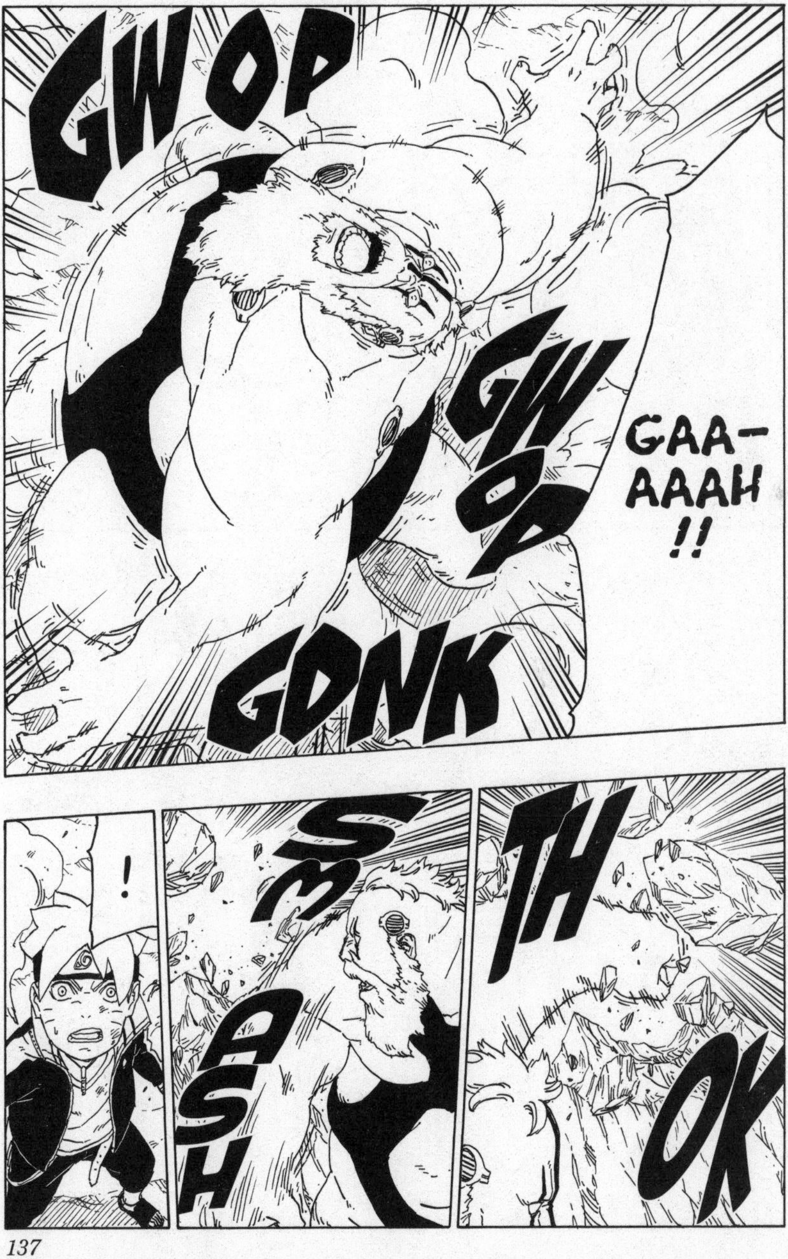
GAA-AAAH!!
GWOP
GWOP
GONK
THOK
SMASH
!

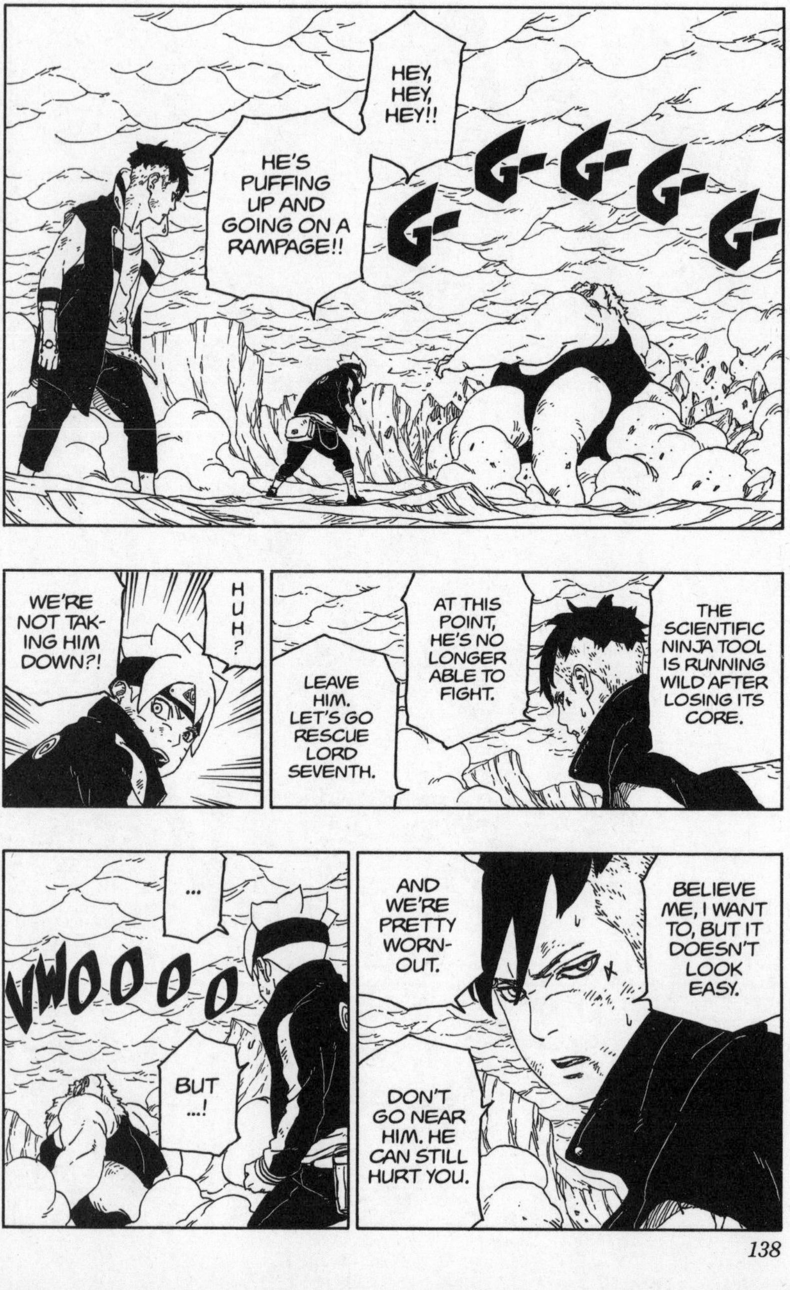
HEY, HEY, HEY!!
G-G-G-G-G-G-
HE'S PUFFING UP AND GOING ON A RAMPAGE!!
THE SCIENTIFIC NINJA TOOL IS RUNNING WILD AFTER LOSING ITS CORE.
AT THIS POINT, HE'S NO LONGER ABLE TO FIGHT.
LEAVE HIM. LET'S GO RESCUE LORD SEVENTH.
HUH?
WE'RE NOT TAKING HIM DOWN?!
BELIEVE ME, I WANT TO, BUT IT DOESN'T LOOK EASY.
AND WE'RE PRETTY WORN-OUT.
DON'T GO NEAR HIM. HE CAN STILL HURT YOU.
...
VWOOOO
BUT ...!

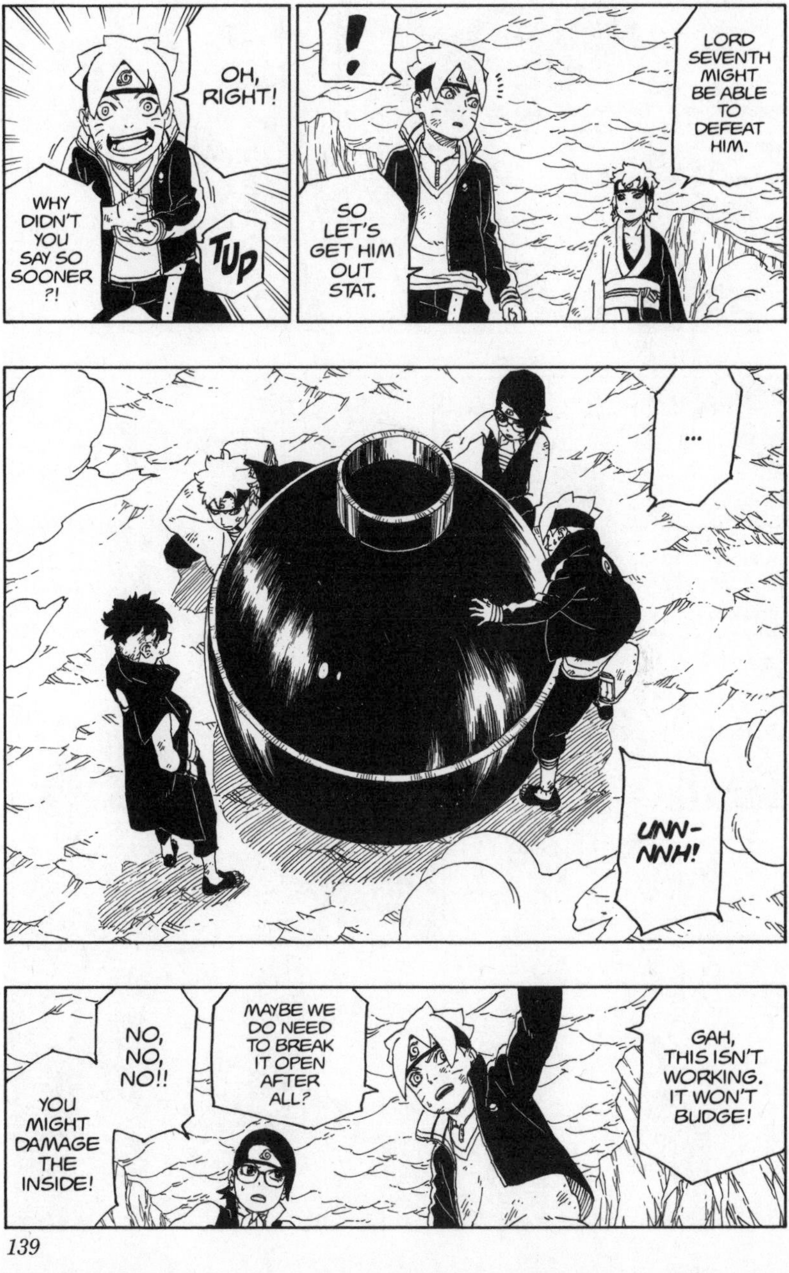
LORD SEVENTH MIGHT BE ABLE TO DEFEAT HIM.
!
SO LET'S GET HIM OUT STAT.
OH, RIGHT!
TUP
WHY DIDN'T YOU SAY SO SOONER?!
...
UNN-NNH!
GAH, THIS ISN'T WORKING. IT WON'T BUDGE!
MAYBE WE DO NEED TO BREAK IT OPEN AFTER ALL?
NO, NO, NO!!
YOU MIGHT DAMAGE THE INSIDE!

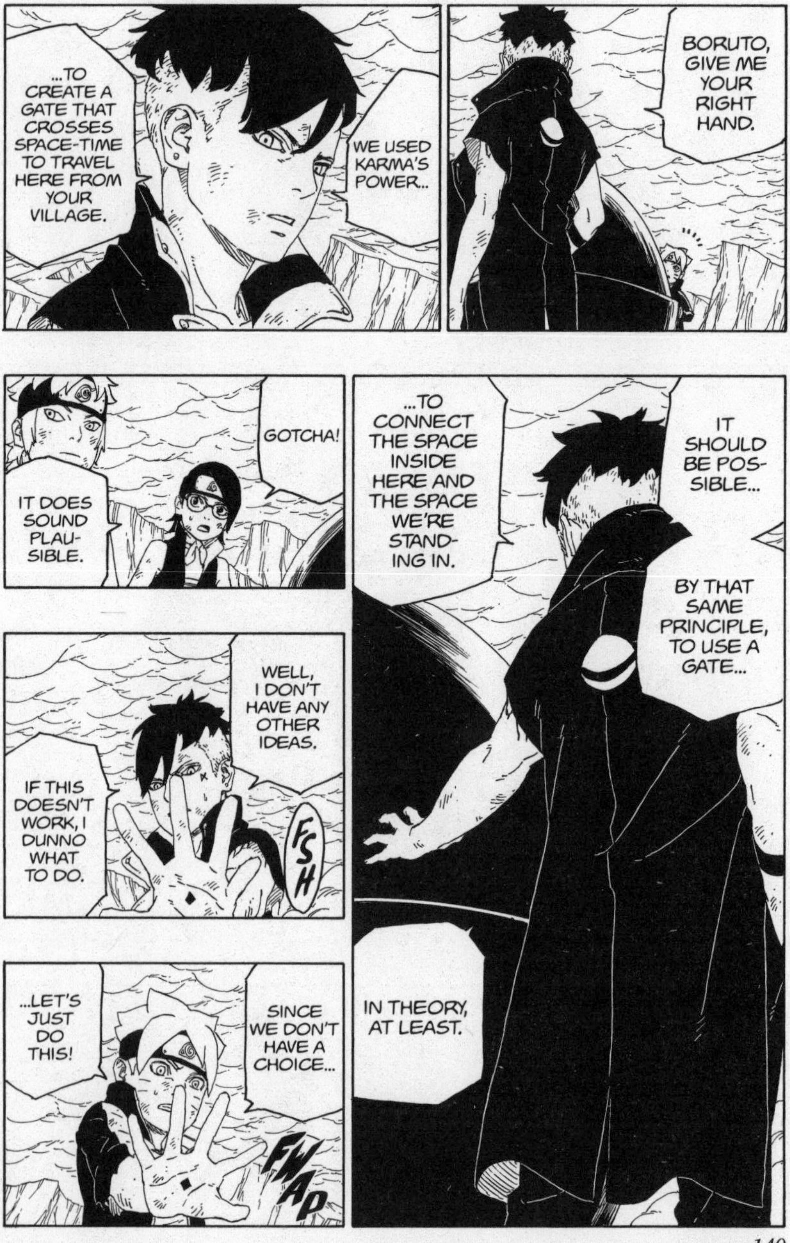
BORUTO, GIVE ME YOUR RIGHT HAND.
WE USED KARMA'S POWER...
...TO CREATE A GATE THAT CROSSES SPACE-TIME TO TRAVEL HERE FROM YOUR VILLAGE.
BY THAT SAME PRINCIPLE, TO USE A GATE...
...TO CONNECT THE SPACE INSIDE HERE AND THE SPACE WE'RE STANDING IN.
IT SHOULD BE POSSIBLE...
IN THEORY, AT LEAST.
GOTCHA!
IT DOES SOUND PLAUSIBLE.
WELL, I DON'T HAVE ANY OTHER IDEAS.
IF THIS DOESN'T WORK, I DUNNO WHAT TO DO.
FSH
SINCE WE DON'T HAVE A CHOICE...
...LET'S JUST DO THIS!
FWAP

SKWEEEE
ZWG-
ZW...

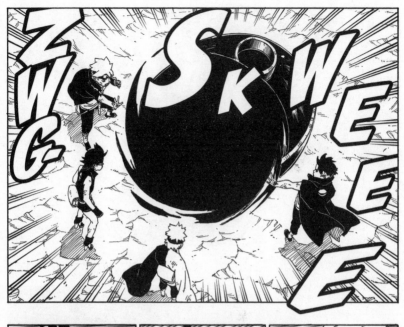

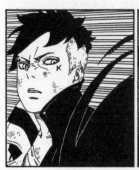

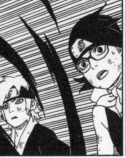

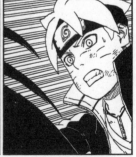

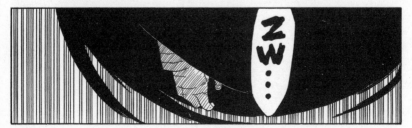

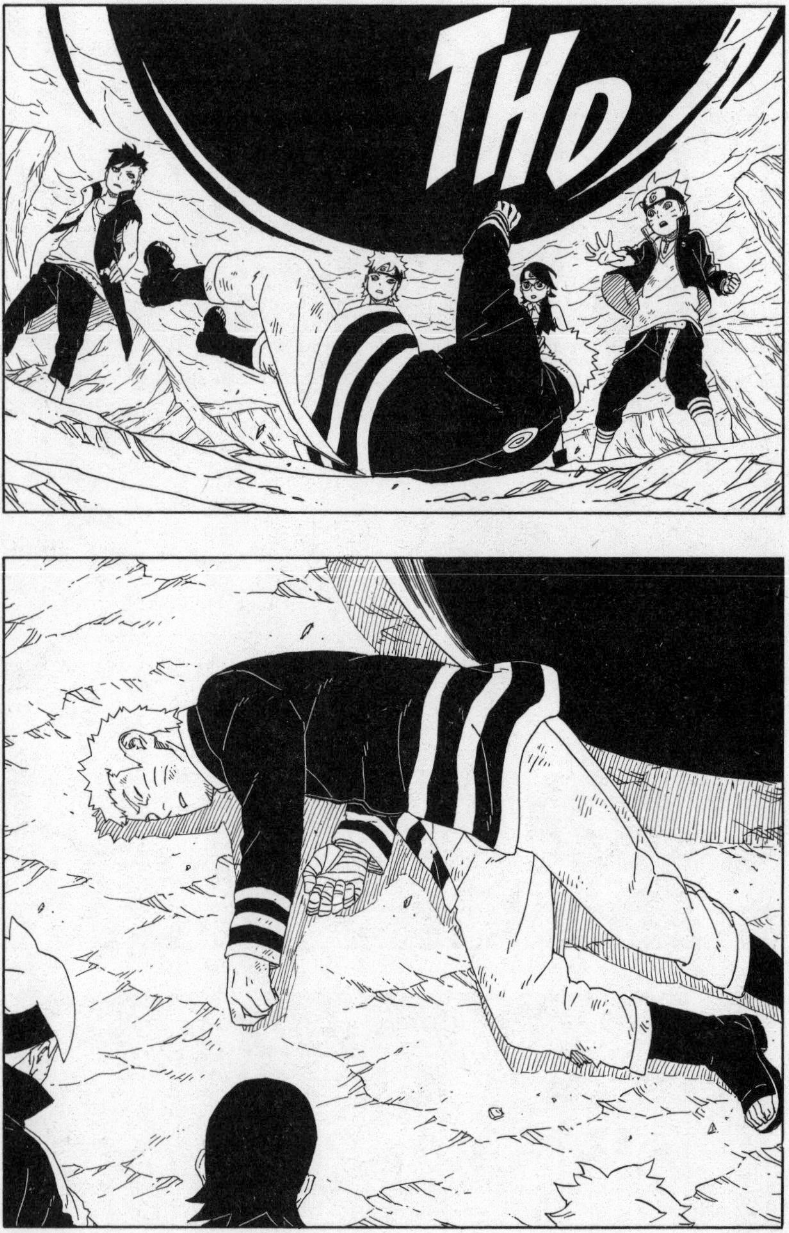
THD

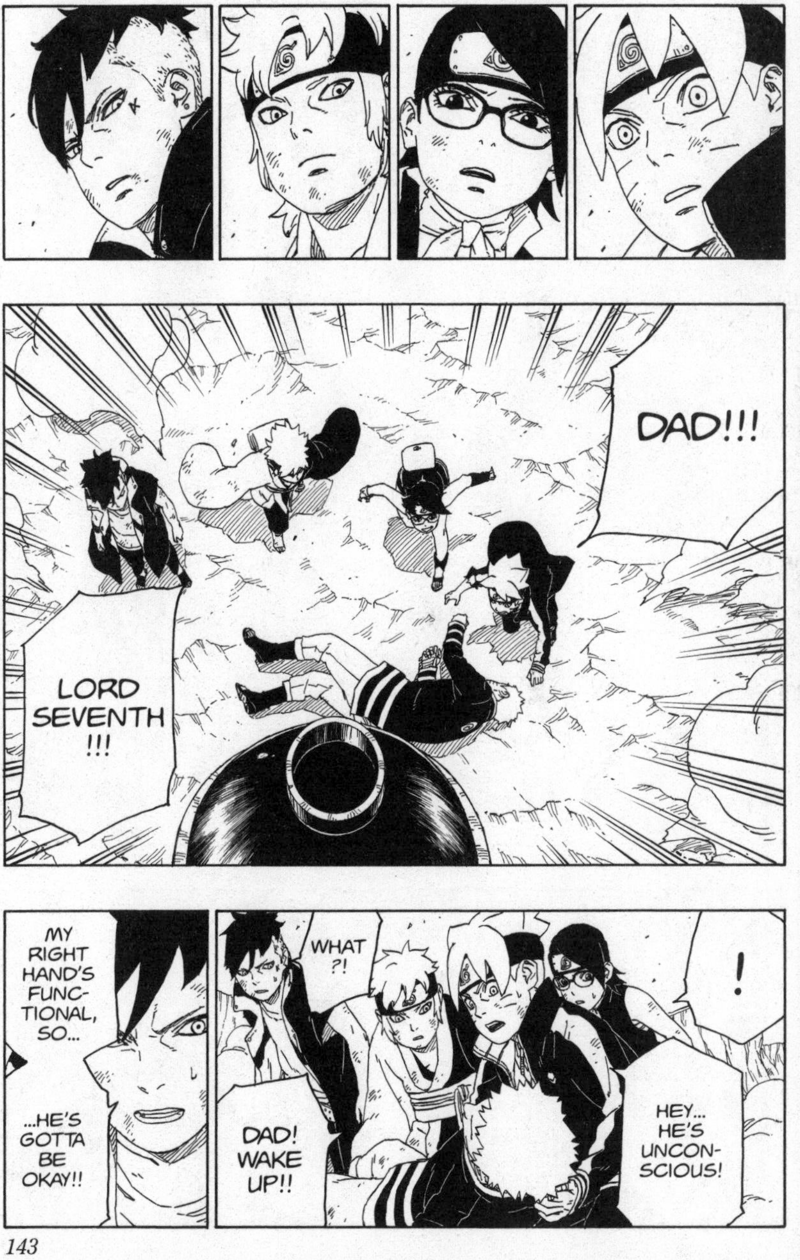
DAD!!!
LORD SEVENTH !!!
!
WHAT ?!
HEY... HE'S UNCONSCIOUS!
DAD! WAKE UP!!
MY RIGHT HAND'S FUNCTIONAL, SO...
...HE'S GOTTA BE OKAY!!

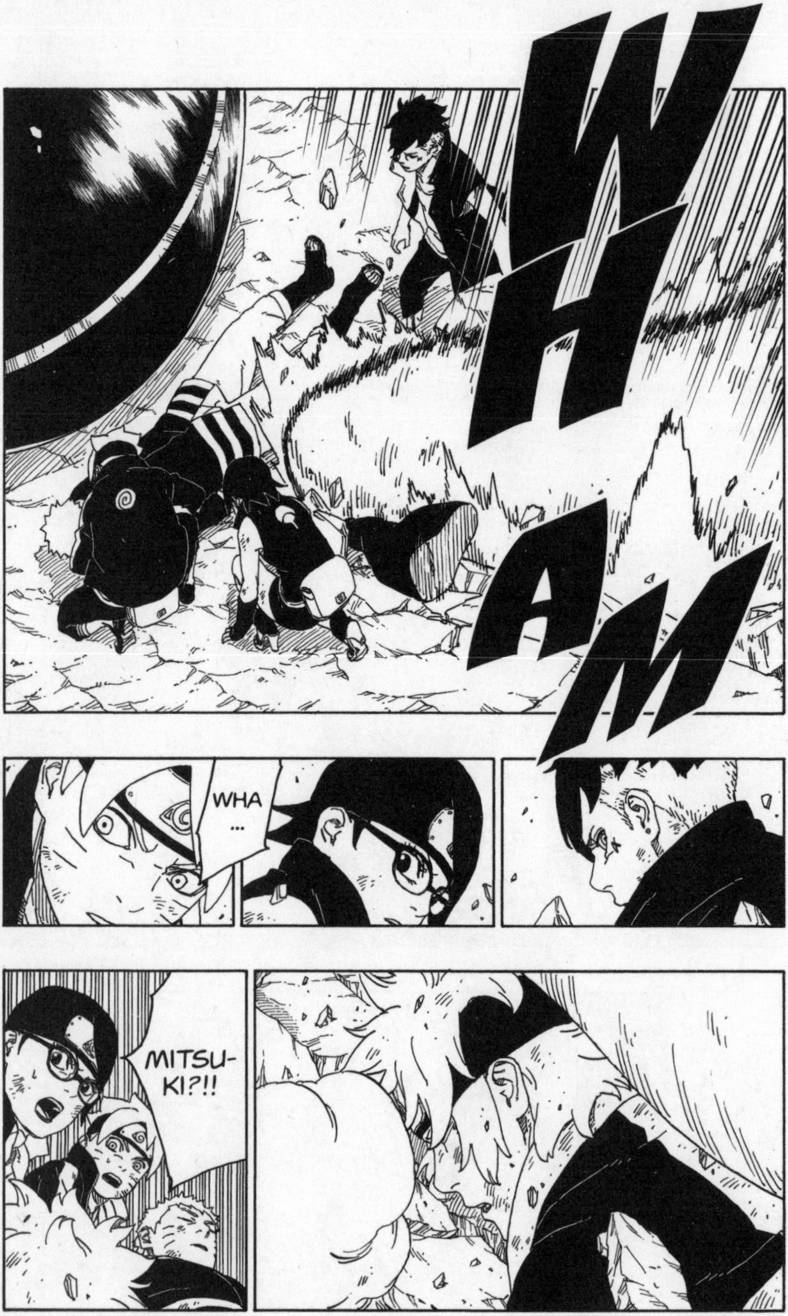
WHAM
WHA ...
MITSU-KI?!!

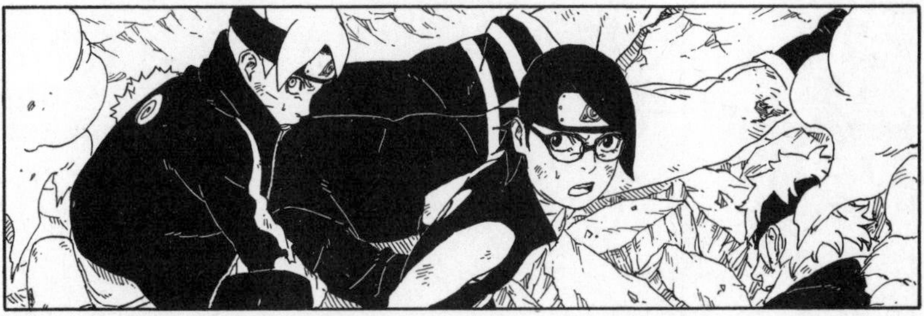
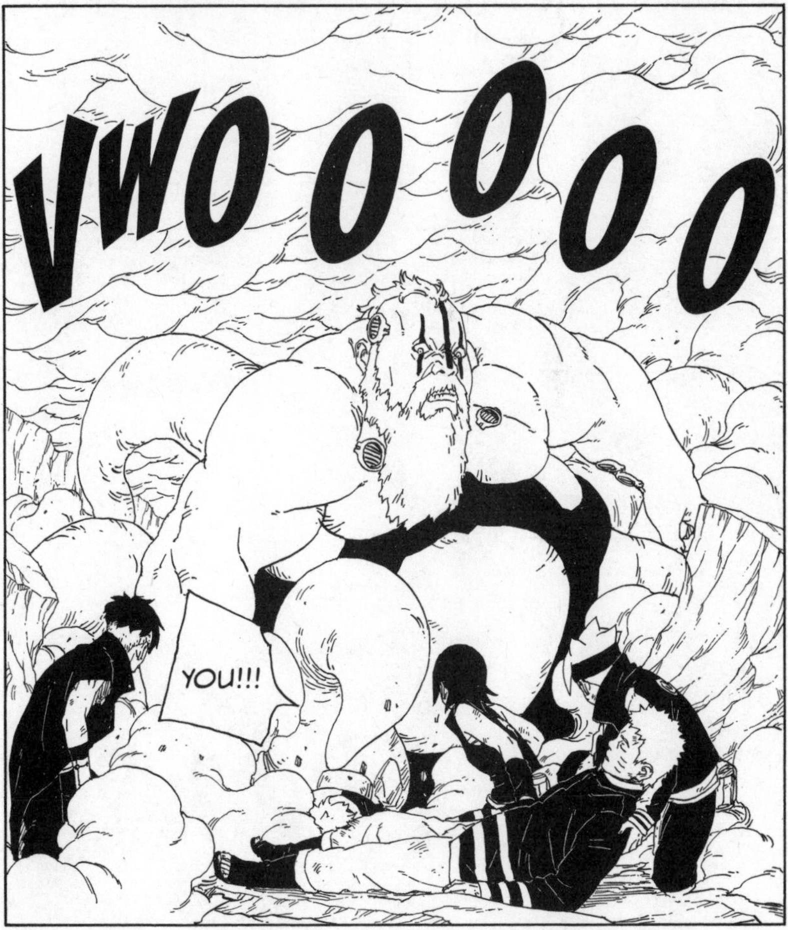
VWOOOOO
YOU!!!

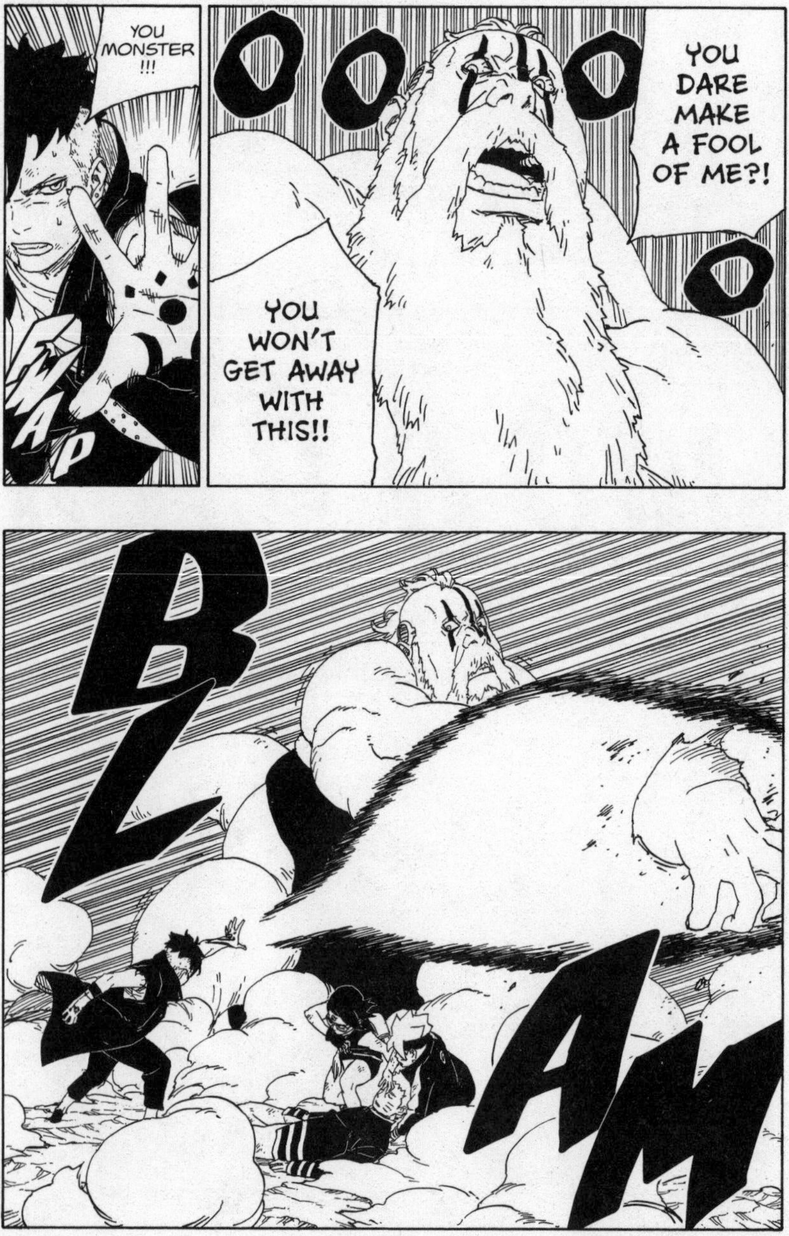
YOU DARE MAKE A FOOL OF ME?!
OOOOO
YOU WON'T GET AWAY WITH THIS!!
YOU MONSTER!!!
WHAP
BLAM

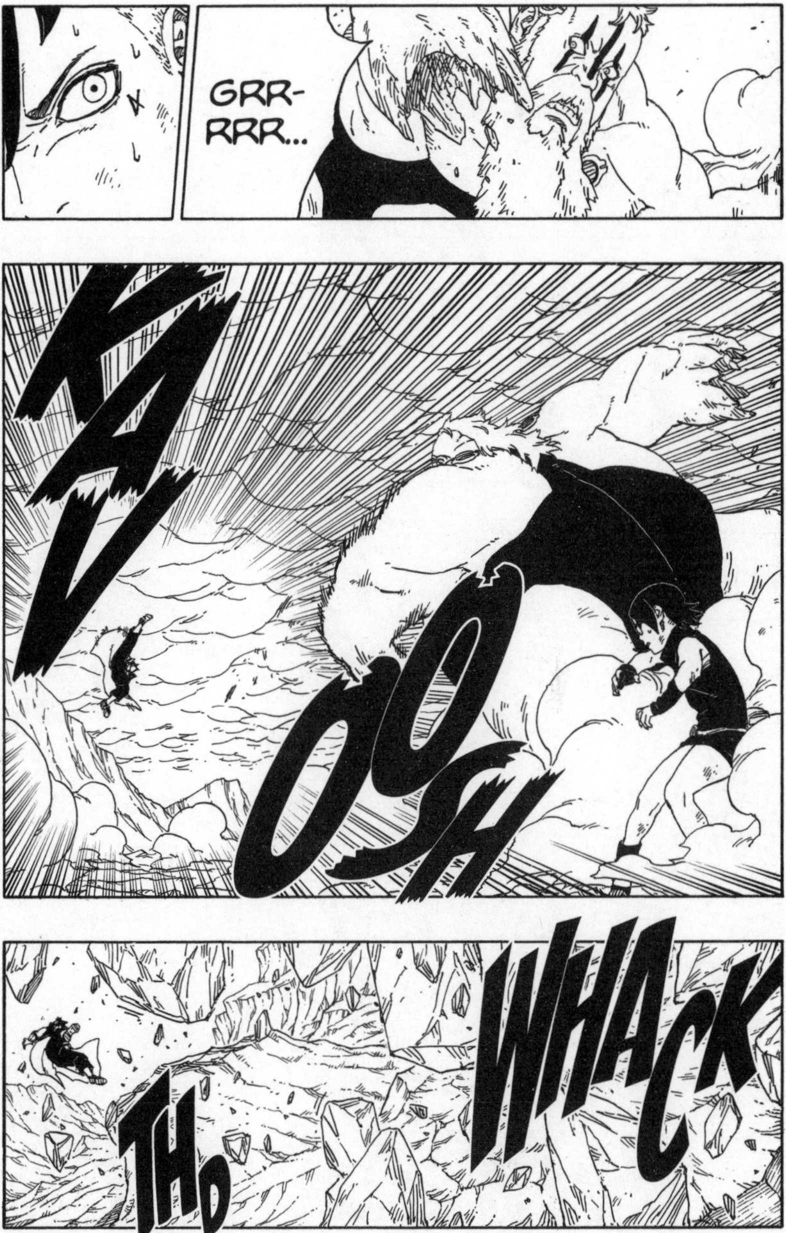

GRR-
RRR...
WHOOSH
WHACK
THD

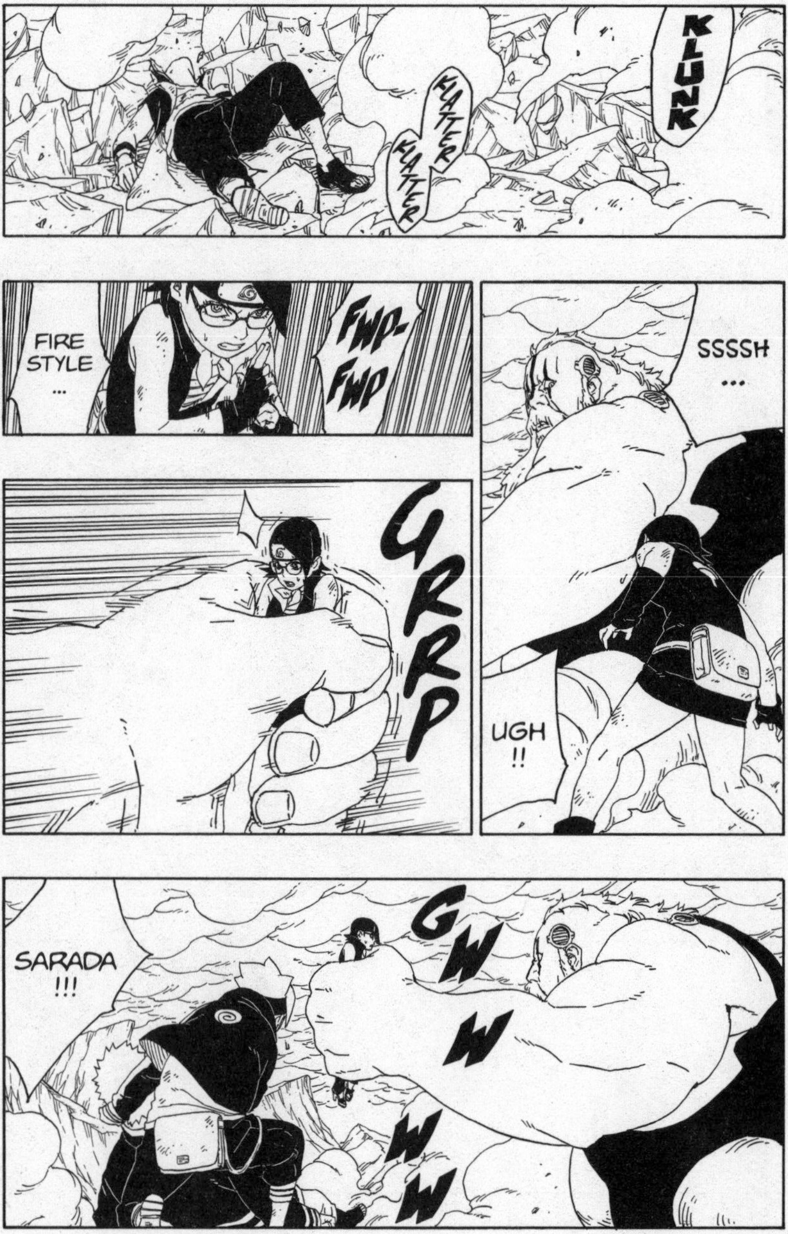
KLUNK
KLATTER KLATTER
SSSSH ...
FWP-FWP
FIRE STYLE ...
UGH !!
URRP
GWWWWW
SARADA !!!

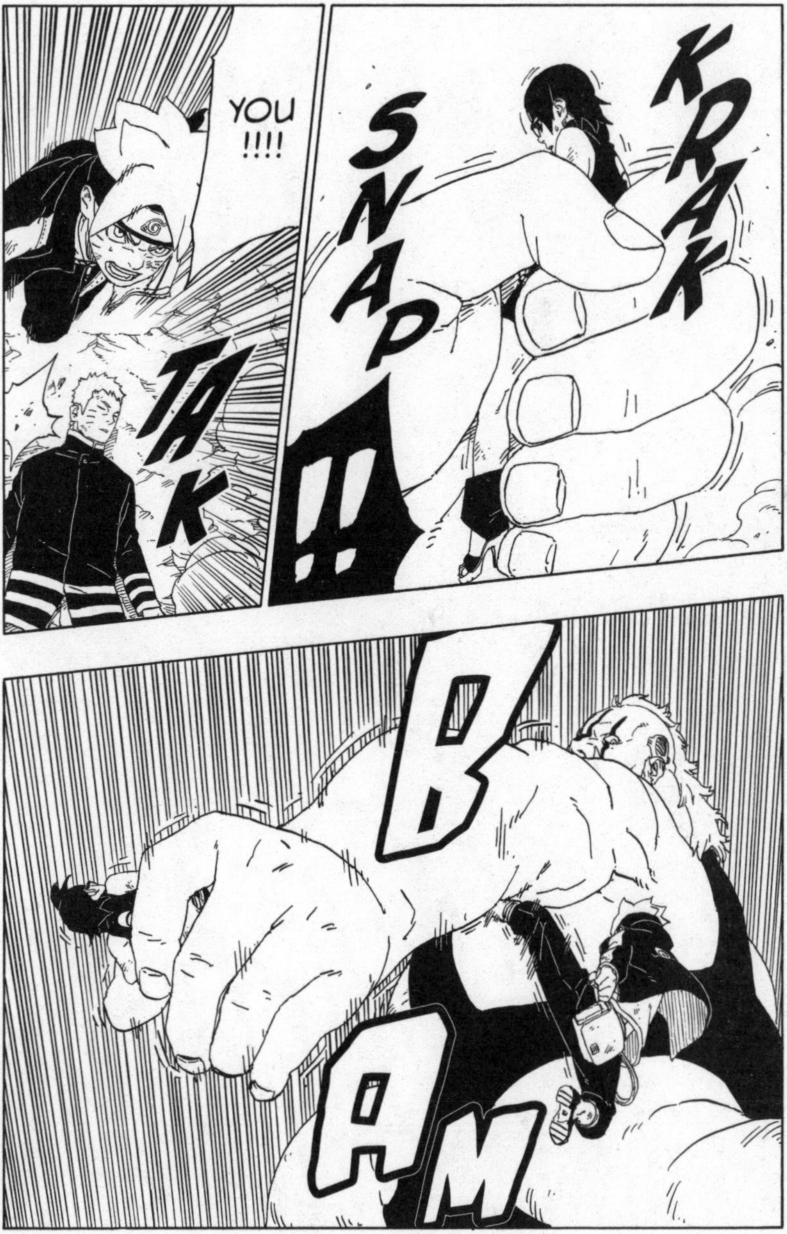
KRAK
SNAP!!
YOU !!!!
TAK
BAM

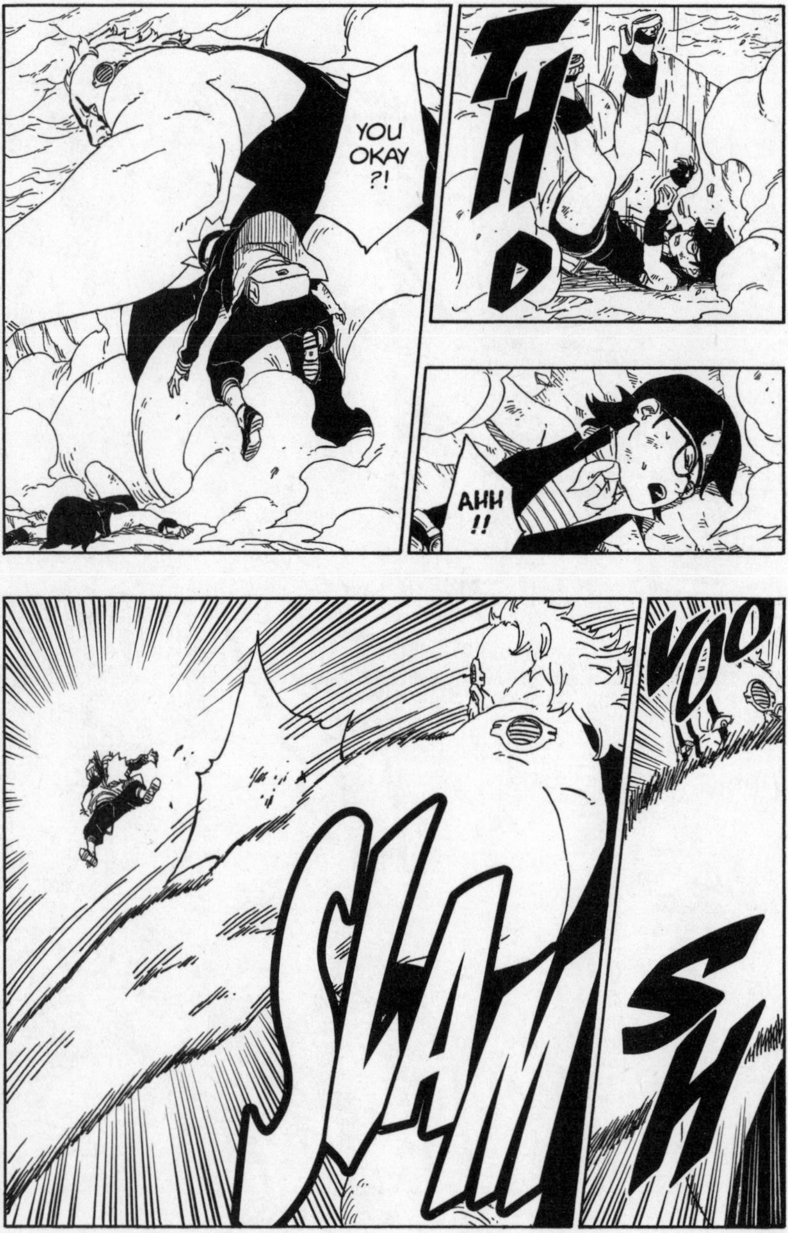
THD
AHH !!
YOU OKAY ?!
VOOO
SLAMSH

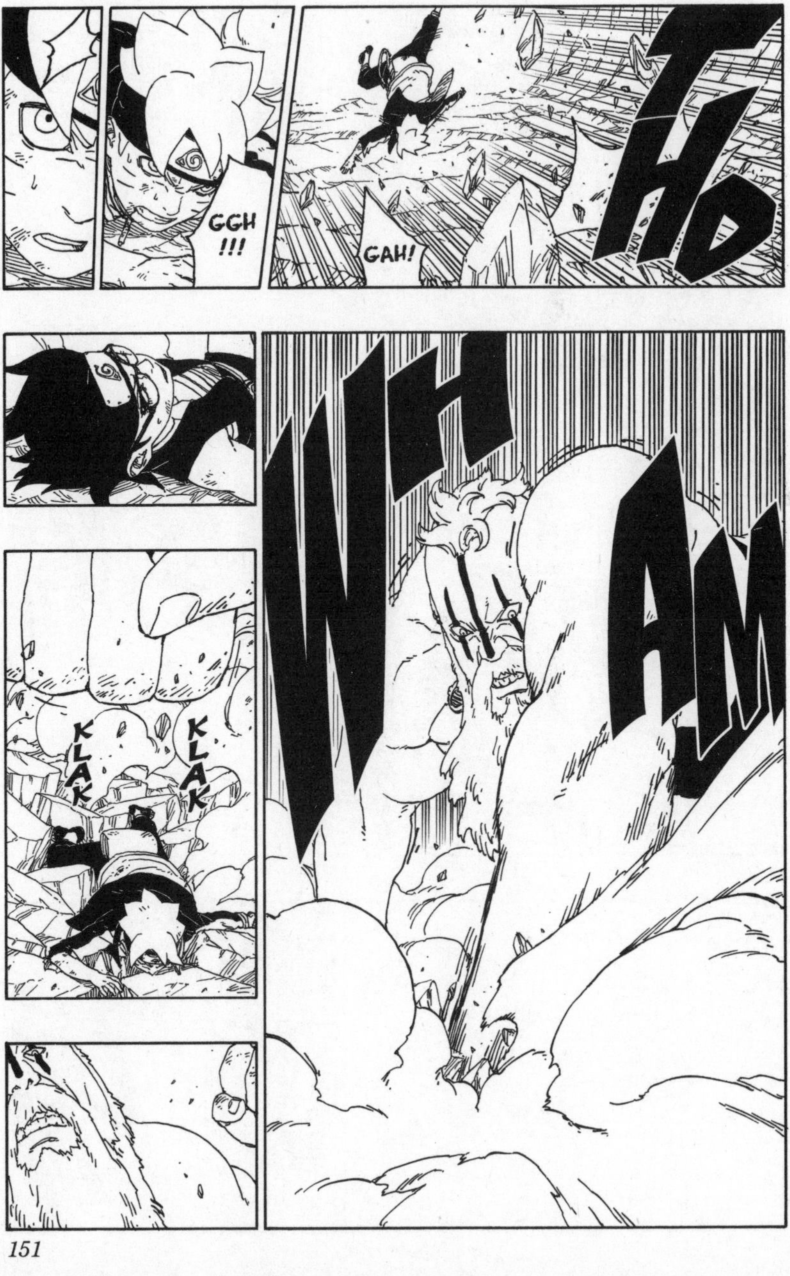
GAH!
GGH !!!
WHAM
KLAK
KLAK

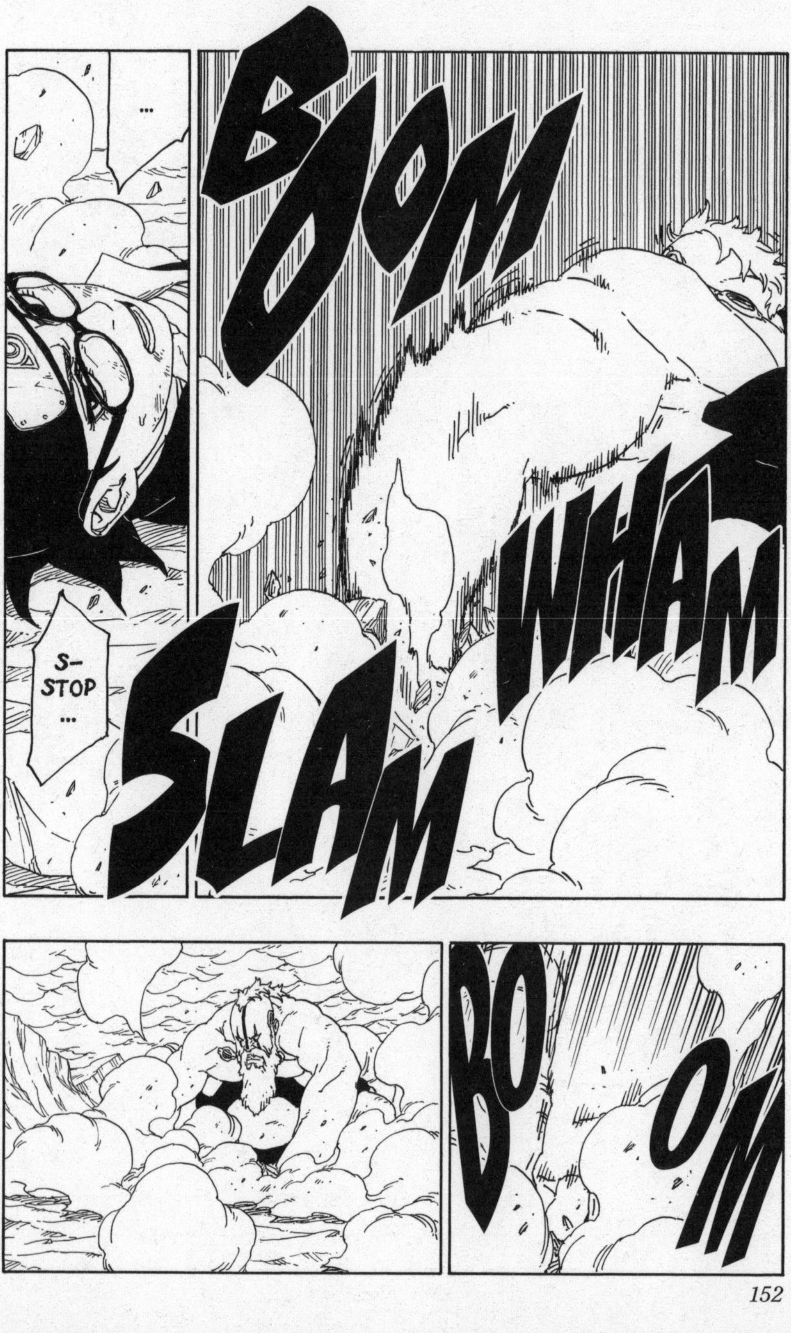
BOOM
WHAM
SLAM
...
S-STOP ...
BOOM

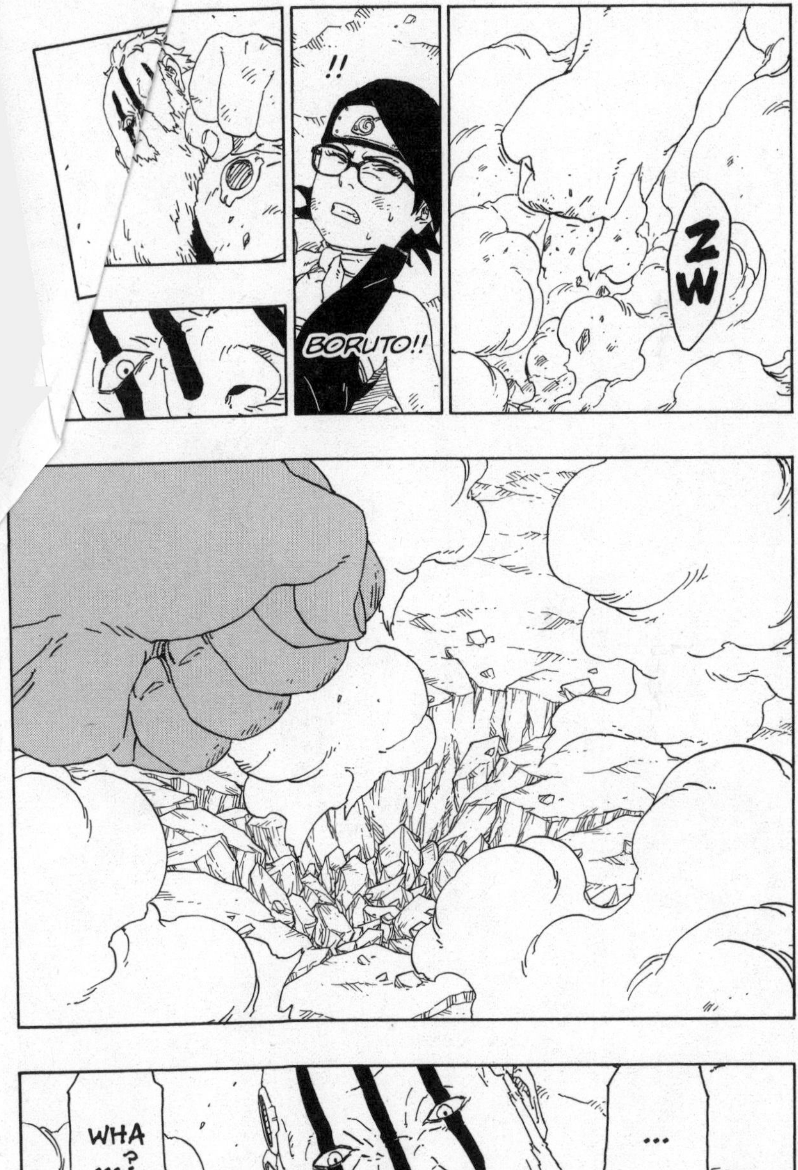
ZW
!!
BORUTO!!
...
WHA ...?

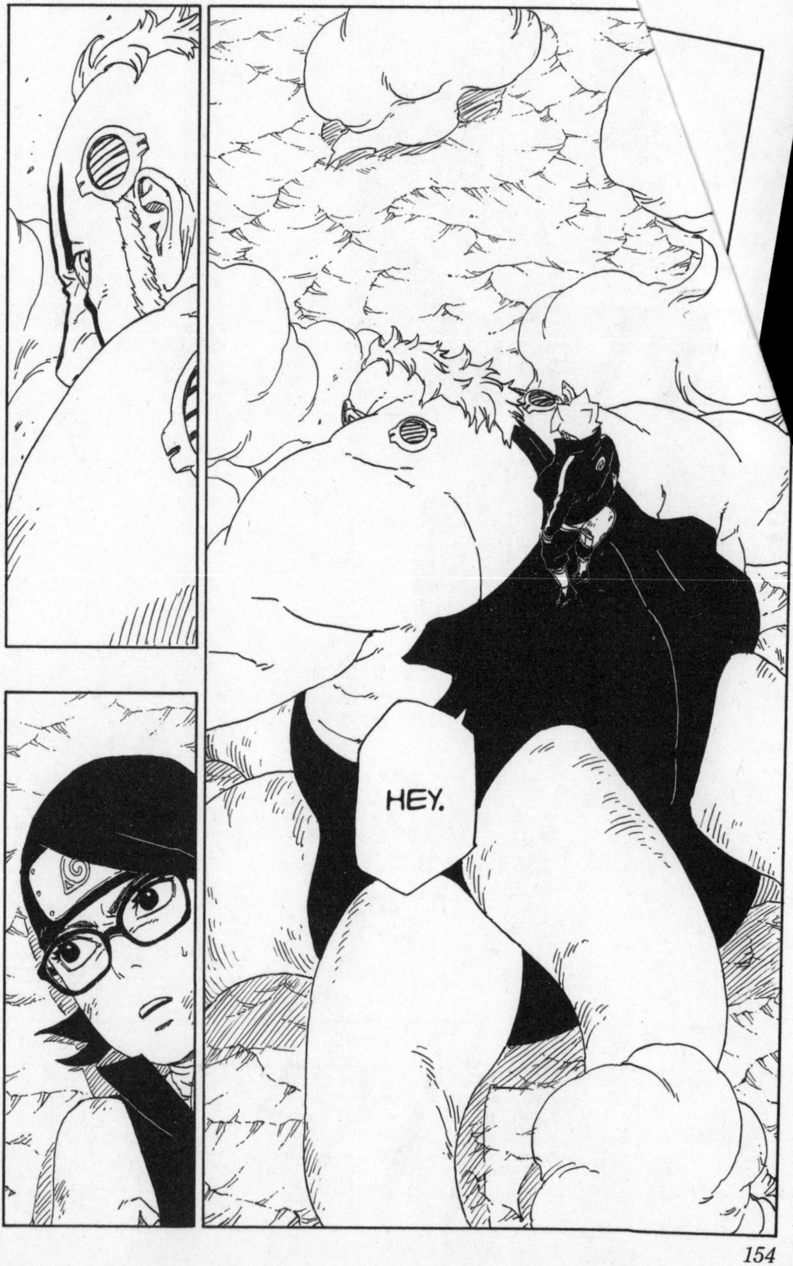
HEY.

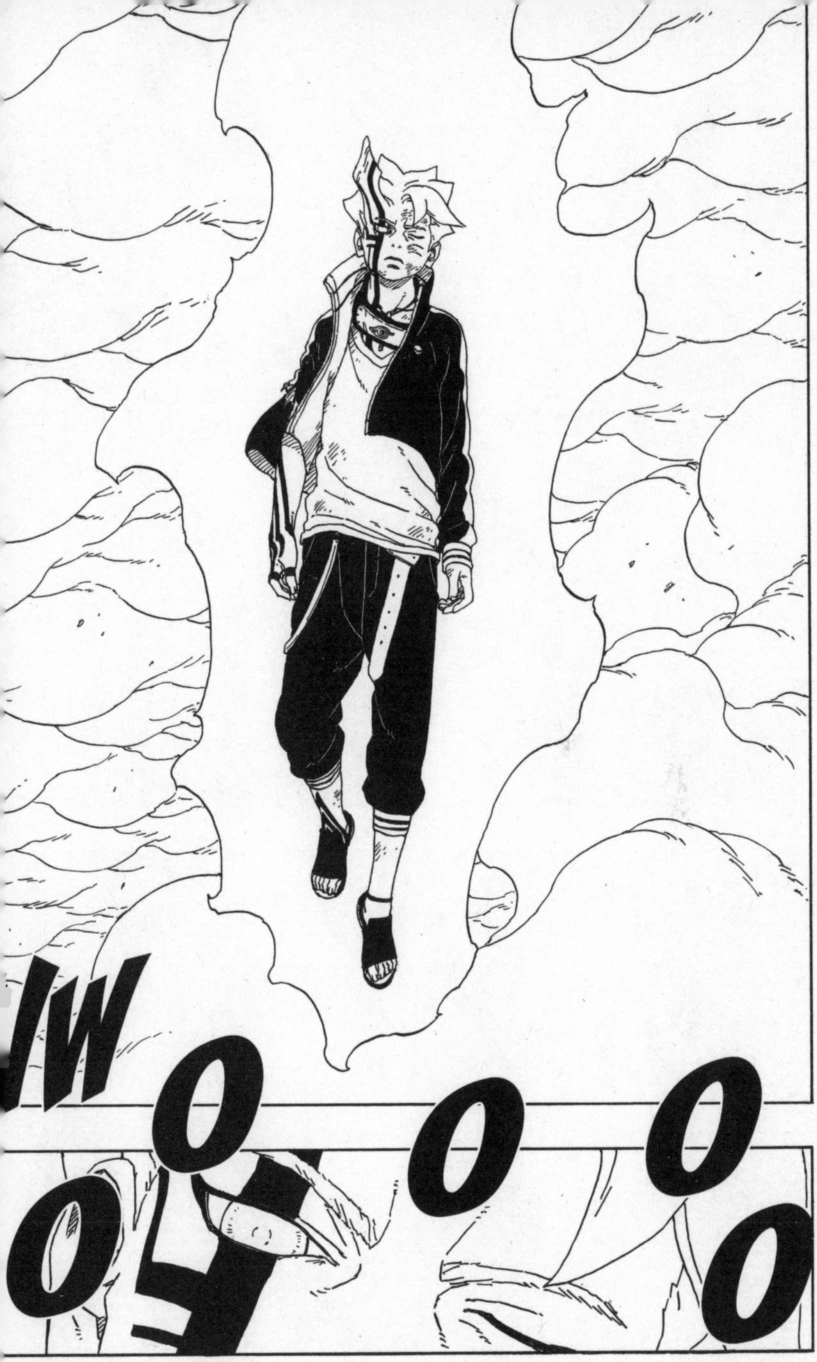
WOOOOO

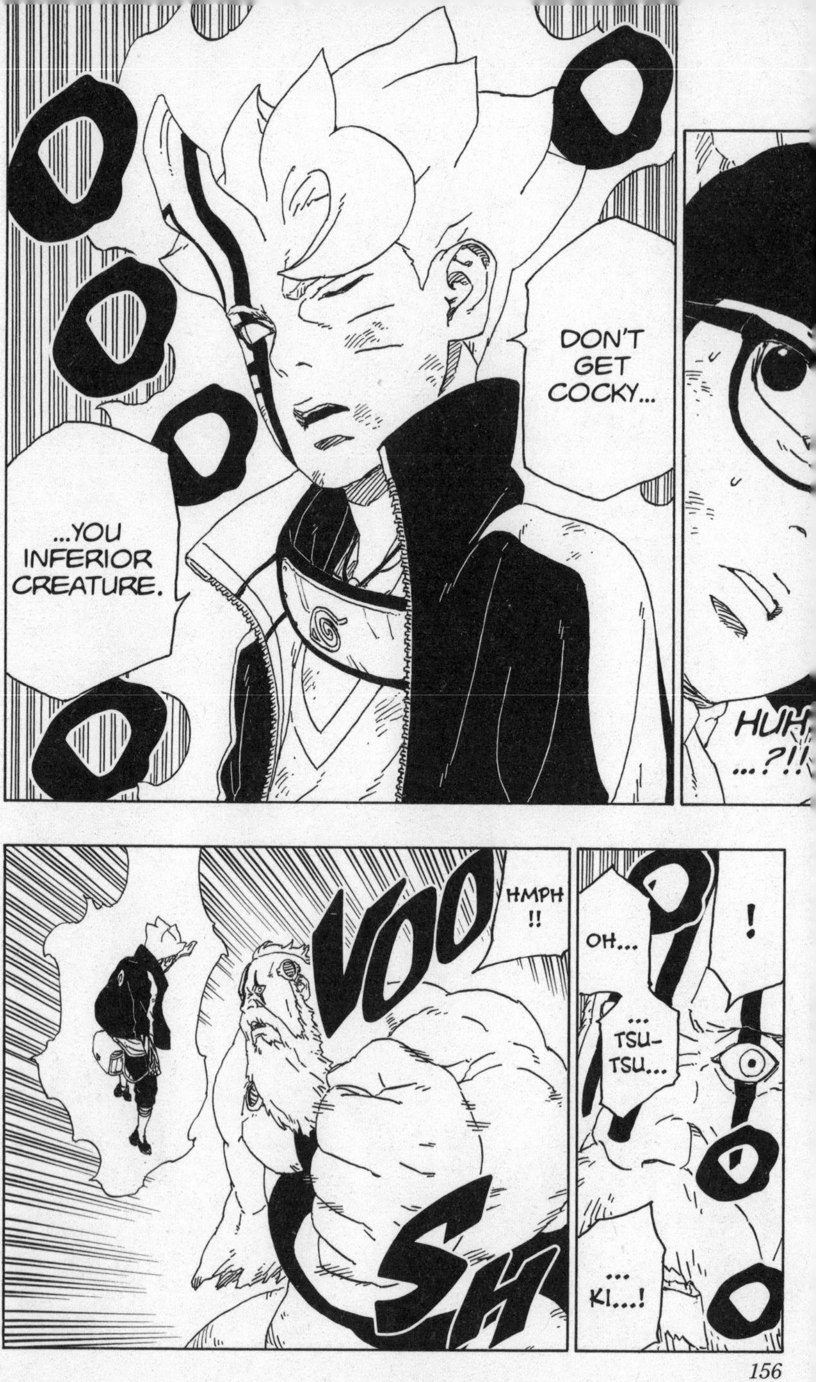
HUH ...?!!
DON'T GET COCKY...
...YOU INFERIOR CREATURE.
!
OH...
... TSU-TSU...
... KI...!
HMPH !!
VOOSH

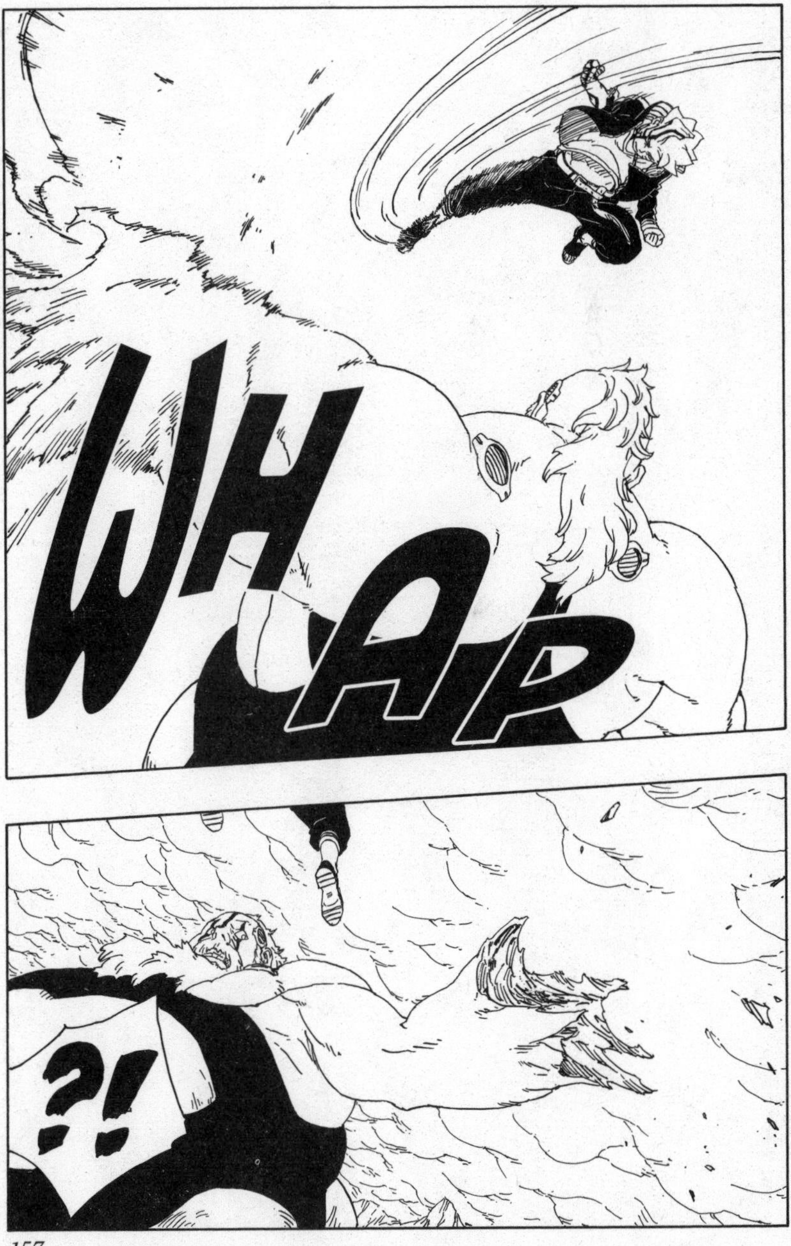
WHAP
?!

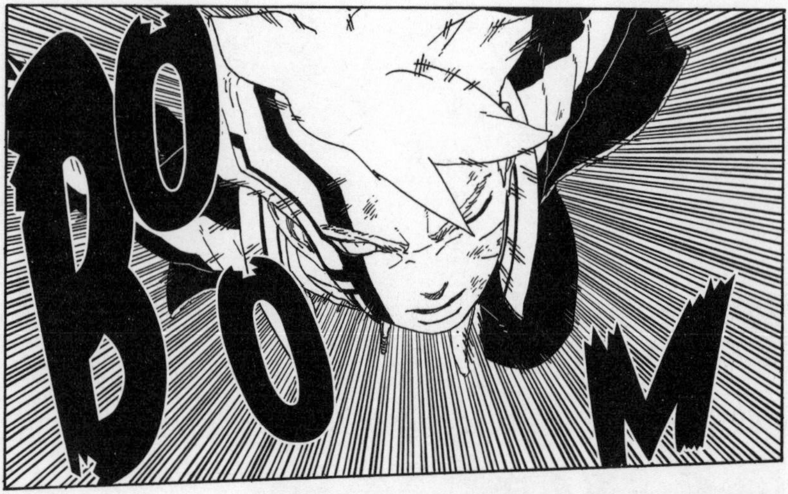
BOOOM
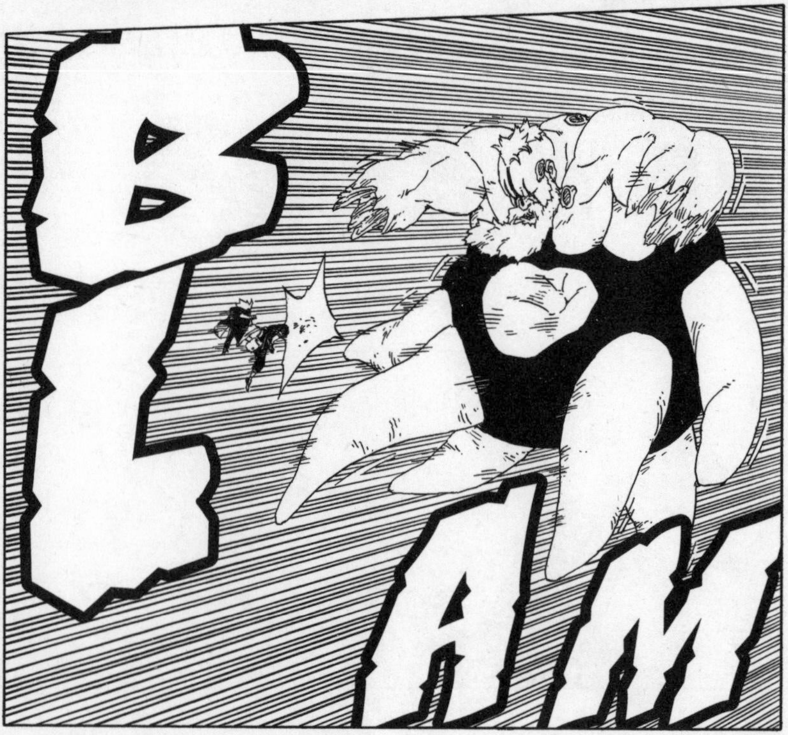
BAM

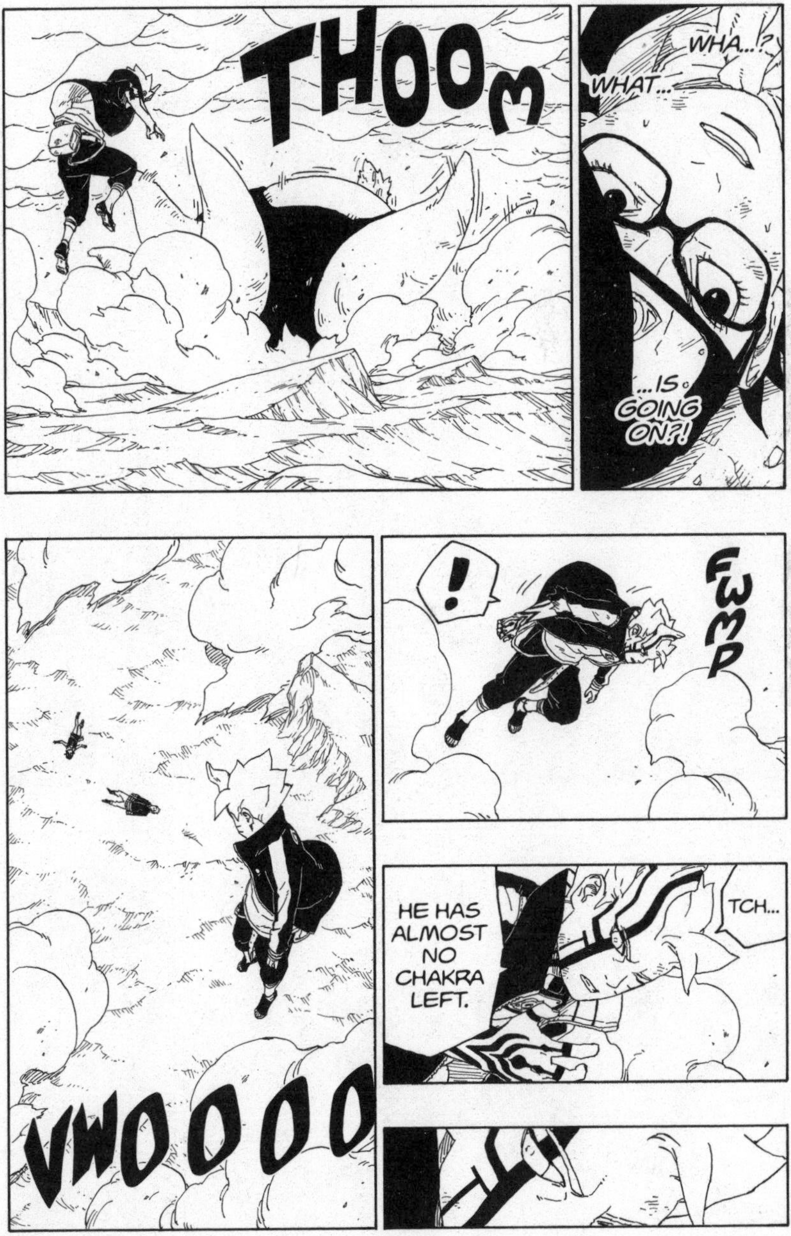
WHA...!?
WHAT...
...IS GOING ON?!
THOOM
FWMP
!
TCH...
HE HAS ALMOST NO CHAKRA LEFT.
VWOOOO

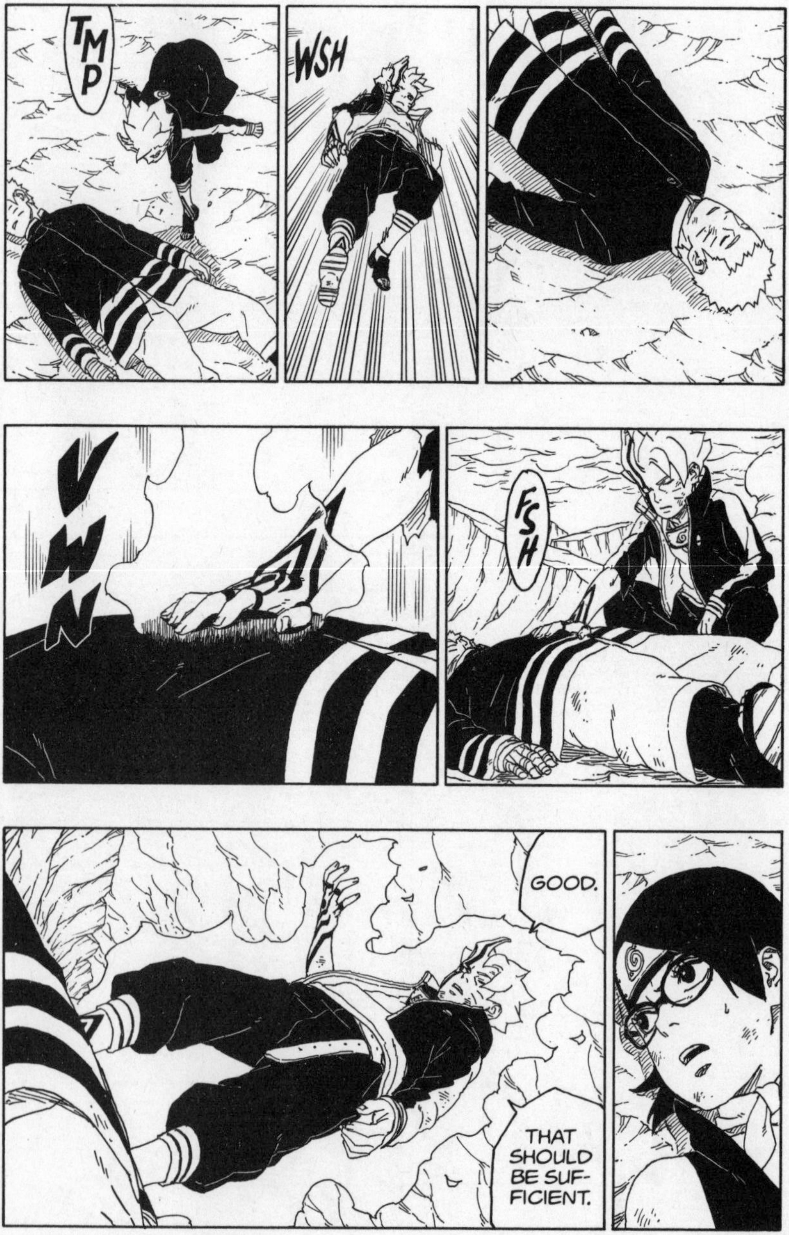
WSH
TMP
FSH
VWN
GOOD.
THAT SHOULD BE SUF- FICIENT.

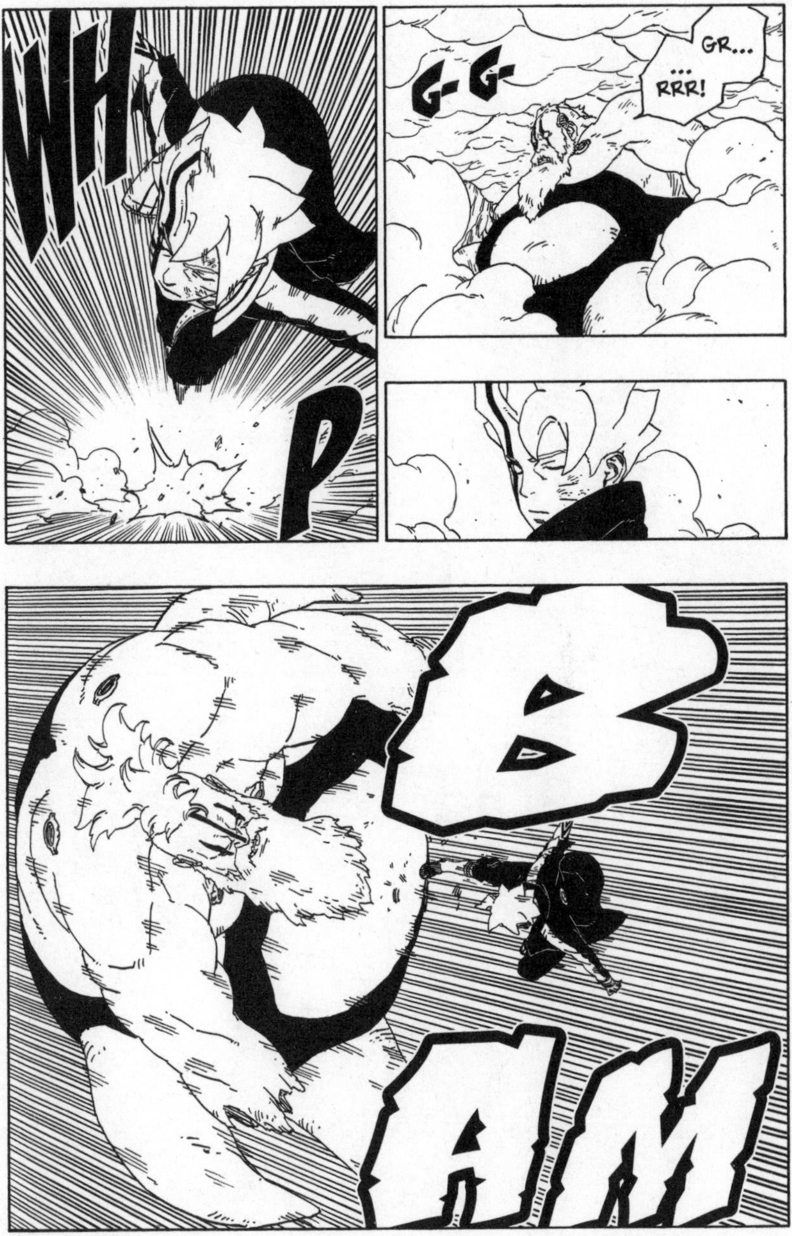
G-G-
GR...
...RRR!
WH
P
BAM

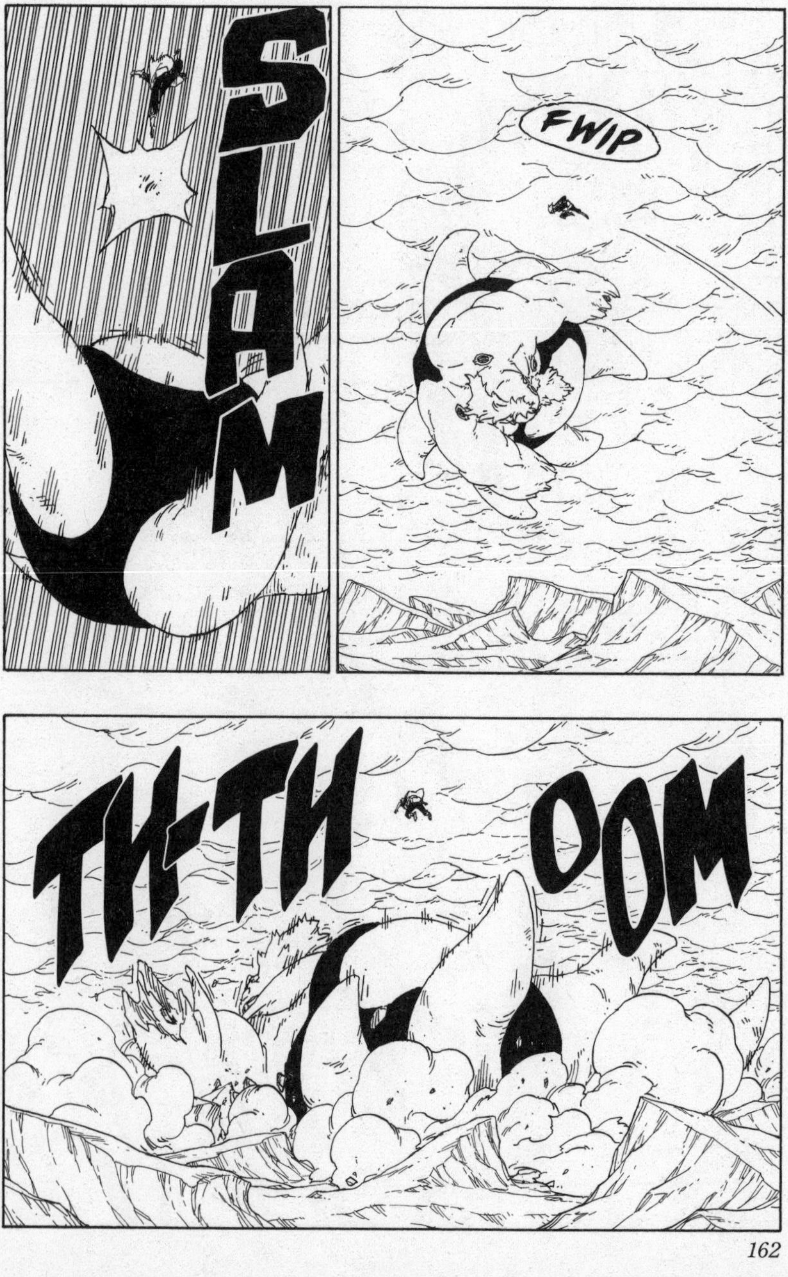
FWIP
SLAM
TH-TH
OOM

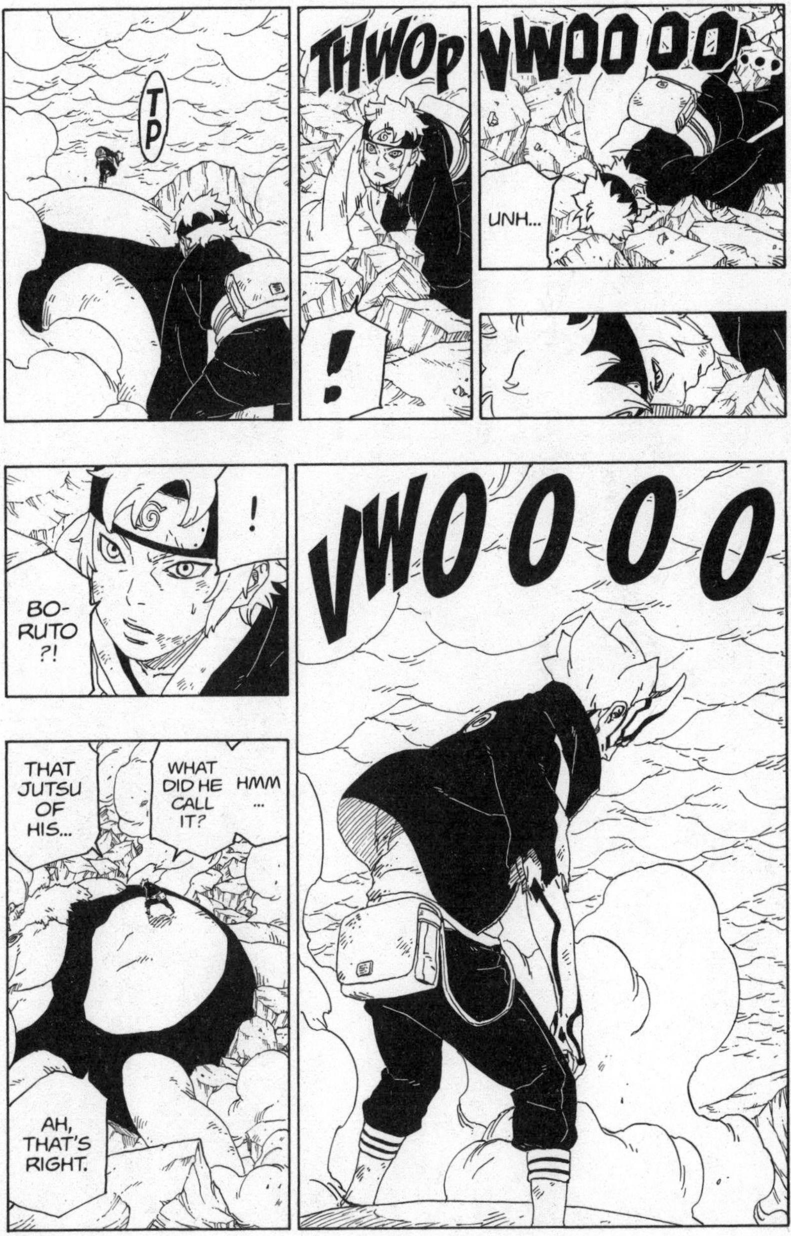
VWOOOO
UNH...
THWOP
!
TP
VWOOOO
!
BO-RUTO?!
HMM...
WHAT DID HE CALL IT?
THAT JUTSU OF HIS...
AH, THAT'S RIGHT.

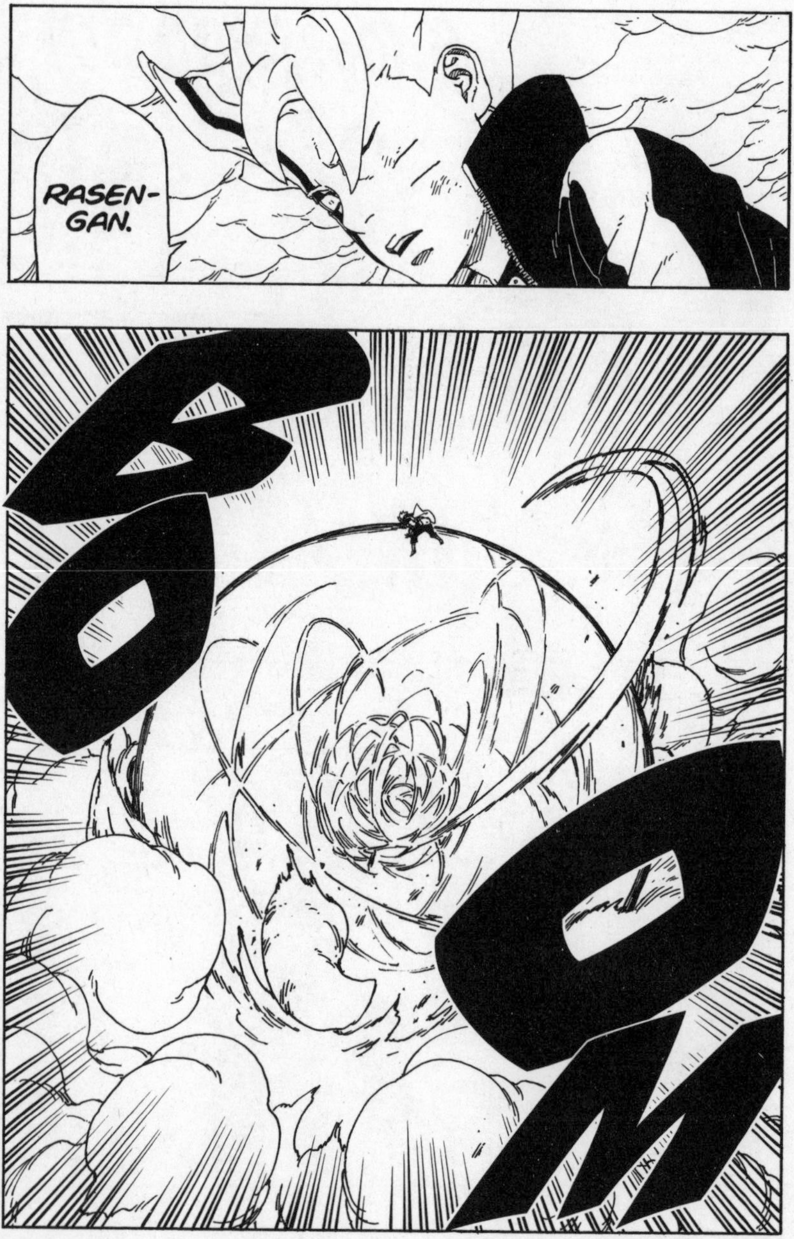
RASEN-
GAN.
BOOM

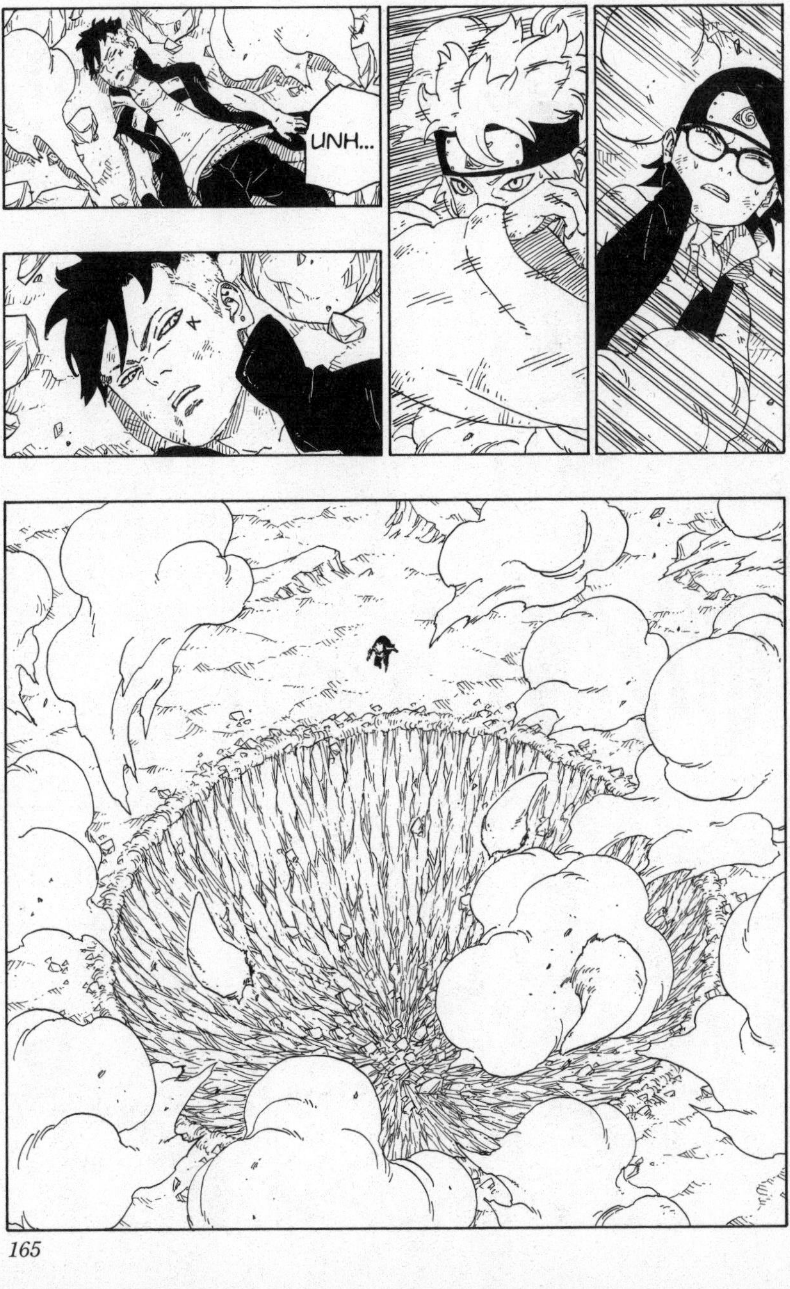
UNH...

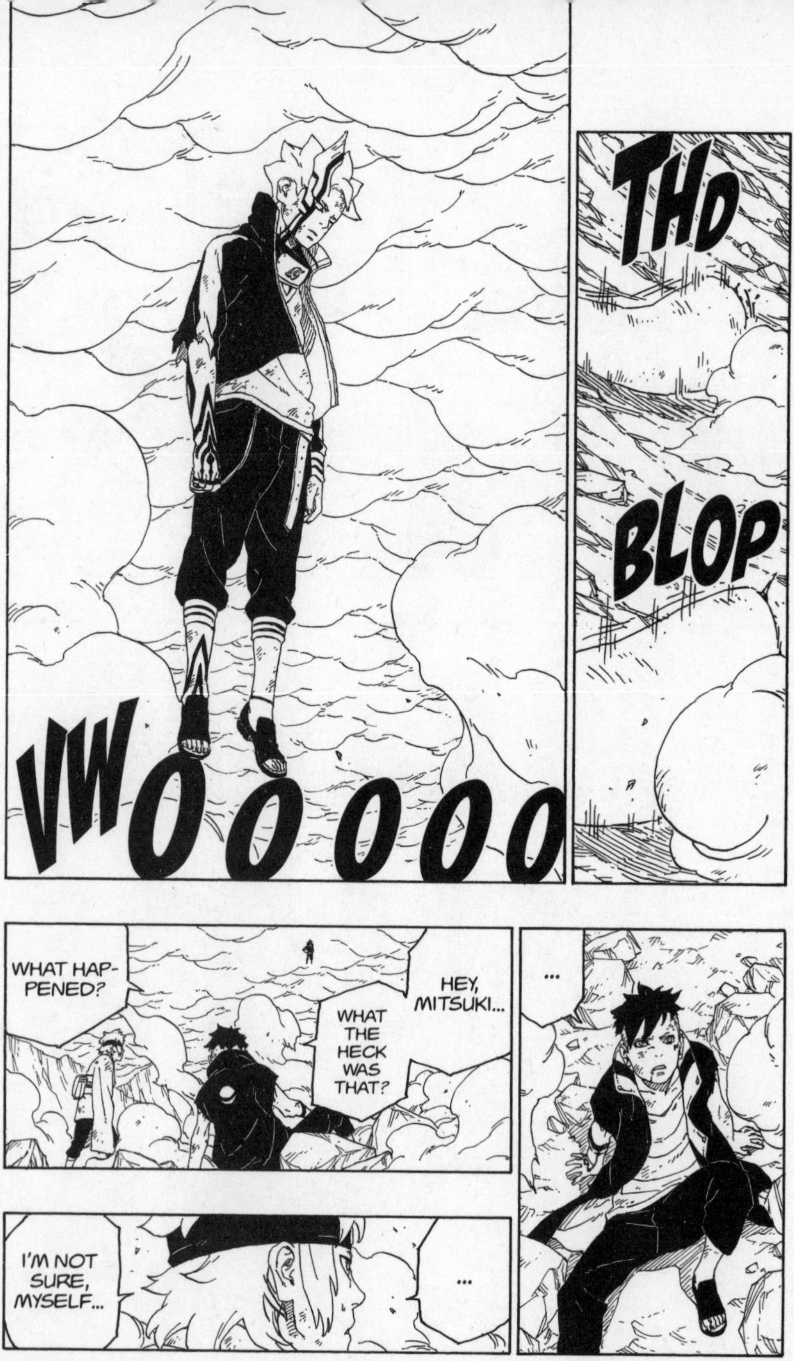
THD
BLOP
VWOOOOOO
...
HEY, MITSUKI...
WHAT THE HECK WAS THAT?
WHAT HAP-PENED?
...
I'M NOT SURE, MYSELF...

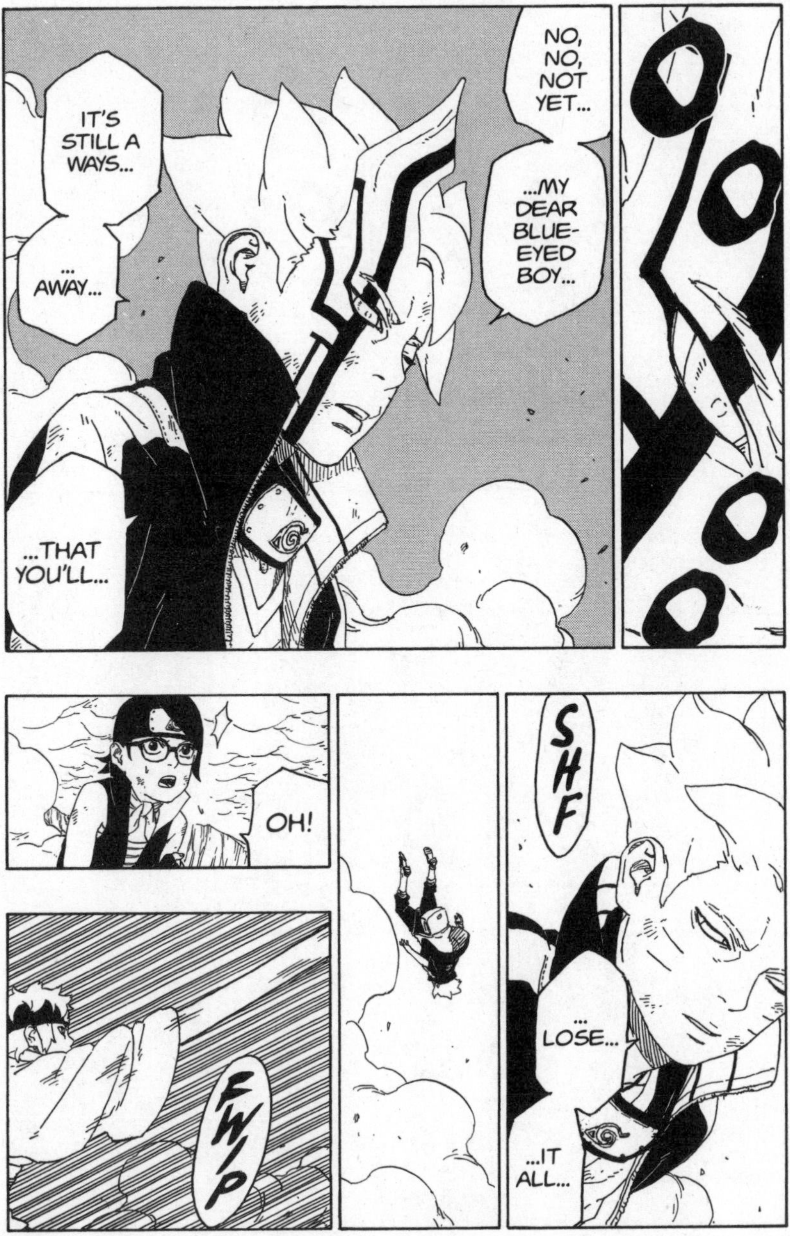
NO, NO, NOT YET...
...MY DEAR BLUE-EYED BOY...
IT'S STILL A WAYS...
...AWAY...
...THAT YOU'LL...
SHF
...LOSE...
...IT ALL...
OH!
FWIP

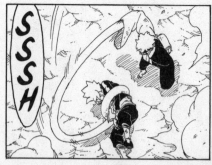

FWAP
SSSH
...
...N ...
...NH ...
SHUP
HUFF
HUFF
HUH?
MI-TSUKI?
I... WHAT ...
!
HE DOESN'T REMEMBER?
JUST NOW...
HE SEEMED LIKE SOMEONE ELSE.
KARMA...
IT MIGHT BE EVEN MORE DANGEROUS THAN WE THOUGHT...

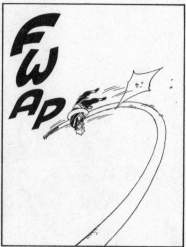

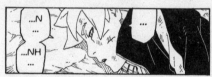

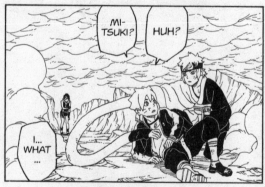

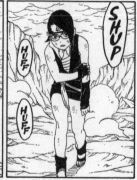

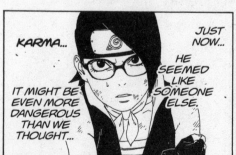

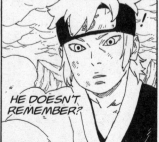

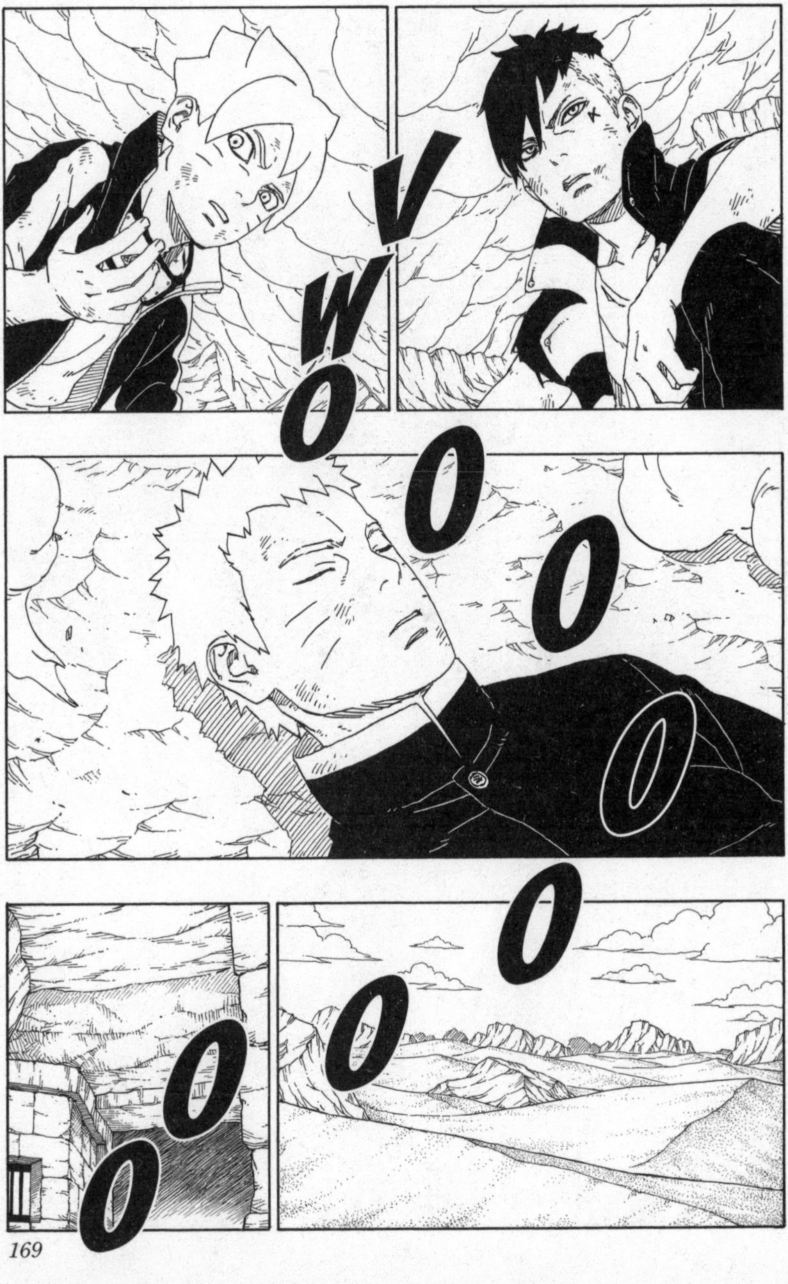
VWOOOOOOOO

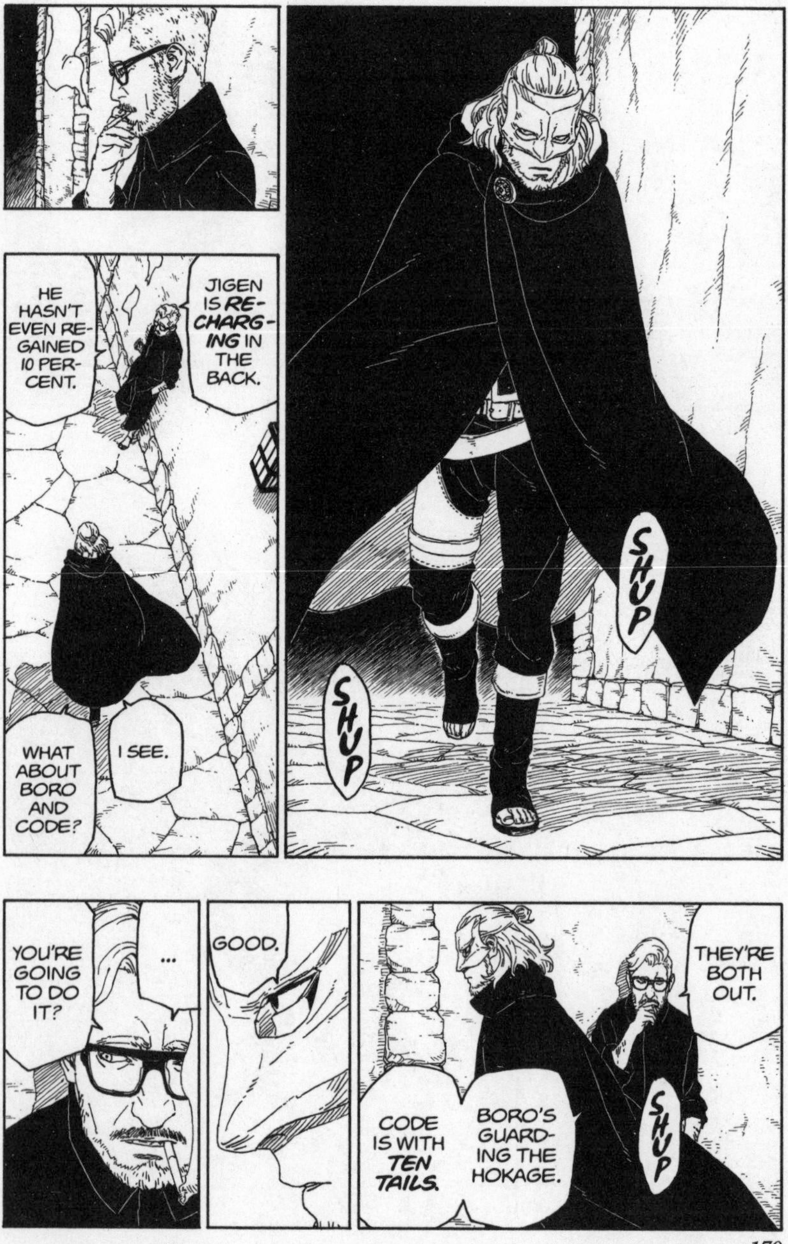
SHUP
SHUP
JIGEN IS **RECHARGING** IN THE BACK.
HE HASN'T EVEN REGAINED 10 PERCENT.
I SEE.
WHAT ABOUT BORO AND CODE?
THEY'RE BOTH OUT.
BORO'S GUARDING THE HOKAGE.
CODE IS WITH ***TEN TAILS.***
SHUP
GOOD.
...
YOU'RE GOING TO DO IT?

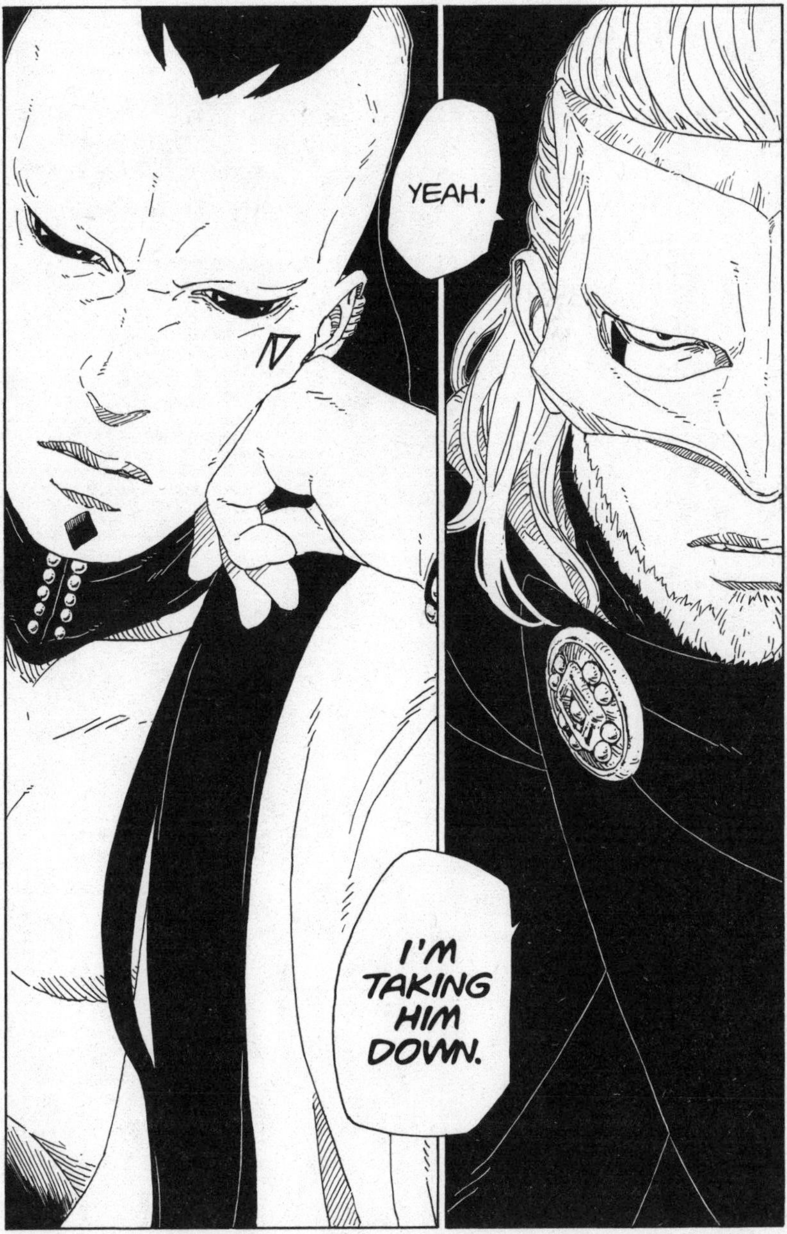
YEAH.
I'M TAKING HIM DOWN.

# BORU-FANS!!!

Graphic Novel Edition!!

## No. 4

### The Ties Between Kara and Konoha

Kara's Leader

## JIGEN

HAS EXTRAORDINARY POWER AND THE ABILITY TO SHRINK AND INSTANTANEOUSLY RESTORE THE SIZE OF OBJECTS. IS HE SOMEHOW CONNECTED TO OHTSUTSUKI OR THE DIVINE TREE?

THE BATTLE AGAINST NARUTO AND OTHERS TO RECOVER HIS VESSEL!!

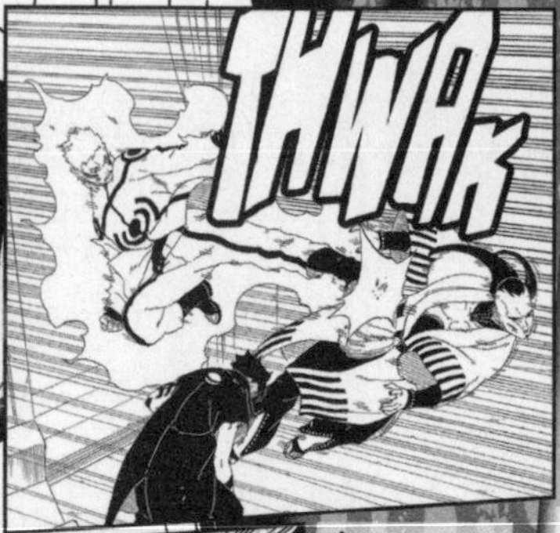
THWAK

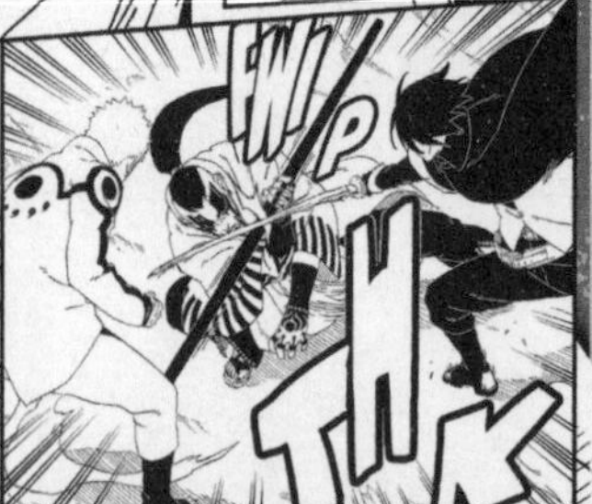
FWIP
THK

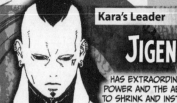

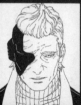

⬆ ⬅ Shows up in Konoha using Karma in order to take back Kawaki, who is being guarded at the Uzumaki home. Faces off against Naruto and Sasuke, who resist.

## THOSE MARKED WITH KARMA

Momoshiki's Karma

### UZUMAKI BORUTO

THE SON OF SEVENTH HOKAGE UZUMAKI NARUTO. HE WAS IMPLANTED WITH KARMA WHEN HE STRUCK A MORTAL BLOW ON OHTSUTSUKI MOMOSHIKI DURING THEIR BATTLE.

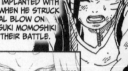

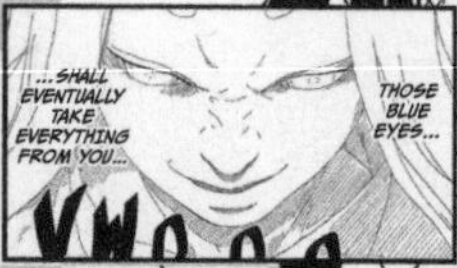
THOSE BLUE EYES...
...SHALL EVENTUALLY TAKE EVERYTHING FROM YOU...
VWOOO

Jigen's Karma

### KAWAKI

A YOUNG MAN WHO WAS BOUGHT IN EARLY CHILDHOOD BY JIGEN. HE SURVIVED HUMAN EXPERIMENTS THAT SOUGHT INDIVIDUALS COMPATIBLE WITH JIGEN'S KARMA AND WAS RAISED BY JIGEN AND THE OTHERS TO BECOME HIS VESSEL. WAS FORTUITOUSLY DISCOVERED BY TEAM KONOHAMARU DURING A MISSION AND WAS TAKEN INTO PROTECTIVE CUSTODY.

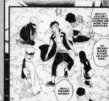

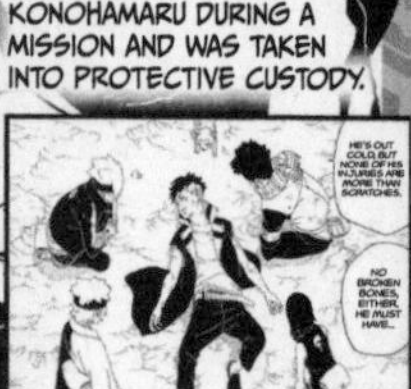
HE'S OUT COLD, BUT NONE OF HIS INJURIES ARE MORE THAN SCRATCHES.
NO BROKEN BONES, EITHER. HE MUST HAVE...
...REALLY DRAINED HIMSELF.

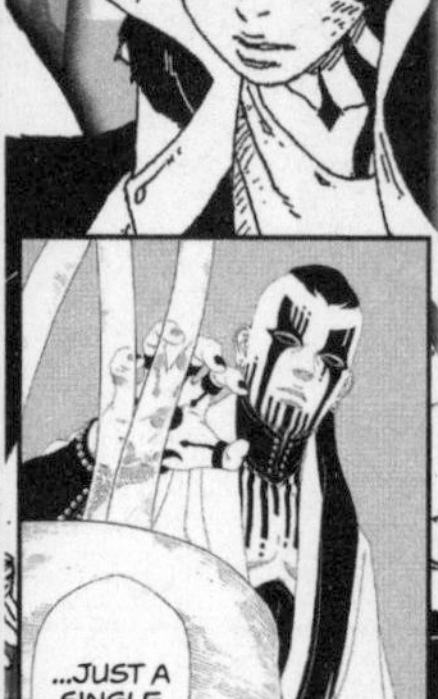
...JUST A SINGLE VESSEL.

## KARA'S ORGANIZATIONAL STRUCTURE

### OUTERS

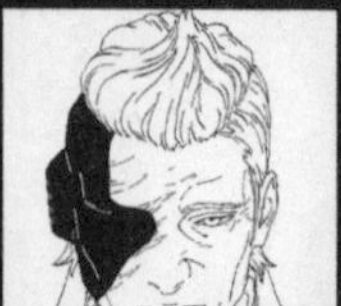

Kara's external collaborators. They are commissioned by Inners to engage in combat, etc.

### INNERS

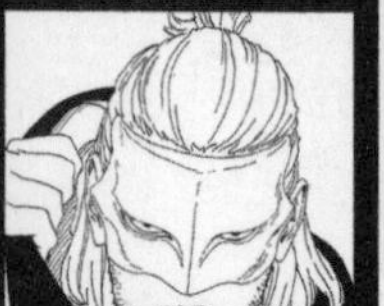

Kara's key members. Each has a division they are in charge of called a Sector.

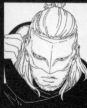

# THE INNERS WHO FOLLOW JIGEN!!

**Possessor of Super Regenerative Ability**

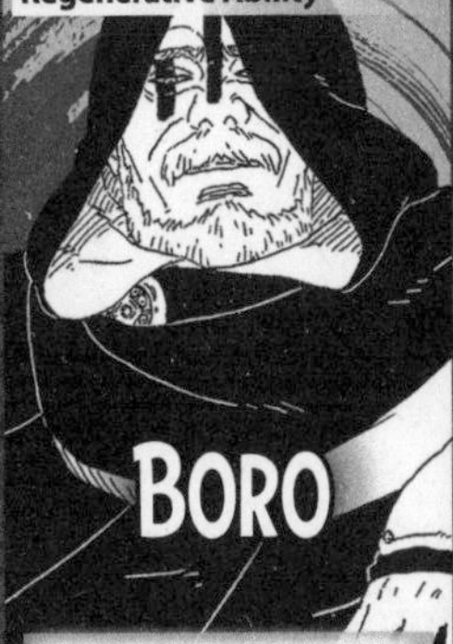

## BORO

FIGHTS USING HIS REGENERATIVE ABILITY AND VIRUSES. SO LONG AS HE DOESN'T LOSE HIS INTERNAL CORE, HIS BODY WILL KEEP REGENERATING FULLY, WITHOUT LIMIT.

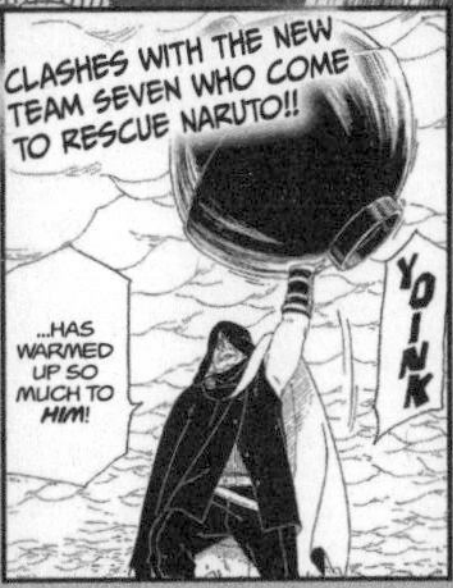
CLASHES WITH THE NEW TEAM SEVEN WHO COME TO RESCUE NARUTO!!
...HAS WARMED UP SO MUCH TO *HIM*!
YOINK

⬆ With his core extracted, the Scientific Ninja Tools inside his body go wild!! Afterward, he is erased by a transformed Boruto.

**Destructive Urges Incarnate**

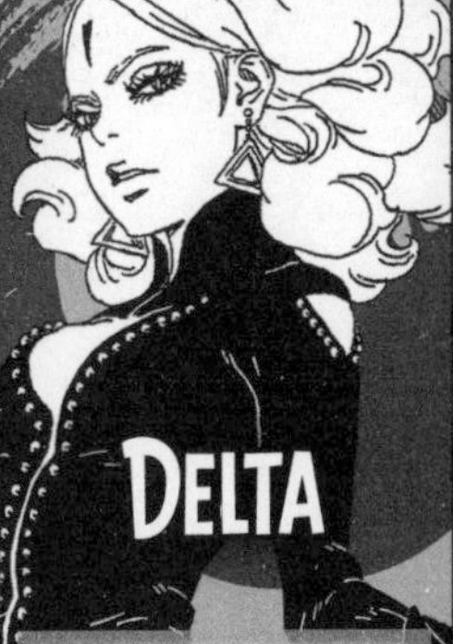

## DELTA

A CYBORG WHOSE ENTIRE BODY IS FITTED WITH SCIENTIFIC NINJA TOOLS. THERE ARE MULTIPLE DELTAS STOCKED AT KARA'S STRONGHOLD.

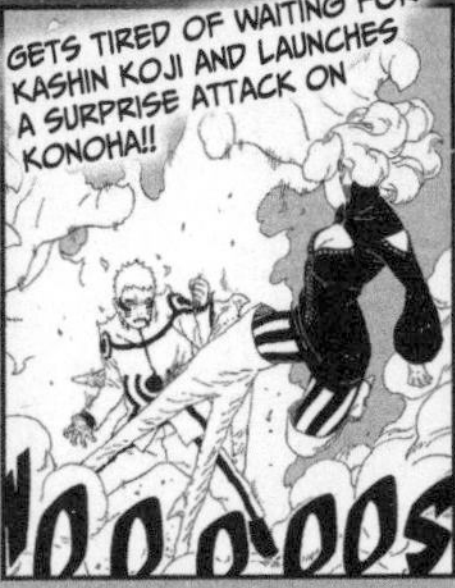
GETS TIRED OF WAITING FOR KASHIN KOJI AND LAUNCHES A SURPRISE ATTACK ON KONOHA!!

⬆ Is soundly defeated by Naruto and blows herself up, but transfers her memory to another Delta at Kara HQ and returns to life right away.

**The Masked Toad User**

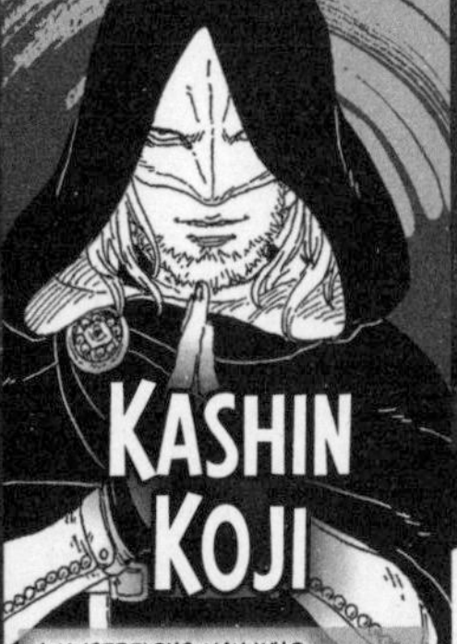

## KASHIN KOJI

A MYSTERIOUS MAN WHO USES POWERFUL NINJUTSU SUCH AS SUMMONING TOADS AND UNQUENCHABLE FLAMES. APPEARS TO HAVE SOME TIE TO KONOHA VILLAGE.

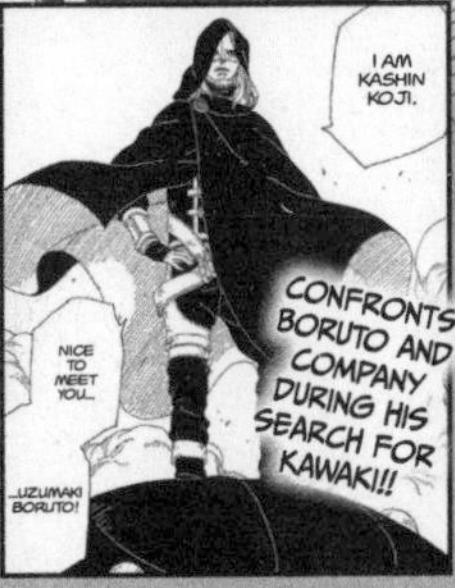
I AM KASHIN KOJI.
NICE TO MEET YOU...
...UZUMAKI BORUTO!
CONFRONTS BORUTO AND COMPANY DURING HIS SEARCH FOR KAWAKI!!

⬆ Retreats once he confirms Boruto bears a Karma. Was keeping watch on Konoha after that.

## AMADO

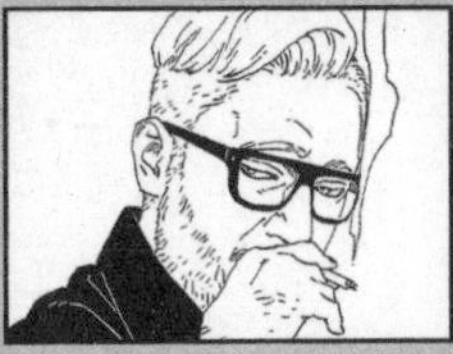

⬆ A noncombatant scientist who is indispensable to fulfilling Kara's dearest wish. He sustains the astounding scientific power and Karma research held by Kara.

## CODE

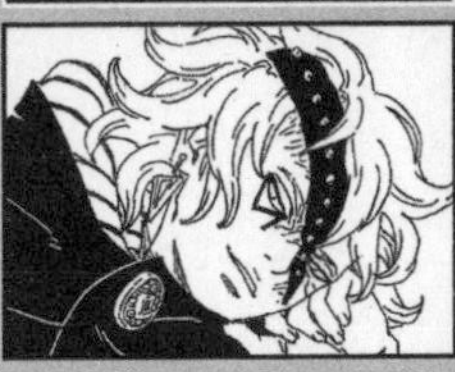

⬆ A member of Inner who has the appearance of a young male. According to him, among the Inners he has more ability than Delta and about the same as Boro.

## VICTOR

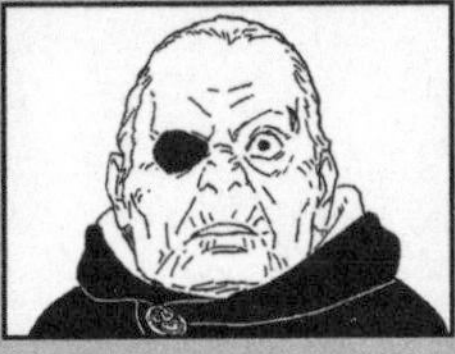

⬆ The old man Inner who was overseeing Kawaki's transport mission. He was erased by Kashin Koji for failing in his responsibility and on suspicion of betrayal.

# Black ✤ Clover

### STORY & ART BY YŪKI TABATA

Asta is a young boy who dreams of becoming the greatest mage in the kingdom. Only one problem—he can't use any magic! Luckily for Asta, he receives the incredibly rare five-leaf clover grimoire that gives him the power of anti-magic. Can someone who can't use magic really become the Wizard King? One thing's for sure—Asta will never give up!

SHONEN JUMP

VIZ media
www.viz.com

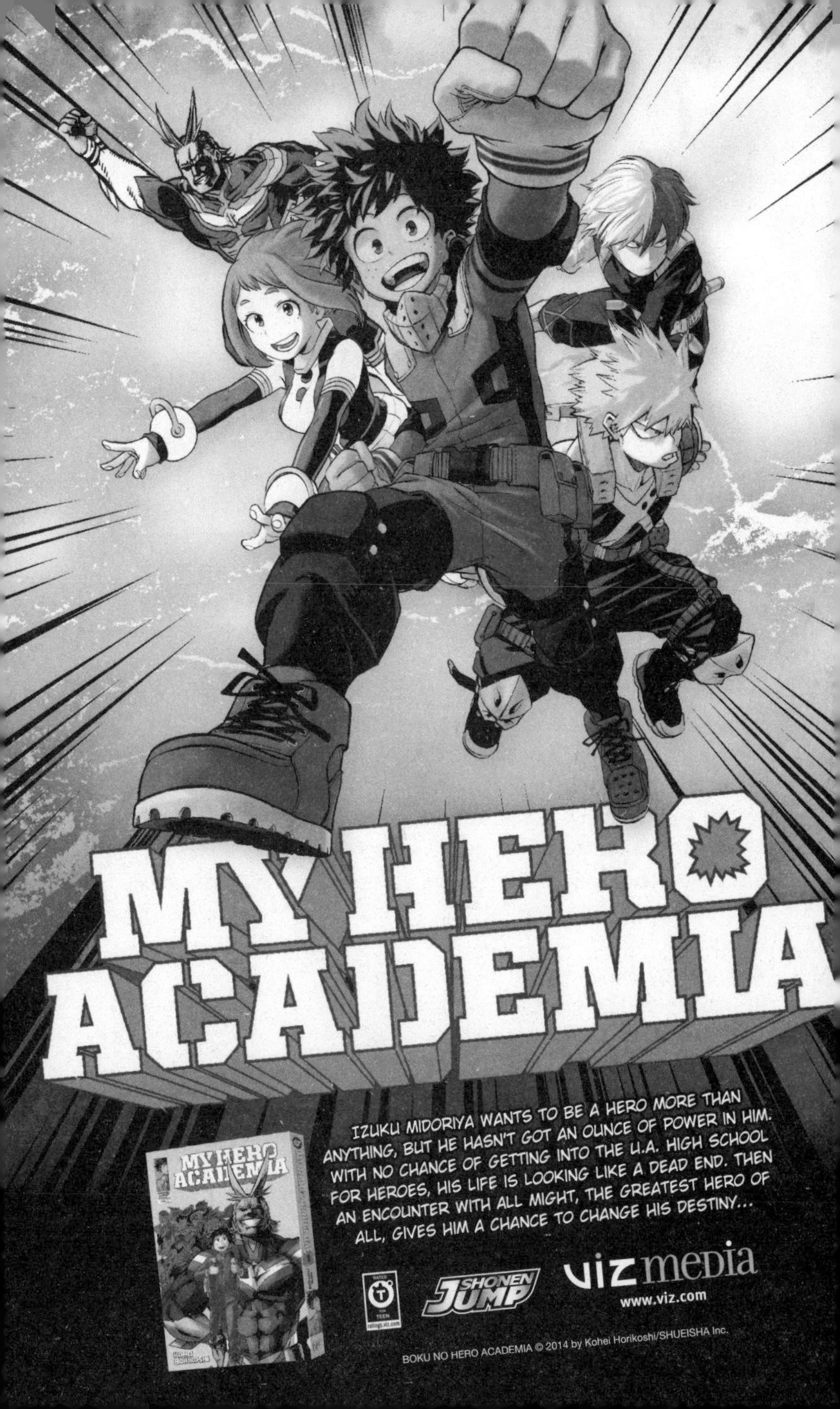
MY HERO ACADEMIA
IZUKU MIDORIYA WANTS TO BE A HERO MORE THAN ANYTHING, BUT HE HASN'T GOT AN OUNCE OF POWER IN HIM. WITH NO CHANCE OF GETTING INTO THE U.A. HIGH SCHOOL FOR HEROES, HIS LIFE IS LOOKING LIKE A DEAD END. THEN AN ENCOUNTER WITH ALL MIGHT, THE GREATEST HERO OF ALL, GIVES HIM A CHANCE TO CHANGE HIS DESTINY...
RATED T FOR TEEN
ratings.viz.com
SHONEN JUMP
viz media
www.viz.com
BOKU NO HERO ACADEMIA © 2014 by Kohei Horikoshi/SHUEISHA Inc.

# YOU'RE READING
## IN THE
# WRONG DIRECTION!!

**W**HOOPS! Guess what? You're starting at the wrong end of the comic!

...It's true! In keeping with the original Japanese format, **Boruto** is meant to be read from right to left, starting in the upper-right corner.

Unlike English, which is read from left to right, Japanese is read from right to left, meaning that action, sound effects and word-balloon order are completely reversed... something which can make readers unfamiliar with Japanese feel pretty backwards themselves. For this reason, manga or Japanese comics published in the U.S. in English have sometimes been published "flopped"—that is, printed in exact reverse order, as though seen from the other side of a mirror.

By flopping pages, U.S. publishers can avoid confusing readers, but the compromise is not without its downside. For one thing, a character in a flopped manga series who once wore in the original Japanese version a T-shirt emblazoned with "M A Y" (as in "the merry month of") now wears one which reads "Y A M"! Additionally, many manga creators in Japan are themselves unhappy with the process, as some feel the mirror-imaging of their art alters their original intentions.

We are proud to bring you **Boruto** in the original unflopped format. Turn to the other side of the book and let the ninjutsu begin...!

—Editor

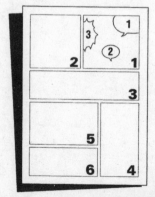